A Massacre in Mexico

A Massacre in Mexico

*The True Story Behind
the Missing Forty-Three Students*

Anabel Hernández

Translated with an Introduction by John Washington

VERSO
London • New York

First published in English by Verso 2018
First published as *La verdadera noche de Iguala. La
historia que el gobierno quiso ocultar* 2017
© Vintage Espanol 2017
Translation © John Washington 2018
Introduction © John Washington 2018

1 3 5 7 9 10 8 6 4 2

Verso
UK: 6 Meard Street, London W1F 0EG
US: 20 Jay Street, Suite 1010, Brooklyn, NY 11201
versobooks.com

Verso is the imprint of New Left Books

ISBN-13: 978-1-78873-148-5
ISBN-13: 978-1-78873-536-0 (EXPORT)
ISBN-13: 978-1-78873-151-5 (US EBK)
ISBN-13: 978-1-78873-150-8 (UK EBK)

British Library Cataloguing in Publication Data
A catalogue record for this book is available from the British Library

Library of Congress Cataloging-in-Publication Data
A catalog record for this book is available from the
Library of Congress. The LCNN is 2018016253

Typeset in Fournier MT by Hewer Text UK Ltd, Edinburgh
Printed in the US by Maple Press

To all the victims of that interminable night: those who were disappeared, the survivors, the tortured, and the witnesses who had the courage to speak out.

To Roberto Scarpinato, whose capacity to fall in love with the destiny of others is a source of inspiration and hope.

They sought to bury them, not knowing that they were seeds

Anon.

Contents

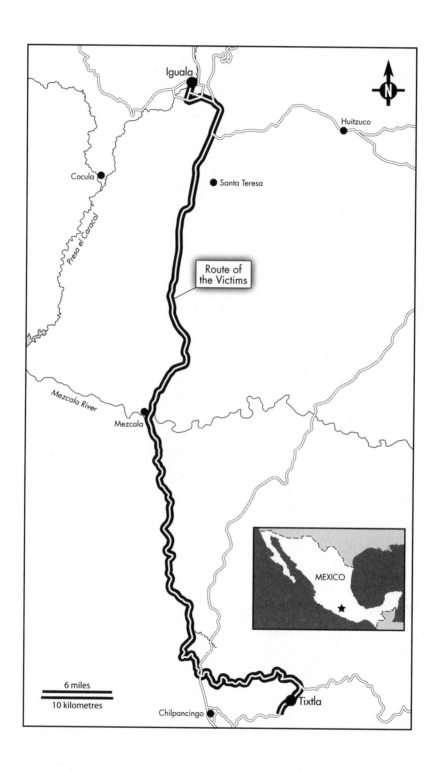

Introduction

by John Washington

W ith no clear end, and no obvious beginning, this is a story that bleeds beyond linear timelines or basic geography. In the fall of 2014, a group of students from the Ayotzinapa teacher training school, mostly in their early twenties, commandeered passenger buses in the small city of Iguala, Guerrero. They took the buses—an established, if, to some locals, annoying practice—to travel to Mexico City to commemorate the 1968 Tlatelolco Massacre, in which Mexican soldiers and police gunned down hundreds of innocent protesters. On that fall night in 2014, following a standoff earlier in the day, local, state, and federal security forces hunted down the unarmed students, shot and killed six people, injured dozens, and disappeared forty-three, all under the watchful and directive eye of the Army. After the disappearance—as news of the slaughter began to break across the world—the government tampered with evidence, fabricated stories, lied to the international press, and brutally tortured the innocent men and women on whom it tried to pin the attacks. Tens of thousands of Mexicans took to the streets, chanting "*¡Fue el estado!*"

They were right, it was the state, and the demonstrations pushed the administration to the brink of collapse. Four years later, after weathering the storm with obfuscation, hollow promises, and a distracting onslaught of other scandals, the government remains in contempt of truth and in contempt of life. This is the endlessness of the story, the unhealing wound: no clarity, no justice. And every time or place you think you've found the beginning of the thread—tracing the story back days, weeks, or decades—you come across another tangle. Anabel Hernández doesn't unsnarl all these shambles; rather, she presents the facts and history such that we glimpse an institution of cruelty and injustice that reaches far beyond that single night.

The massacre and disappearance of the students was different from other state-enacted slaughters of civilians only in degree, not in kind. Just months before the students were hunted down, twenty-two people were summarily executed by soldiers in Tlatlaya, in the state of Mexico. Their deaths stood out from the over 200,000 people killed in the decade of the drug war, as, despite government claims they had died in a standoff, the Army lined the victims up against a wall and shot them point-blank. They then tortured the sole surviving witness. Later, information was leaked that the soldiers hadn't merely been acting in wrath, they had been following *orders*.

Follow the thread, prod at another tangle—blood feeds into Guerrero's fertile soil. 2011: two Ayotzinapa students killed by police during a protest. 1995: the Aguas Blancas massacre, at least seventeen farmers slaughtered as they protested, among other things, for their right to clean water and against the disappearance of one of their leaders. These sorts of cold-blooded killings became common practice during the Dirty War, during which, from the late sixties to the eighties, the government killed and disappeared thousands, most notoriously in the 1968 Tlatelolco Massacre—the crime that the students were planning to commemorate in Mexico City. The violence seems to feed off itself, but that's not how violence works. There's always someone—in this case, *el estado*—holding, aiming, and firing the gun.

The students killed and disappeared that night were *normalistas*, studying at the Raúl Isidro Burgos Normal Rural School in the small community of Ayotzinapa, in Guerrero state. The system of Normal Rural schools, based on pedagogy developed in seventeenth-century France, was initiated after the Mexican Revolution to train teachers in remote and mostly indigenous areas that the government had long neglected—and continues to neglect. Situated in areas of extreme poverty, with little to no infrastructure and high infant mortality rates, the Normal schools—offering free tuition and board—stand out as enclaves of opportunity and empowerment. The Normal schools afford alternatives to the local youth, those who want to remain in their communities.

The other options, which are few, include succumbing to the centripetal maw of Mexico City, signing up as pawns in the drug trade, or crossing the Arizona desert into *el otro lado*, where they would become prey for another violent paramilitary organization—the US Border Patrol. For decades, Mexico's normal schools, though underfunded, politically undermined, and occasionally shuttered by the state, have been struggling to continue offering self-empowerment, indigenous pride, and the basic staples of education and community ethics to populations often relegated to cultural and economic attrition. It wasn't only those students who were attacked that night—their way of thinking, being, and even speaking have been tyrannized by the state for decades.

In the late sixties, Lucio Cabañas, the most famous alumnus of the Ayotzinapa Normal School, after witnessing and suffering multiple assaults from the police and the military, joined a nascent guerrilla group and ended up forming the Party of the Poor. As Omar García, a third-year student at the school and survivor of the 2014 attacks, explained, "Cabañas and the others didn't think it was enough, because teachers shouldn't only care about what goes on in class. A teacher needed to see what the whole community was struggling with, get involved in the issues—not ignore the kid who comes to school with rags for pants, underfed, belly bloated from hunger. We need to get involved in the issues, that's the essence of the rural normal schools."

The *campesinos* "are the ones who help the Earth," Lucio Cabañas says in Carlos Montemayor's masterful (and still untranslated) 1991 novel, *Guerra en el Paraíso*. "The ones who sweep the streets. We are the ones who work for the wealth of all the places. Which is why we say that this is the fight of the poor, we say that it's the cleanest fight."

Cleanliness was not an attribute of the Dirty War. It was, Hernández explains, "waged primarily by the military, whose officers raped, sent to secret prisons, disappeared, summarily executed, and threw out of planes into the sea men, women, senior citizens, boys, and girls from peasant families around [Guerrero] state." Over the decades these tactics have not ceased; they have been honed.

Today, the pretext for Mexico's military presence in the streets—domestically entrenched since the Dirty War—is no longer to quash rebellion. The pretext for unleashing the failed and failing state violence machine is the so-called War on Drugs, which overwhelmingly targets poor, brown, and black people. But it is only a pretext. Hernández reveals that as President Peña Nieto was coming into office in 2012, the transition team listed the Ayotzinapa *normalistas* as one of the top national security priorities, even above the notorious, heavily accoutered paramilitary drug cartels. How could a vivacious bunch of students pose more of a national security threat than paramilitary cartels that wield the firepower of some standing armies? The answer is that the students actually did pose a threat, but not to national security. They threatened, rather, to derail the extractive, exploitative, despoiling neoliberal narrative that ruling administrations have long been riding on.

Author Dawn Paley acutely explains the underlying motivations of the decades-long War on Drugs: it isn't really about prohibition or the control of illicit substances, but a campaign in which terror is wielded against poor and indigenous populations. "The war on drugs," Paley writes, "is a long-term fix to capitalism's woes, combining terror with policymaking in a seasoned neoliberal mix, cracking open social worlds and territories once unavailable to globalized capitalism."

It is a hallmark of our era that capital flows across borders. So do guns. And so do drugs. Though the US has been meddling, to varying degrees, in Mexico's domestic politics for over a century, the most recent iteration captures a particularly disturbing irony. The scourge suffered by US cities struggling with rampant opiate addiction is catalyzed by the US foreign policy that has destabilized Mexican communities, making them increasingly reliant on drug production and trafficking. The US government escalated its security funding to Mexico in the mid-2000s, shortly before President Felipe

Calderón, in an effort to deflect attention from what many consider a stolen election, unleashed a brutal crackdown, Operation Michoacán, in his home state. Desperate to convince the Mexican populace of his legitimacy, Calderón pounded his fist and deployed the Army into the streets.

The Mérida Initiative, modeled after a similar paramilitarization of Colombia, was a whopping weapons coupon and torture-training package from the US government. It boosted Mexico's security forces as they nationalized the Michoacán strategy and oligopolized the drug trade to the cartels in cahoots with the government. Over the past decade, as a direct result of US addiction and binational violent interdiction efforts, more than 200,000 Mexican civilians have been killed, at least 30,000 have been disappeared, and some states have become littered with mass graves. It is at least possible—if ultimately unprovable—that the very weapons wielded by police and the Army against the students that night were purchased through Mérida Initiative funds.

Though there are tens of thousands of murders a year in Mexico, it is not every day that state forces disappear forty-three students. What was it about that night that provoked such a crackdown? The most likely explanation, as described to Hernández by one of her key informants, is that the students had unwittingly commandeered a bus carrying a load of heroin worth a couple-million dollars. That heroin was likely on its way north to Chicago, or some other hub city, where it would then be distributed to Columbus, Wilmington, or Terre Haute—or to any of the communities equally ravaged by addiction and by the state's violent crackdown on addiction. The syringes plunged in the US have turned Guerrero into the hemisphere's primary area of poppy cultivation and a state rife with homicide. In 2017, there were 2,500 murders, or nearly seven a day, in Guerrero alone. Across the country, there were over 29,000 murders. Meanwhile, in the US, over twice as many people—over 64,000—died from drug overdose, mostly from opioids. As SWAT-style, tanks-in-the-streets, punitive policing continues to be one of the state's—both states'—consistent answers to poverty and addiction, more poppy blooms will dot the hills of Guerrero, more loads will head north on buses, and more communities, on both sides of the border, will be laid to waste. The only winners of the War on Drugs are gun makers, gravediggers, and politicians.

But—beyond motives—how is it *possible* to disappear forty-three people? The answer is betrayed in the one piece of actual evidence that has turned up. The remains of nineteen-year-old *normalista* Alexander Mora were "discovered" by Tomás Zerón, the then head of Mexico's Criminal Investigations Agency and intimate crony of President Peña Nieto, one month after the attacks. Hernández reveals the pathetic tragedy of errors that was staged on video as Zerón pretended to find a plastic bag containing Mora's remains—along with attending evidence that was also tampered with—by the side of a river. If Zerón planted the remains, he must have had access to the body. If not exactly the method, this unmasks the actors. And there is only one actor with the capacity to disappear forty-three people, chase down multiple buses, "clean up" enough evidence to forge plausible deniability (barely), scare witnesses into silence, and immediately launch a flailing national disinformation campaign.

"It was the Army," is how Hernández succinctly puts it. Or, as tens of thousands of Mexicans preferred, *¡Fue el estado!*

Anabel Hernández has herself been a target of state violence. After her investigation of the inner workings of what she calls the *narcogobierno*, published in 2010 and translated into English as *Narcoland* (2013), she began receiving credible threats on her life, especially from Genaro García Luna, the controversial former secretary of public security with seemingly blatant ties to the Sinaloa cartel. "The only thing I could do to protect myself," Hernández has said about the threats, "was to keep investigating." But, after decapitated animals were repeatedly left in front of her house, and her home was broken into by a commando unit of eleven federal police officers, she and her children fled to the US. "If it's the state that's killing us, then who's going to protect us?" she asked.

It is a question that Hernández implicitly raises throughout *Massacre in Mexico*. In her detailed, sometimes microscopic retelling of the attacks against the *normalistas*, Hernández does so much more than recreate a scene: the discarded sandals, human finger fragments, and bullet shells littering the darkened streets of Iguala. She lifts the curtain to reveal a world of state violence, murder, torture, falsehood, and impunity—all the necessary ingredients for a mass disappearance.

As pointed out by Ryan Devereaux, who, along with the intrepid John Gibler, is one of the few American journalists to delve deep into the Ayotzinapa case, under international law enforced disappearance is a crime that is ongoing from the moment subjects are taken until they are found. That means that the massacre in Guerrero has been *being continuously committed* for four years. Gibler describes the ongoing cover-up as "the administrative stage of forced disappearance." The Army and the police who carried out the disappearance, along with the politicians who covered it up, have left a suppurating wound, both bloody and bureaucratic, in Guerrero. Hernández's book doesn't purport to close or heal the wound. It exposes it. US drug addiction, US drug policy, and US foreign policy not only are salting that wound—they're making it deeper.

Preface

They say that in investigative journalism you don't choose the stories, the stories choose you. They fall into your hand like a burning ember, come at you like a gust of wind that opens your eyes and forces you to ask yourself: what's going on here?

In this job it's indispensable to care about the fate of others.

The story that gave rise to this book came to me on September 29, 2014, while I was drinking coffee at the University of California, Berkeley. I had recently arrived in the Bay Area and was beginning to try to find a way to return to Mexico, the place of my home and my life, and yet a place that was at the same time—little by little—killing me. As has happened to dozens of Mexican journalists, the federal government forced me to flee by negligently tolerating an increasing number of aggressions against me, my family, and my sources. After four years of harassment, threats, and more harassment, the night of December 21, 2013 was the last straw: eleven armed men, dressed in civilian clothes but organized like a military squadron, violently burst into my home. They first identified themselves to my neighbors as members of the drug cartel, Los Zetas, and then as federal police, forcing them at gunpoint to tell them where I lived. A few members of the group, speaking on radios, took control of the street for more than half an hour, during which time they dismantled the thick metal gate to my garage and entered my home with the utmost ease. Along with my family, I was elsewhere on that day, though it is possible that the presence of the external security guards led them to believe that they would find me inside.

This happened despite the fact that I was supposedly shielded by the Ministry of the Interior's Civil Protection Mechanism for defenders of human rights and journalists. The men didn't steal a thing, they only took the hard drive on which the security cameras—uselessly installed by the Ministry of the Interior—stored footage. My neighbors and a security guard helped the Attorney General's Office (PGR, for its Spanish acronym) create composite sketches of the intruders. To this day there has not been a single arrest.

It wasn't an easy decision to leave Mexico. I didn't want to go into exile, as some people were advising, nor was I about to lock myself in my house, without family, without life, without journalism. I came to Berkeley as a fellow of the Investigative Reporting Program (IRP) run by the journalists Lowell Bergman and Tim McGirk. They accepted my proposal for an investigation into a Mexican cartel operating in the United States. But then my project took an unexpected turn. On the night of September 26, 2014, forty-three students from the Raúl Isidro Burgos Normal (teacher training) School of Ayotzinapa, near Iguala, Guerrero state, disappeared; the earth seemed to have swallowed them, and all searches had turned up nothing. The images of their abandonment were shocking; the testimonies of their mothers and fathers were heartrending.

The official version of these terrible events began rapidly to unfold, based on nonsensical evidence. The case smelled so rotten that when you got near enough it felt hard to breathe; it seemed emblematic of Mexico's level of political decomposition, and it wasn't possible to remain indifferent. The federal government's immediate reaction was to explain that they weren't even aware of the case until a few hours afterwards. But why the self-justification, if nobody was accusing them of anything? Were they involved? From the tone of the government's statements, you'd have thought that Iguala was some distant, lawless land on the confines of the Mexican state, when in reality it's a city lying less than 120 miles from the capital.

From the beginning, the federal and Guerrero state authorities followed one single line of investigation, focusing on the criminal organization Guerreros Unidos and on the mayor of Iguala, José Luis Abarca, along with his wife, María de los Ángeles Pineda Villa—members of the oppositional Party of the Democratic Revolution (PRD). The pair turned out to be a perfect fit for the hasty framing: she was the sister of two presumed drug traffickers, Alberto and Mario Pineda Villa, accused of being lieutenants in the Beltrán Leyva cartel, both of whom were assassinated in 2009. According to the office of Ángel Aguirre Rivero, governor of Guerrero, on the night of September 26 the mayor and his wife had ordered municipal police to attack five buses in which the *normalistas* (students attending the training college) were riding, as well as one other bus occupied by a soccer team, the Avispones (the Hornets, whom they mistook for students), in order to defend "the territory," the city's drug market controlled by Guerreros

Unidos. The results were six dead (including three *normalistas*), more than twenty wounded, and forty-three disappeared students.

Between October 3 and 4, the Guerrero state government, in collaboration with federal authorities, arrested the first suspects; subsequently, the state prosecutor's office recused itself from the case and transferred competence to the Federal Attorney General's Office. It fell to Tomás Zerón de Lucio, director of the PGR's Criminal Investigations Agency (AIC), to follow leads that were brimming with inconsistencies from the outset: the names of the culprits who had allegedly confessed and the scenes of the crime fluctuated wildly, even while the central claim and the official story remained the same. Together the state and federal authorities had scripted the final outcome: the same night that the forty-three students went missing, their dead bodies were incinerated. It didn't matter what new killer confessed, the conclusion was always the same.

On November 7, the then attorney general Jesús Murillo Karam, along with Zerón, announced that, according to the statements of the presumed members of Guerreros Unidos who had been apprehended, on the night of the attacks, municipal police officers from the cities of Iguala and Cocula handed the forty-three students over to Guerreros Unidos, who then transported them to the Cocula garbage dump where they were executed and burned in an immense bonfire lasting for more than fifteen hours. Later, to substantiate the claim, they alleged that members of the marines found bone fragments pertaining to the *normalistas* in plastic bags in the San Juan River, at the location where the "confessed murderers" had dumped them. The PGR put forth this story as the "historical truth," maintaining that the crime had been solved.

The official version, pushed by the PGR, the Secretariat of

the Interior, and Los Pinos (the presidential residence), was presented as indisputable—notwithstanding the absence of expert evidence supporting it and the manifest incoherence of the so-called confessions. Meanwhile, the great majority of the national and international media reproduced the government's avalanche of information without doing their own independent fact-checking.

In October 2014, when I noticed the first signs that the PGR was dealing out questionable information, I plunged deep into the case with financing from the IRP, as well as with support from my colleague, Steve Fisher, who helped me with the technical aspects of video recording and editing the various interviews that I conducted in the course of the investigation. The story that I was able to reconstruct after two years of work points to a very different truth than the one claimed by the Mexican government.

The attack against the *normalistas* of Ayotzinapa became, for me, an enormous journalistic challenge, not only because of the complexity of the case—the government has heaped stones and mud onto the facts, onto the truth, and tireless digging was required to unearth them—but also in the human sense, which is what matters most in the end. This is an investigation conducted not only by a journalist, but by a citizen who was forced out of her country by violence and impunity, and who then returned to Mexico because of the violence and impunity meted out to others.

Confidential official records and dossiers that I accessed served as the entrance into the labyrinth of a crime that has provoked Mexico's largest political crisis of recent years; the dozens of first-hand testimonies, videos, photographs, and audio recordings that I was able to collect have been the tools by which I've attempted to find an exit.

In December 2014 I published the first part of this investigation as "The True Night of Iguala: The Unofficial History," in *Proceso* magazine, describing my discovery of the existence of the Center for Control, Command, Communications, and Computers (C4) in Iguala, through which the Army, the federal police, the state police, and the state government, as well as Iguala's local police department, all coordinated and shared information. Through the C4 the government knew, in real time, of the ambush against the students and had indeed been monitoring their movements since 18:00, three hours before the first assault. In the same article I documented that the federal police, with the support and outright complicity of the Army, were present during the attack; I also obtained medical accounts that proved that the first suspects to be arrested showed signs of having been tortured.

Jesús Murillo Karam's reaction was emphatic: he immediately denied the existence of documents and testimonies that were, in fact, in the PGR's possession. Worried about the repercussions of my research and the imminent start of the investigation by the Interdisciplinary Group of Independent Experts (GIEI, by its Spanish acronym) set up by the Inter-American Commission of Human Rights, the Attorney General's Office did everything in its power to close the case.

President Peña Nieto's government was becoming desperate. With every arrest of another alleged suspect, the torture turned ever more brutal. The perpetrators of this abuse came from each of Mexico's law enforcement agencies: federal investigative police, federal police, Secretariat of National Defense, and the Navy. Rather than isolated abuses committed by a few twisted agents, this was the method the state used to impose its own version of the night of September 26.

In early 2015, a high official of the federal government

suggested, amicably, that I drop my investigation: without offering the slightest evidence, he assured me that the students were dead because they were involved in drug trafficking. I went on digging and shared my information with GIEI and the UN.

On September 6, 2015, the GIEI released its first report: it contained the same information I had revealed in my articles months before.

Despite being internationally shamed and lacking even the most basic credibility, for the first anniversary of the massacre, in 2015, the PGR decided to open a tranche of its evidence for review. Yet it redacted the most important data, including names, phone numbers, and addresses of the presumed suspects or victims, information indispensable for anybody looking to corroborate the official version of the story. What had actually occurred that night, however, was not to be found in the case files of the prosecutor, but on the streets of Iguala.

The first day I arrived in the city, it still smelled of terror. I had to knock on a lot of doors, some of them repeatedly, before witnesses overcame their fear, before the memories of the pain of others gave them the courage to speak.

The reader of this investigation will traverse a labyrinth, with all its traps, darkness, and flashes of light. You will walk down Juan N. Álvarez Street, see the bullet shells and sandals strewn over the ground. You will enter the Raúl Isidro Burgos Normal School and hear the vividness of the students' voices, sometimes filled with courage and pride, other times with fear and desolation. You will step into those sordid corners where the government tortured people to manufacture suspects and extract confessions, as well as into the government offices in

Mexico where the lies were concocted. You will hear the voices of people who were offered generous sums of money to incriminate themselves or to shut down unsettling leads. Through witnesses' voices you will hear the panic of the victims during the protracted massacre, the indignation of the survivors, and the fading cries of those who were disappeared. You will feel the grief of neighbors who heard or saw the attacks through their windows and were too afraid to open the door when the students begged for succor, as well as the solidarity of those who, despite imminent danger, saved some of the students—enabling them to recount what happened on that night. And you will discover, name by name, those who participated in the attacks and those who participated in the subsequent cover-up.

The infamy of September 26, 2014 doesn't reside solely in the fact that six people were killed and forty-three were disappeared: these acts unleashed a host of further crimes and wove a net of complicity that served to obscure the truth and protect the perpetrators. After two years' research, it's difficult to decide which of the two phases was the more brutal.

The events in Iguala force us to reflect on the current conditions of Mexico. They paint a crude portrait of the degradation of the institutions that should dispense justice and protect us, and, at the same time, they paint our portrait as a society—revealing both our deepest fears and highest hopes. In the midst of Mexico's polarization and loneliness, people have forgotten that the pain caused by injustice against another should also be our own pain. At any moment, that other could be oneself.

1

Red Dawn

It's 03:20, September 27, 2014. In the middle of Juan N. Álvarez Street, only a few blocks from the main square in the city of Iguala, the rainwater runs red down rivulets and into the cracks in the asphalt; the cracks absorb the blood, drinking it in. On the ground are the bodies of Daniel Solís and Julio César Ramírez, students from the Raúl Isidro Burgos Normal School of Ayotzinapa whose contingent had become, on that night, the target of five armed attacks. They lie sprawled at the intersection of Juan N. Álvarez and Periférico Norte. The water on the pavement reflects their lifeless faces.

Daniel, eighteen years old, from the port town of Zihuatanejo, was in his first year of teacher training; his face—a shadow of a beard, a thin mustache—is turned to the east. He's wearing a red sweatshirt, navy-blue pants, and, like most of his fellow *normalistas*, brown leather sandals. The bullet entered his back on the right side, traveled through his body, and exited through the left side of his chest.

Julio César, twenty-three years old and another first-year student, was from Tixtla. His face is turned to the southeast.

He is dressed in a green sweatshirt, blue pants, and black shoes. A bullet, fired at point-blank range, entered on the right side of his face and exited through the back of his neck, to the left. The rest of his face remains undisturbed.

Here and there in the street are tokens of the massacre that played out a few hours ago. Close to a water purification station lies a pair of sandals made of tire tread and leather straps; slightly further on, a checkered sandal with a black sponge sole, and then its twin. There are pieces of finger torn from a hand and walls and benches spattered in blood. All about the street are spent cartridges, the majority .223 or 7.62 caliber, along with others piled in places hard to make out in the darkness.

In the middle of the road, three buses, inside of which a few hours ago almost sixty *normalistas* were riding, are beached. Drops of rain fall on the windshields, trickling through the bullet holes that have left the vehicles looking like colanders: it has been raining all night. The lead bus is a Costa Line, license plate 894 HS, registration number 2012, one of its windows shattered by gunfire. The middle bus—the least damaged—is another Costa Line, license 227 HY 9 and registration 2510, with a shattered back window. The third bus is a white Estrella de Oro with green trim, registration number 1568.

In the photographs a few of the survivors had taken with their phones—and which later contributed to my investigation—further details arise. The bullet holes riddling the Estrella de Oro 1568 show that it was the principal target of the attack, with the holes concentrated at the level of the windows and, in order to stop the bus, its wheels; inside there is blood on the driver's seat, in the aisle, and on a number of the passenger seats.

When agents from Guerrero's State Prosecutor's Office arrive at Juan N. Álvarez Street, the scene of the crime has already been cordoned off by members of the 27th Infantry Battalion under command of Captain José Martínez Crespo, along with officers of the Public Ministry (the organ of the Attorney General's Office, or PGR, tasked with the investigation and prosecution of federal crimes, locally attached to the State Prosecutor's Office, or Fiscalía). José Manuel Cuenca Salmerón, a lawyer working for the Public Ministry of the Hidalgo Judiciary District, has been assigned to this crime scene. He is accompanied by Luis Rivera Beltrán, expert in field criminalistics, and María Guadalupe Moctezuma, expert in chemical forensics. The notes from their examination of the scene still have not been released to the public.

Cuenca Salmerón has been traveling to Iguala to investigate homicides for years, long before the jewelery retailer, José Luis Abarca, was elected mayor of Iguala. In 2010, for example, he was assigned to a case concerning a homicide victim discovered in the industrial zone of the city, whose body was found beaten, stabbed, and without hands. Next to the cadaver was the message: "Dear people of Iguala, don't do what I did, this happened for making anonymous accusations, and the worst of it is that the soldiers themselves handed me over." The body of Daniel is for Cuenca Salmerón the third corpse of the night; Julio César will be his fourth. More will come in the following hours. The rain doesn't make his work any easier.

Mechanically, the ministerial agent begins to count pieces of evidence, marking them with numbers. "Marker 1" is a Nissan Urvan truck with the side windows shattered and the interior bloodied on the passenger's side. "Marker 2" is a sand-colored Chevy with Mexico City plates, MBC 9797. "Marker 3" is a Yamaha motorcycle, plates F4808W. "Marker 4" is the body of Daniel Solís. "Marker 5" is a pair of glimmering .223-caliber shells. "Marker 6" is the body of Julio César Ramírez. "Marker 7" is a cluster of five .223-caliber shells; another collection of ten shells of the same caliber constitute "Marker 8." The first Costa Line bus is given "Marker 9," the second Costa Line is "Marker 10," and the Estrella de Oro is "Marker 11."

"Marker 11-a" is used to identify the pool of blood in the Estrella de Oro bus; presumably a sample was taken for analysis and to determine whose blood it was. "Marker 11-b" is a group of rocks, of various sizes, inside the bus. "Marker 12" corresponds with a Volkswagen Pointer, plate number HBR 3525. "Marker 13" comprises four .223-caliber shells. The pool of blood measuring one meter by eighty centimeters that the cracks have partially swallowed, along with three more .223 shells, constitute "Marker 14." Markers "15" and "16" are more gleaming .223 shells. "Marker 17" corresponds to the last pieces of evidence to be identified: a red Ford Explorer, with plates HER 8831 and with bullet holes in the rear.

There are some confusing errors in the labeling of evidence, which raises a question: if they weren't even able to correctly categorize the evidence, how were they able to transfer the evidence down the chain in such a way as to ensure that these essential facts were not mixed up as the investigation proceeded? These are such fundamental errors that, from an early point in my own research, they began to appear intentional.

Rivera Beltrán takes photos and packages what evidence he's able to transport, while Moctezuma Díaz extracts samples of blood from the Urvan truck, the Estrella de Oro bus, and the pool of blood in the street. Nobody marks the fifty shells that the *normalistas* piled together at the base of an electricity post before the third attack; nor are the sandals or the finger fragments registered.

Considering his work for the night done, Cuenca Salmerón notes in his four-page report that he has ordered the company Mejía Meta Towing to take into their custody the vehicles tagged as evidence. The company, however, doesn't tow the vehicles until the next day.

When the agents depart, there's nobody left to guard the scene of the crime. The rain finally stops. As the sun begins to rise, curious neighbors begin showing up, immediately horrified by what is obviously the site of a massacre. Some will later say that they heard screams and shots during the night, others that they witnessed part of the event through their windows but got frightened and hid. They didn't grasp what had happened until seeing the remnants of the attack in the light of day.

"There were dozens of bullet shells in the street. The third bus was completely shot up. The gunfire came from outside, you could tell by how the metal was bent where the bullets entered. Everything was covered in blood," a woman who glanced inside the bus would later recall with horror. For her safety, she didn't want her name printed. "The steering wheel was covered in blood, the floor also covered in blood, pieces of flesh, even the wall of one of my neighbor's houses was smeared in blood."

She didn't know it at the time, but of the twenty occupants of the Estrella de Oro 1568, only the driver and one student would survive. The rest were disappeared.

The work of the Public Ministry on Juan N. Álvarez Street was so inadequate that at eight the next morning, the Prosecutor's Office sent forensic expert Martín Cantú López to perform another survey of the site. Cantú found more .223

and 7.62 caliber shells, part of a finger, stray sandals, and another car—a Jetta that had been abandoned on a street perpendicular to Juan N. Álvarez. It was riddled with bullet holes, with its windows shattered.

In this second inspection, Cantú López failed to take samples from the blood spattered on the wall of the wood-worker's shop, where some *normalistas* had been lined up on the ground in submission. If those samples had been collected it would have at least been possible to determine who had been taken away from that location—and ultimately disappeared. Cantú López also missed other finger pieces and more shells which local residents had seen, and some had even photographed.

The three buses were towed away by Mejía Meta Towing around eleven in the morning of September 27. At that hour, with the permission of state authorities, residents of Juan N. Álvarez Street—the cries and sobs of the victims still echoing in their ears—began to clean the street. One person took a piece of a finger and later buried it. Another neighbor, with a somber gaze, tossed a bucket of water on the wall and the bench to wash away the blood. He felt like he could still hear the machine-gun fire. Before sweeping up dozens of scattered shells, a woman asked a few officers still hanging around if she could start tidying up and, lazily, they told her that she could.

The Hours of the Massacre

On the night of September 26, 2014, the trainee teachers of the Raúl Isidro Burgos Normal School of Ayotzinapa were attacked five separate times over the course of four hours in Iguala, a city located three hours from Mexico City and one hour from Chilpancingo, the capital of the state of Guerrero.

Earlier that evening the students had traveled to Iguala intending to commandeer buses so as to join the annual protest in Mexico City, commemorating the Tlatelolco massacre, in which the Mexican military and police killed hundreds of student and civilian protesters on October 2, 1968.

The first armed ambush of the *normalistas* occurred around 21:30 on the corner of Juan N. Álvarez and Emiliano Zapata, one block from the main square in Iguala. The incident is not registered in the dossiers kept by the State Prosecutor's Office (Fiscalía) or the Attorney General's Office; there were no casualties.

The next attack took place between 21:30 and 23:00 on the corner of Juan N. Álvarez and Periférico Norte, where three students suffered gunshot wounds.

A few kilometers from there, on the Iguala–Mezcala federal highway, close to the Palacio de Justicia, or state courthouse, another attack was launched against two buses full of students—the Estrella de Oro, number 1531 and Estrella Roja, 3278. At 23:40, a few kilometers down the same highway, the bus carrying the soccer team, the Avispones (Hornets), was shot at: unluckily, this Castro Tours bus, white with green stripes down the side, resembled the Estrella de Oros that the *normalistas* were riding in. After midnight, once more at the intersection of Juan N. Álvarez and Periférico Norte, Daniel Solís and Julio César Ramírez were shot and killed.

In total, the wave of armed attacks resulted in the death of six people: the *normalistas* Daniel Solís, Julio César Ramírez, and Julio César Mondragón, who was aged twenty; Blanca Montiel, aged forty; the Avispones player David Josué García, aged fifteen; and the driver of the Avispones bus, aged fifty.

Of the twenty-four people who received gunshot wounds, seven were students. Aldo Gutiérrez was shot in the head and remains, as of this writing, in a coma. The left forearm of Fernando Marín was shattered by a bullet; he almost lost a hand. Edgar Andrés Vargas was shot in the mouth. A volley of gunfire amputated four of Jonathan Maldonado's fingers on his left hand.

The signature barbarity of that night was the disappearance of forty-three *normalistas* between the ages of seventeen and twenty-one; all were first year students, except for Bernardo Flores Alcaraz, who led the group to commandeer the buses.

No police force intervened to stop the attacks or prevent the disappearance of the students, despite the fact that each level of government maintained its own security base near where the attacks occurred. The municipal police had a small station amidst the private homes on Rayón Street, in the center of Iguala. The state police had its Regional Police Training Center on the Iguala–Tuxpan highway, a group of large buildings isolated from the urban zone. The PGR ran its Center for Strategic Operations on Nicolás Bravo Street, close to the corner of Bandera Nacional in the Centro neighborhood. The federal police ran its operations from Highway 95, on the Iguala–Mezcala stretch, and the Secretariat of National Defense (SEDENA) had a military base that occupied at least eight blocks on the Periférico Oriente highway, home to the Army's 27th and 41st Infantry Battalions.

All of these bases and stations with their military or police presence were within a short radius of the attacks that occurred on September 26, and all of them were active and vigilant twenty-four hours a day, 365 days a year. And yet, none of them reacted to the shootings or came to enforce public security. Furthermore, a security surveillance mechanism was operational and may have played a key role in what occurred on that night. The C4 system was built in 1995 during the presidential term of Ernesto Zedillo and was part of the first general security law to establish the National System of Public Security (SNSP). The law mandates that states, municipalities, and Mexico City—as part of the Federal District—create a communications service to receive calls related to accidents, emergencies, and crimes. This was when the country launched the national emergency line, 066.

The proposal behind the creation of the C4 was for municipal, state, and federal authorities to act in a coordinated manner to combat crime and share information through the central 066 phone system, with the intent of making emergency response more rapid and efficient. The Secretariat of the Interior web page states that the system's "technological development of interconnection and telecommunications correlates all the networks of the departments related to public security, updates the national telecommunications grid and develops the concept of computers, communications, control, and command (C4), scaling it for nodes of telecommunication interconnection (NIT)."

In all major cities in Mexico, the C4 tracks incidents involving the police, controls strategically located security cameras, and responds to emergency calls through a central telephone system connected to the National Telecommunication Network and the National System of Information, both run by the Ministry of the Interior. The system responds to medical emergencies, rescues, vehicular accidents, assaults, fires, disturbances, and shootings.

The C4 stations are part of the SNSP public security system, which since December 2012 has operated under the National Security Council and is staffed by federal, state, and municipal agents monitoring security cameras—basically, they are the nerve center of public security in each state and in the capital. The C4s are run by the governor's offices of each state, but for funds and equipment rely largely on the federal government, which receives emergency information in real time.

In July 2013, the governor of Guerrero, Ángel Aguirre Rivero, met with the secretary of the interior, Miguel Ángel Osorio Chong, the secretary of finance and public credit, Luis Videgaray Caso, and the secretary of the economy, Ildefonso Guajardo Villareal. After the meeting it was announced that Osorio Chong had promised to build C4 security stations in Chilpancingo, Iguala, Ciudad Altamirano, and Taxco, along with installing more security cameras.

In the C4 station in Iguala, the Guerrero state police, the local police, civil protection agents, and Army officers all coordinate with the federal police station and the offices of the PGR, which are both located in Iguala. The Iguala C4 hosts frequent meetings with representatives of all the security branches to evaluate the efficacy and capacity of response to emergencies coming in through the 066 line.

The unavoidable conclusion is that on the night of September 26, 2014, all the law enforcement branches converging in C4 knew, in real time, everything about the attacks that were occurring in the streets.

The First Reports

At 23:00 on September 26, Iguala's Public Ministry of common law attached to the State Prosecutor's Office of the Hidalgo Judicial District received a call from Dr. Jacobo Ruiz Moreno, the on-call medic at the city's General Hospital, to report the arrival of three men, two of whom—Daniel Martínez and Erick Santiago López—suffered from gunshot wounds, with the third in such a critical state that he was unable to give his name. The call officially obligated the Prosecutor's Office to open a preliminary inquiry, HID/SC/02/0993/2014, under which they would initiate proceedings.

According to the first page of the report, officers were requested to immediately go to Dr. Jorge Soberón Acevedo General Hospital to take down information from the victims and investigate the violent attacks that caused their injuries. None of the authorities complied; they didn't even go to the hospital.

It wasn't until 00:04 on the 27th that the Prosecutor's Office undertook their first actions, as the Iguala C4 informed them that on the Mexico–Acapulco highway, at the Iguala–Mezcala section, specifically under the bridge in front of the state courthouse, was an "abandoned" Estrella de Oro bus that showed signs of gunfire damage; Cuenca Salmerón was the first to go, arriving at 00:20. It had begun to rain. His shift would be long and hard: he had just arrived at the scene of the third attack, and he would continue on to the scenes of the second, fourth, and fifth attacks, skipping the scene of the first.

He was accompanied by field expert Luis Rivera Beltrán and ministerial police under the orders of Javier Bello Orbe. Almost directly in front of the state courthouse, close to the sign "Come back soon, Iguala is waiting for you," they saw the Estrella de Oro bus, white with green stripes, registration number 1531: the front tires were punctured, the door was open, and the glass windows and windshield were shattered.

Stepping onto the bus they saw, lying on the steps by the driver's seat and along the aisle, rocks of different sizes. The air still stank of tear gas. Five meters away from the bus was a pile of clothes: among them they found three white shirts with bloodstains, four black t-shirts, an Arsenal soccer jersey, a gray sweater, and a faded red handkerchief. The records in the preliminary inquiry and in the court files indicate that the ministerial officer and the forensic expert confirmed in their report that the clothing was collected and packed as evidence, but neither the State Prosecutor's Office nor the PGR, which later took over the investigation, refer to any garments used as evidence.

On December 21, 2014, the magazine *Proceso* published my own investigation in which I noted the existence of these garments. On September 6, 2015, the Interdisciplinary Group of Independent Experts, sent by the Inter-American Commission on Human Rights, again referred to my article in its "Ayotzinapa Report: Investigation and Initial Conclusions on the Disappearances and Homicides of the Students of Ayotzinapa," confirming that the items were never subjected to analysis or forensic testing.

Almost twenty *normalistas* who were riding in the Estrella de Oro bus were taken away and disappeared; only the driver survived. According to the official record, the bus was taken into the custody of the ministerial police of Iguala, which operates under control of the state government. Other documents and testimonies, however, reveal that it is unclear through whose custody the bus passed and who had access to it.

Almost immediately after the ministry's Cuenca Salmerón signed the report on the clothing, his office received another call from C4 reporting that two victims had been discovered on the Iguala–Chilpancingo highway, close to the Santa Teresa turn-off: an adolescent male and a woman, killed by gunfire.

According to the report, part of case file HID/SC/02/0993/2014, Cuenca Salmerón and Rivera Beltrán, along with officers of the Medical Forensic Team, arrived at the location at 01:20. Under the rain, they discovered the bodies of the two people shot during the fourth attack, when the passenger bus that the Avispones soccer team (whose players were about the same age as the Ayotzinapa students) were riding in was attacked.

There were already two federal police officers on the spot, as that section of the Iguala–Mezcala highway is within federal police jurisdiction; also present was a squadron of the 27th Infantry Battalion, though their presence wasn't mentioned, for unknown reasons, in the initial ministerial report. Curiously, nobody had offered assistance to the victims.

On the highway, in the direction heading from Chilpancingo to Iguala, taxi number 0972 sat riddled with bullet holes. Two meters away lay Blanca Montiel, forty years old, face down on the wet pavement. She wore a blouse with black and white stripes, gray pants, and black shoes. She had been riding in the taxi with her husband when, as gunfire broke out all around, they tried to escape. The husband managed to jump out and make it to safety, but Blanca was shot three times: in the jaw, the hand, and the chest.

After the forensic team had taken the standard photographs, Cuenca Salmerón ordered them to recover the corpse. It was only then that the federal police informed the ministry that there were other dead and wounded victims. Fifty meters away they saw another taxi, a Nissan Tsuru, also shot up, and another fifty meters beyond that there were seventy-one shells; after photographing them, they collected them as evidence. The rain started to come down harder; a storm was rolling in, with heavy winds.

In a ditch by the entrance to the small town of Santa Teresa was the overturned Castro Tours bus used by the soccer team; like the two commandeered by the *normalistas*, it was white with green stripes. Federal police agents—the first law enforcement officers to arrive—were already on the scene, along with the chief of their Iguala station, Luis Antonio Dorantes Macías.

Inside the bus Cuenca Salmerón found the body of a fifteen-year-old boy, David Josué García. He remained sitting, his head resting on the right inside wall of the vehicle. He was wearing a blue short-sleeve shirt with white stripes and light blue jeans. He had been shot in the chest and one leg, and bore multiple cuts from the glass shards sent flying during the shootout.

At 02:40, as the Public Ministry was taking statements from the Avispones players, Dr. Ruiz Moreno phoned again from the General Hospital to report that more gunshot victims were coming in, at least eleven so far, including one woman. They had been injured in the most recent attack, committed under the noses of the numerous authorities deployed around the city and its outskirts.

Only then did the Prosecutor's Office send a ministerial official, José García, to the hospital to investigate. Valuable hours had been wasted: when García arrived in the emergency room, the wounded were already hooked up to IVs.

The Misfortune of the Avispones

On the night of the attacks the Avispones football team, playing in Mexico's third division, defeated the local Iguala club by three goals to one. The game took place on the field of one of the city's sports complexes; the city police officers in charge of security at the game were Hugo Hernández Arias, Zulaid Marino Rodríguez, Josefina López Cornelión, and Lucía Verónica Núñez Núñez. They reported no incidents.

The lurch from a spirit of triumph to one of horror is best conveyed through the declarations of the twenty-two players and the team's coach, Pablo Rentería, which were made before the state prosecutor on the morning of September 27: the individual stories are corroborated by subsequent interviews with the players, the coaches, and family members.

Facundo Serrano, a member of the coaching team, recalled that at 22:30, after the players had showered and changed, the team wanted to go and eat in Iguala, but Rentería decided that they would leave town, as he had heard rumors of a shootout in the city center and preferred to go straight back to Chilpancingo. The team boarded their Castro Tours bus and started watching a movie—the windows were closed and the interior lights turned off.

When the bus was already on the Iguala–Chilpancingo highway and leaving the city, at approximately 23:00, they received information that the highway had been taken by *ayotzinapos*—a pejorative term for the *normalistas*. Félix Pérez, the team doctor, said that upon passing the state courthouse, they saw an Estrella de Oro bus (1531) with broken windows; the driver slowed down, Dr. Pérez told the Public Ministry, but continued past the stationary vehicle. The players were too scared to speak up about what they'd seen. It wasn't until a year and five months later, in March 2016, that passengers in the Castro Tours bus explained that after passing the shot-up bus the *normalistas* had been traveling in, they saw that the federal police had set up a checkpoint.

The players' family members were traveling separately, in their own cars. Some of them described how the federal police let trucks and cars go through the checkpoint but initially stopped the team bus, whose livery resembled that of the Estrella de Oro. Shortly after they finally let it through, however, it would receive a barrage of gunfire.

Luis Enrique Romero, aged nineteen, was sitting in his reclined seat in the second to last row of the bus, his head against the window and his feet in the aisle; he was listening to music on his headphones when, suddenly, he noticed the horrified faces of his teammates as they dived to the floor. Romero quickly did the same. For a moment he took off his headphones, but after hearing the gunshots, he put them back on, hugged his knees to his chest, and shut his eyes tightly.

Dr. Pérez related that at 23:40 he noticed people blocking the highway at the Santa Teresa turn-off; he thought it was the *ayotzinapos*. The driver asked him to tell the boys to relax and not make a fuss. The doctor stood up to make the announcement, but then heard the first burst of gunfire exploding into the air and shattering the windows.

Aureliano García, the taxi driver who survived the attack in which Blanca Montiel was killed, took a bullet in the ankle. He testified that upon attempting to drive around the scene of the attack, men began firing at the taxi from both sides of the highway: he managed to get out of the car and hide, later limping back to the highway where another taxi took him to the hospital.

The inside of the Castro Tours bus had turned into a hell:

amidst the gunfire the players and coaching staff threw themselves instinctively down in the aisle or hid under the seats. Jorge León, the team trainer, saw armed men firing at them. "Don't shoot! Don't shoot!" he cried out. "We're a soccer team."

The first gunshots wounded the driver, Víctor Manuel Lugo, in the head, causing him to lose control and drive the bus into a ditch. Its right side was slammed against a dirt wall, sealing off the door. Another blast rang out.

"Get out, motherfuckers!" one of the shooters screamed.

"We can't open the door; it's stuck," the coach yelled back.

Fifteen-year-old Alan Osvaldo Castañón thought he was going to die: "I was really scared. What I did was cover my ears and start to pray."

"Get out!" ordered the attackers, trying to open the door themselves. They threatened them and then fired off another volley.

"They got me in the eye," shouted Rentería.

Just as suddenly as the assailants had opened fire, they retreated. At once Dr. Pérez, heroically, started helping the players out of the windows and directing them to hide in the nearby cornfield. Many of them had been wounded by bullets or shattered glass. Finally he was able to pull out Rentería, who had also been shot in the stomach, as well as the driver— who was fatally injured and died in hospital at four in the morning. "After pulling the two wounded men out I went back to the bus and found a kid in agony . . . [who] had been shot several times. I took his pulse, it was very weak. I tried my best to staunch his wounds, but that made things worse, and sadly he died right there," Dr. Pérez said in his declaration before the state prosecutor on September 27. The terrified players remained hidden in the fields.

The first to arrive on the scene of the attack were federal police officers based in Iguala. The survivors later confirmed that the commander, Luis Antonio Dorantes Macías, was with them; and yet, instead of calling ambulances to assist the wounded, they intimidated the victims as they took control of the scene. Later, agents from the State Prosecutor's Office arrived, followed by soldiers.

The statements the prosecutors took from the Avispones at the hospital, however, are suspicious. In reviewing the documents, I found that at least five of the testimonies were identical, meaning that they were copied, changing only the name of the subject providing the testimony.

None of the players or staff of the Avispones understood what had happened to them—they had won the game, and there was no trouble afterwards. Why were they attacked? Why them?

The answer is that the Avispones' Castro Tours bus had been confused with two of the buses taken by the *normalistas*. All the students in those two Estrella de Oro buses were driven off and disappeared, except for the one student who was taken to the hospital. The fact that all three buses were white with green stripes explains why the federal police stopped the Castro Tours as well as the Estrella de Oros. The Costa Line buses, the target of lesser aggressions, were beige with blue stripes, and the Estrella Roja that the *normalistas* took that night from the Iguala bus station, which was not fired upon when it was stopped, had blue and white stripes. Later in my investigation, I found out why the Estrella de Oros were of particular interest.

Inexplicably, in the General Hospital, priority was given to the injured soccer players over the *normalistas*, who had been there longer and also suffered from gunshot wounds.

One of the last victims to be interviewed that night was the Ayotzinapa student Fernando Marín, who reached the hospital in a state of terror, and, fearing for his life, gave the false name of Erick Santiago López. He had lost a lot of blood and was barely able to say that, after they had seized a few buses from the terminal in Iguala, as he was riding with about twenty-four other students, the municipal police started shooting at them.

He also said that the police took the students off the bus and beat them. He and others were badly injured, and he later filed a formal complaint for attempted homicide. Marín was the only survivor of the Estrella de Oro bus that was stopped on Juan N. Álvarez, and though his admission to the hospital was reported by Dr. Ruiz Moreno at 23:00 to the state prosecutor, no one from that office went to investigate.

When state prosecutors took Fernando Marín's statement in the emergency room of the General Hospital in Iguala, Governor Ángel Aguirre Rivero already knew what was happening: his officials, as well as those of President Enrique Peña Nieto, had been monitoring the students before, during, and after the attacks. At 17:59 on the 26th, the C4 in Chilpancingo had notified the state and federal police forces that the *normalistas* were on their way to Iguala.

The state and federal officials later hid from the public that on that night the municipal police of Iguala and Cocula, just like the federal police, were armed with R-15 and G36 automatic rifles using .223-caliber ammunition, as well as 9mm pistols, while the troops from the 27th Infantry Battalion carried G3 assault rifles firing 7.62 × 51-caliber ammunition. Shells of all these calibers were found on Juan N. Álvarez Street, where two attacks were carried out, as well as on the Iguala–Mezcala highway, at the Santa Teresa turn-off.

According to the "Report from the General Prosecutor of the State of Guerrero on the investigation related to the events of the night of September 26 and the morning of September 27, 2014, in the city of Iguala, Guerrero," the ministry removed 193 shells from the crime scenes, while many more remained on the ground. Of the registered shells, seventy-seven were 7.62 × 39mm, eighty-six were .223-caliber, eighteen were 7.62 × 51mm, six were 9mm, one was .22-caliber, one was .38 Super, and six were .380-caliber.

Between 22:30 and midnight, as officers from federal and state law enforcement agencies descended into the streets of Iguala, guarding the entrances and exits to the city, forty-three Ayotzinapa *normalistas* vanished into the rainy night as if it had swallowed them.

Below is a list of the names and nicknames of each disappeared student, grouped according to the bus they had been riding in. Unfortunately, I have not been able to determine with certainty in which of the two buses eight of the students were riding.

Bus 1568, stopped on Juan N. Álvarez Street

1. Abelardo Vásquez Penitén (*El Abe*)
2. Antonio Santana Maestro (*Copy*)
3. Bernardo Flórez Alcaraz (*Cochiloco*)
4. César Manuel González Hernández (*Panotla, Marinela Tlaxcala, Pinky*)
5. Cristian Tomás Colón Garnica (*Oaxaco, Reloj*)
6. Cutberto Ortiz Ramos (*Komander*)
7. Dorian González Parral (*Kinder*)
8. Emiliano Alen Gaspar de la Cruz (*Pilas*)
9. Everardo Rodríguez Bello (*Shaggy*)

10. Giovanni Galindes Guerrero (*Spider*)
11. Jonás Trujillo González (*Beny*)
12. Jorge Álvarez Nava (*Chabelo*)
13. Jorge Luis González Parral (*Kinder, Charras*)
14. Jhosivani Guerrero de la Cruz (*Coreano*)
15. Leonel Castro Abarca (*Magueyito*)
16. Luis Ángel Abarca Carrillo (*Amiltzingo*)
17. Marcial Pablo Baranda (*El Indígena, Magallón*)
18. Marco Antonio Gómez Molina (*Tuntún*)
19. Miguel Ángel Hernández Martínez (*Botitas*)
20. Miguel Ángel Mendoza Zacarías (*Miclo*)
21. Saúl Bruno García (*Chicharrón*)

Bus 1531, stopped in front of the state courthouse

22. Adán Abraján de la Cruz (*El Ñero*)
23. Alexander Mora Venancio (*Pericón, La Roca, Randy*)
24. Carlos Lorenzo Hernández Muñoz (*Frijol*)
25. Christian Alfonso Rodríguez Telumbre (*Hugo, La Huga*)
26. Israel Jacinto Lugardo (*Chukyto*)
27. Jesús Jovany Rodríguez Tlatempa (*Churro, Jovany*)
28. Jorge Aníbal Cruz Mendoza (*Chivo*)
29. Jorge Antonio Tizapa Legideño (*Perezoso*)
30. José Ángel Navarrete González (*Pepe*)
31. José Eduardo Bartolo Tlatempa (*Bobby*)
32. Julio César López Patolzín
33. Luis Ángel Francisco Arzola (*Cochilandia*)
34. Magdaleno Rubén Lauro Villegas (*El Magda*)
35. Martín Getsemany Sánchez García (*Zunpango, Cabe*)

The other disappeared normalistas (unidentified bus)

36. Abel García Hernández
37. Benjamín Ascencio Bautista (*Dormilón*)
38. Carlos Iván Ramírez Villareal (*El Diablito*)
39. Felipe Arnulfo Rosas Rosas
40. Israel Caballero Sánchez (*Aguirrito*)
41. José Ángel Campos Cantor (*Tío Tripa*)
42. José Luis Luna Torres (*Pato*)
43. Mauricio Ortega Valerio (*Espinosa*)

2

The Week Before: The Key Days

The morning of September 20, 2014 was a busy one at the Raúl Isidro Burgos Normal School, located in the Ayotzinapa community in the municipality of Tixtla, Guerrero state. It was a Saturday, and the second- and third-year students were preparing to leave for the state capital, Chilpancingo, to seize passenger buses. Their mission was to get hold of twenty buses in only ten days, which, despite their experience, would be a difficult task.

They had no room to fail. In the assembly for the Federation of Rural Socialist Students of Mexico, which took place on September 18 in Amilcingo, Morelos state, the general secretaries of the seventeen rural normal schools of the country decided that the Raúl Isidro Burgos would be in charge of providing transportation for all *normalistas* who would be attending the October 2 traditional protest march in Mexico City, which commemorates the 1968 massacre. That date generally marks the kick-off of an annual campaign or "days of struggle" to obtain more resources for their various schools. The mobilizations last until March.

Students Omar García and Ángel de la Cruz, along with lawyer Vidulfo Rosales of the NGO Center for Human Rights of Tlachinollan Mountain, which represents the forty-three disappeared students, as well as other *normalistas*, describe the days leading up to September 26, 2014. The year before they were also in charge of obtaining buses for the Lázaro Cárdenas del Río Normal Rural School, located in San José Tenería, in the State of Mexico: hundreds of representatives from the seventeen rural teacher training schools had gathered on that campus to travel together to Mexico City. This year it was Ayotzinapa's turn to host, provide accommodation for their colleagues in the Federation, and have the buses ready. It wasn't up for discussion—it was a task assigned by the Amilcingo assembly. On September 20 they started both projects, finding the buses and collecting funds to provide for their colleagues' stay and the trip to Mexico City.

In Ayotzinapa, the operation to commandeer busses was led by twenty-one-year-old Bernardo Flores Alcaraz, originally from Atoyac, and an embattled veteran of the process. With a round face, clear brown skin, bright eyes, short hair, and a plump figure, fellow students nicknamed him *Cochiloco* (Crazy Pig). He was in his second year and current chair of the *Comité de Lucha*, the Committee for Struggle, one of the most important roles in the Student Executive Committee, the highest governing organ of the school. *Cochiloco*'s primary job was to coordinate the taking and fueling of the buses for the protests. His polemical, even combative, spirit contrasted with his generous and friendly character. Those who knew him confirmed that he was never abusive or aggressive. He was elected to his position because his fellow students simply saw him as an ideal fit.

The standard procedure was to get the buses in Chilpancingo, which is close by and, because it's the state capital, there are more buses and more terminals for passenger lines like Estrella de Oro and Estrella Blanca. Typically, the *normalistas* travel in groups of twenty; they don't need more, since they have commandeering down to an art. They stop two buses at a time, preferably ones that are traveling the same route. The first they stop for about a half an hour, or until the second one catches up, and then they transfer the first bus's passengers onto the second bus—so they still arrive at their destination—and then continue on with the first bus and its driver.

In defense of these acts the *normalistas* argue that the government doesn't provide them with a budget allowing them to buy or rent transport for their professional necessities, and so, in order to comply with their state-required academic program, they need to take matters into their own hands.

When a bus is commandeered, the driver reports to the company that it has been taken. Usually, the company then tells the driver to stay on board to make sure that nothing happens to the bus itself. The students claim that they don't damage the buses and do take good care of the drivers, giving them whatever they want to eat, and, when they no longer need them, giving them a letter of "liberation."

Some sectors of the local community don't understand or support the students' actions, including the roadblocks they set up to collect donations, the commandeering of buses, or the theft of fuel. For decades the local and federal government took advantage of the disapproval to undermine their protests and associate the *normalistas* with organized crime.

On September 20 and 21, *Cochiloco* got lucky: he and a group of second- and third-year students were able to take a couple of buses in Chilpancingo, which alerted local and federal law enforcement. Then, on September 23, things got complicated: on board the school's only bus, some students arrived in Chilpancingo to seize more but found that the terminals were being closely guarded by state and federal police, who began to follow the students.

They changed strategy. At around 15:00, the second-year students attempted to block the Chilpancingo–Iguala high-way, close to Tierras Prietas, to take the buses they still needed, but very soon about a dozen state and federal police vehicles arrived, heavily armed and in riot gear. Student Ángel de la Cruz and lawyer Vidulfo Rosales described how the police encircled the *normalistas*, who kept them at bay with sticks and rocks. The confrontation was covered by the *Diario de Guerrero* in articles published on September 23 and 27.

The second-year *normalistas* called their third-year *compañeros* for help. The third-years had just been issued their school supplies and were still in gala uniform of black pants and white shirts. Even so, they put bandannas and ski masks on their faces and rapidly came to the rescue. With a quick maneuver they broke the police line and were even able to take two buses: two Estrella de Oros, white with green stripes, registration numbers 1568 and 1531. Federal and state police were left thwarted in the middle of the highway.

"It was kind of funny, is one way of putting it: in formal dress, but wearing bandannas, the students came and rescued us. It was the entire third-year cohort," said de la Cruz, a second-year student who survived the later attacks.

The confrontation was recorded on video by the Chilpancingo C4, where municipal, state, and federal police, as well as the Army, were all coordinated. Though in the course of my investigation I learned of the existence of these recordings, the government has worked to cover up these initial confrontations, along with the videos that reveal the various law enforcement agencies' rising level of irritation towards the students.

On September 24 the *normalistas* attempted to take more buses from the central station in Chilpancingo but found state and federal police ready with a stronger encirclement. The students returned empty-handed. *Cochiloco* had so far obtained only eight of the twenty buses he needed, the majority belonging to the Estrella de Oro line. On September 25, the day before the attack, and a day of frustration for the *normalistas*, the Estrella de Oro company filed a formal criminal complaint (BRA/SC/05/2374/2014) against the students with the state prosecutor, for their commandeering, in that year, of seven of their Mercedes Benz buses.

For the government of Guerrero headed by Aguirre Rivero, as well as for the federal government, the *normalistas* had turned from a perpetual headache into a public enemy—a target they believed they could rid themselves of with impunity.

Bullets and Torture from the Federal Police

Prior to September 26, 2014, the most brutal episode of repression experienced by the Ayotzinapa *normalistas* occurred on the morning of December 12, 2011, the same year Aguirre Rivero became governor.

As part of their annual mobilization to demand more state funds to improve their school, the students asked to meet personally with Aguirre Rivero. Around 300 *normalistas* blocked the Mexico–Acapulco highway, at the Palo Blanco toll booth. Sixty-one federal police officers, seventy-three state security officers, and thirty-four ministerial police—a total of 168 men—confronted the students. In a report on the incident compiled by the National Commission on Human Rights (CNDH), CNDH/1/2011/1/VG, the federal officers carried fifty-nine guns, the state police had six, and the ministerial police had twenty-six. The federal police launched a tear gas grenade, and simultaneously a fire started on the side where the students were.

Then the federal police began shooting, followed by the local police, killing Gabriel Echeverría and Jorge Alexis Herrera. Echeverría, twenty-one years old, and the leader of the Political and Ideological Guidance Committee, the most important political organ in the Raúl Isidro Burgos Normal Rural School, received a bullet to the neck. Herrera was shot in the head. Three other students were injured.

During and after the attack, the federal police used extreme violence to arrest students and persons not involved with the confrontation. Twenty-three people were handed over to the ministerial police, which then transferred them to facilities of the then State Attorney General's Office (now State Prosecutor's Office); another eighteen were taken directly to the Federal Police Regional Headquarters. In both locations the detainees were manhandled and beaten, and some of them were even tortured, according to the CNDH.

Student Gerardo Torres, who was detained in the State Attorney's Office facility, was tortured in an attempt to incriminate him in the murder of his two fellow students.

According to the CNDH, "Six officers . . . grabbed him and transferred him by pickup truck with his head covered under a wooden plank, they beat him and threatened to end his life if he didn't pull the trigger of a rifle. The victim explained that his aggressors forced one of his fingers onto the trigger of a gun and fired. He added that ministerial police took the discharged shells and threw them back in the place where the confrontation with the students had taken place."

In the same document, the CNDH states that the wounded were not assisted by federal police, but by civilians: "a situation that evidences not only a disinterest in aiding victims of the crime, but a fundamental lack of sensitivity and dignity on behalf of the federal police . . . whose officers not only didn't help [the victim] but threatened to harm him further if he didn't leave."

The CNDH finds in the federal police's conduct a clear tendency to criminalize the Ayotzinapa students: "The public servants from the Secretariat for Public Security, the Guerrero Secretariat of Public Security and Civil Protection, and the Guerrero Attorney General's Office, criminalized the social protests conducted by the students at the Raúl Isidro Burgos Normal School of Ayotzinapa, Guerrero, as well as other organizations, which took place on December 12, 2011, limiting their right to the freedom of peaceful assembly and, as a consequence, their right to life, security and personal integrity, legality, judicial security, personal liberty, and dignified treatment."

The then delegate to Guerrero from the Attorney General's Office, Iñaki Blanco Cabrera, should have opened an official investigation into the involvement of the federal police in the murders, but he did not. Not a single federal police officer or official was sanctioned for the murders or abuses committed against the *normalistas*. Instead, the government's rancor towards the students exploded again on September 26, 2014, in Iguala.

It's important to clarify that, for decades, the traditionally revolutionary Raúl Isidro Burgos Normal School of Ayotzinapa has been a national security concern for the Mexican government, which has been monitoring it for a long time. The students themselves are well aware that government officials infiltrate them, spy on them, and report on their actions.

In 2011, concern about how people might respond to the murders of Echeverría and Herrera was a red flag for the National Security Council (CNS), the Secretariat of National Defense, the Secretariat of the Navy, the Department of Public Security, the Secretariat of Finance and Public Credit, the Attorney General's Office (PGR), The Center for Investigation and National Security, and the National Center for Analysis, Planning, and Intelligence against Organized Crime, which alerted the PGR about investigations within its jurisdiction. "On January 25, 2012, the PGR concluded an expert's report on the case, in which several irregularities stand out, underlining the fact that the scene of the crime was not properly preserved and evidence was lost and no sodium rhodizonate tests were conducted on the ministerial officers involved," reads one confidential federal document titled "Current Special Report," dated March 2012, which was distributed to the CNS, though never publicly acknowledged.

According to the same report, which I was able to access during my investigation, "the crime scene [where Echeverría and Herrera were murdered] was tampered with, and conclusive evidence disappeared."

In February 2012, a judge issued an arrest warrant for nine Guerrero state government officials, though all of them were eventually released. Impunity reigned: none of the state or federal police who fired on the students on that December 12 were punished, nor did those who beat or tortured the *normalistas* suffer any consequences. On the contrary, such impunity encouraged the subsequent attacks against the *normalistas* and led to the promotion of Iñaki Blanco Cabrera, who, in June 2013, was named state attorney general.

"We're going to burn you alive"

On the morning of November 15, 2012, there was another act of aggression against the Ayotzinapa *normalistas*. Three students and a driver were traveling on the Acapulco–Chilpancingo highway in an Estrella Blanca bus, returning from a march (sponsored by the Raúl Isidro Burgos School) for the coming anniversary of the murders of Gabriel and Jorge Alexis. They had just dropped off a few other participants, when a number of trucks blocked their way. Six armed and masked men signaled them to stop, forcing them onto the side of the road, shooting in the air, and finally boarding the bus. They loudly reprimanded the students for participating in the march and told them to stop engaging with "vandals." If they kept on protesting, they warned them, they were going to "burn [them] alive."

They then allowed the bus to continue, following it all the way to Chilpancingo. As they were entering the city, some of the armed men who had stayed on the bus ordered the driver to turn around and head to Acapulco on the federal highway. When the driver refused, they began beating him. He lost control and rolled the bus. The driver, his wife, and the three students were all injured, with one of them left in critical condition.

After the incident, the Center for Human Rights of Tlachinollan Mountain issued a communiqué that denounced the assault as part of an escalating series of attacks against the Ayotzinapa *normalistas*. "These actions on behalf of the authorities are an attempt to delegitimize and criminalize the Normal School, positioning it in terms of illegality." The document put the blame for these actions on Governor Aguirre Rivero. The Tlachinollan Center was founded in 1994 in response to repeated abuses by the authorities, including violations of human rights and forced disappearances in the La Montaña region, principally against indigenous communities. It has supported the Ayotzinapa *normalistas* during a number of periods of aggression, such as in 2007, when the federal police violently dispersed a student demonstration against the government's bid to stop offering bachelor's degrees in primary education.

Throughout this investigation, in attempting to reconstruct the events that took place prior to the attack on and disappearance of the forty-three *normalistas*, I found that the tension between the students and the authorities (local, state, and federal), which was already high, had been escalating since they began commandeering buses for the October 2 march. To date, none of the confrontations prior to September 26, 2014 have been investigated by the State Prosecutor's Office or the Attorney General's Office. Nor were they taken into account in analyzing the tragedy of the 26th, despite the fact that what happened that night in Iguala is impossible to understand outside the context of prior events.

The Ayotzinapa Students as a National Concern

Since Enrique Peña Nieto assumed power, he and his cabinet have considered the Ayotzinapa *normalistas* a "national security priority." According to documents I was able to obtain in my investigation, these students—almost all children of impoverished peasants living in a region known for its history of resistance and political activism—have been seen by the president and his team as a direct threat.

In November 2012, during the transition between the administrations of Felipe Calderón and Peña Nieto, the advisors of both presidents met multiple times to discuss Mexico's most pressing national security issues, in terms of national stability, governability, and security. The political vice-coordinator of Peña Nieto's team was Luis Enrique Miranda, who would play a key role on that night in Iguala, and who would serve as undersecretary of the interior, later ascending to secretary of social development. Miranda had been secretary general of the interior in the State of Mexico at the time when Peña Nieto was the state governor. The two are firm friends, and Miranda is one of the cabinet members closest to the president. It's common knowledge that he is in charge of matters of political intelligence. In the framework of these meetings, Calderón's team handed over to the president-elect a classified document, dated November 2012 and titled "Priority Areas of Concern for the Start of the 2012–2018 Administration." I was able to gain access to and confirm the authenticity of this seventeen-page text.

Under the category of "priority issues," I found that the activities of criminal organizations such as the Sinaloa Cartel and its boss, Joaquín Guzmán Loera *El Chapo*—considered the most powerful drug trafficker in the world—or the bloodthirsty Los Zetas and their then leader Miguel Ángel Treviño Morales, remained unmentioned. By contrast, the situation in Guerrero, specifically the demonstrations by the students at the Raúl Isidro Burgos Normal School of Ayotzinapa, were listed second in the national security priorities.

The report was divided into five categories, ordered according to importance: first was "governability," followed by "security," "institutional strengthening," "legislative agenda," and "international agenda."

The first concern under the governability category was the situation in Michoacan state, where "illegal logging operations," the presence of organized crime in the towns of Cherán, Nahuatzen, and Paracho, as well as the high public debt of twenty-four cities, were all flagged.

The second concern was Guerrero, with the emphasis on "organized crime" causing increased violence in Acapulco, as well as in the regions of Tierra Caliente, Costa Grande, and Costa Chica.

Another issue in Guerrero were the activities of the Council of Ejidos and Communities Against the La Parota Dam, who were also fighting the Plutarco Elías Calles thermoelectric plant. Among the "governability" concerns in Guerrero was the "activism of the Ayotzinapa *normalistas*" and the persistent activities of the state's subversive groups, also listed as a national security concern. "The Revolutionary Army of the Insurgent People (ERPI), a splinter group of the Popular Revolutionary Army (EPR) remains active," the report warned.

During my investigation I discovered, and was able to document, that during the demonstrations by the Raúl Isidro Burgos Normal School of Ayotzinapa in Chilpancingo between September 20 and 25, the governments of Aguirre Rivero and Peña Nieto were closely coordinating and preparing to quickly respond to and halt the students' commandeering of buses. On the very day of September 26, hours before the armed attacks in Iguala, the *normalistas* were confronted by soldiers and state police in the state capital of Chilpancingo.

3

Ayotzinapa

August 8, 2014: a colorful parade winds through the streets of the county seat of Tixtla, Guerrero. Children and adults of all ages watch from benches: the occasion is the 232nd anniversary of the birth of one of the heroes of Mexican independence, Vicente Guerrero, who was born in this town. In the central square, on an elaborately decorated stage that seems to float above the rest of the crowd, are seated the town's politicians and their distinguished guests, one of whom wears a crisp military uniform—a common sight at these sorts of civic ceremonies.

In a video of the day's parade you can watch groups passing by while performing regional dances to live music; later, a few dancers in headdresses and loincloths move to the rhythm of the shells wrapped around their ankles, followed by others gyrating to salsa beats. A giant green cloth turtle comes down the street mounted on a wire structure carried by tall, dark young men with shaved heads, all wearing black pants and white shirts. Other young men follow, dressed in jeans and white shirts with blue-trimmed sleeves. Most of them look between eighteen and twenty-two years old. Their voices thunder through the streets, but they smile as young kids chase each other underneath the plodding turtle.

By their marching in step and their closely cropped hair you might have thought they were soldiers, or youths completing their military service, but they are first-year students at Raúl Isidro Burgos Normal School of Ayotzinapa, participating in the strict order demanded of them. As they march past the politicians they chant slogans picked up from the older students: "Sorry, people, don't mean to bother you, but this government forces us to protest!" "Not with tanks, not with guns, Ayotzi won't be silent!" "December 12 won't be forgotten, the fight is everybody's!" "Warning, warning, warning, Latin American guerrillas are marching!" "Careful, careful, careful with Guerrero state, state, state of the *guerrilleros!*"

Some of the townspeople look on nervously, while others applaud. On the stage, the master of ceremonies starts talking up the *mole* festival and other upcoming events, trying in vain to drown out the *normalistas'* chanting.

As the students stride past Tixtla's police station, they begin to direct their shouts at the uniformed officers sitting or standing next to their patrol cars: "*¡Policías trabajando y el sancho aprovechando!*" "Police at work, their wives at play!" "*Ay, policía, qué lástima me das: teniendo tú las armas, ¡no puedes protestar!*" "Hey, police, I pity you: you got the guns, but can't protest!"

The 2014–15 academic year for the Raúl Isidro Burgos Normal School commenced in July with "initiation week," in which all incoming first-year students were expected to take part. That year, almost 140 new students were beginning the program, guaranteeing at least three more years of operations for a school—among sixteen other rural teacher training institutions across the country—that the federal government had been trying to shut down for years. The freshmen must adapt quickly to the school's way of life: if they make it through the initiation week and commit to studying there, they enter into a truly unique community.

The campus is situated in a deep valley in the community of Ayotzinapa, municipality of Tixtla, where the hot Guerrero sun bakes the walls of a property resembling an old hacienda. Walking through the wide front gate, flanked by a small guard house, you enter another world: a liberated space that over the years has developed its own administration, its own rules, unique school activities, and, above all, a fraternity based on a concept of socialism that, in the rest of the world, seems bound for extinction.

The educational model of these rural training schools was first developed in 1926, when the Raúl Isidro Burgos and thirty-five similar establishments were created as part of a national program based on the concept of "student governance," with the objective of training teachers who speak Spanish without having to give up their native indigenous languages and who could teach in their own communities. During the presidency of Lázaro Cárdenas (1934–40), the normal rural schools took on a Marxist-Leninist ideology, which is maintained even today. Originally, there were thirty-six of these schools. After the 1968 student movement, President Gustavo Díaz Ordaz ordered the closing of eighteen of them.

The majority of the students come from *campesino* families for whom teaching is the only viable means of social advancement. Students can choose to study for degrees in primary education, primary education with a focus on intercultural bilingualism, or physical education.

The students at the normal rural schools are very different from the typical student attending one of the country's private or public universities: their language, their ideological training, and the way that they organize themselves into a community are unique. Accustomed to the demands of life in the countryside, most of the students adapt quickly to the demands of schoolwork. Their formal uniform consists of black pants and white shirt, though they usually wear colored t-shirts and jeans or shorts. Whether formally dressed or not, they always keep a ski mask handy or are ready to improvise to cover their faces with a bandanna or a shirt.

Inside Ayotzi, as the students affectionately call it, the walls themselves proclaim their ideology and history. One motto is attributed (perhaps apocryphally) to Che Guevara: "If I lead, follow me; if I hesitate, push me; if I am killed, avenge me; if I'm a traitor, kill me." Portraits of Lenin, Emiliano Zapata, and Subcomandante Marcos—the most widely recognized Zapatista figure, now known as Galeano—crowd the walls. The Zapatistas are a political and revolutionary group that erupted onto the national scene on January 1, 1994 in San Cristóbal de las Casas, Chiapas, reminding the federal government and all of Mexican society of its debts to the country's indigenous peoples.

These walls also express an indelible indignation at the murder of the students' comrades. The names Gabriel Echeverría and Jorge Alexis Herrera Pino are blazoned in black paint along with the query "Justice?" over two crypts. Adjacent to the crypts is painted the figure of a young man on the ground, with an evil-looking character holding a pistol to his head while a crowd of protesters—black holes in place of eyes and mouth, fists raised aloft—chant behind them.

The Ayotzi campus has classrooms, dormitories, rocky sport fields, and plots where the students grow crops whose sale supports their educational and political activities. Everything is simple and humble: the lack of resources is visible everywhere, made up for by ingenuity and hard work. In the media room, for example, the students have outfitted the television and radio recording areas by soundproofing the walls with egg cartons.

The Student Executive Committee is the highest governing body in the school, and its members change each year through an internal election, generally held in February. In September 2014, the general secretary was third-year student David Flores, aka *La Parka* (the name of a popular Mexican wrestler).

The school functions according to five basic principles: the academic, which focuses on the preparation to become teachers; the cultural, which offers instruction in dance and music; sports and physical training; agriculture, teaching students about the planting and harvesting of crops in order to sustain the school; and, last, the beating heart of Ayotzinapa—politics.

On September 26, 2014, the head of the Political and Ideological Orientation Committee was third-year student Omar García. He would survive the attacks and become one of the recognizable faces, after dozens of interviews, of the tragedy. He is brown-skinned, with a rectangular face and prominent cheekbones, strong-looking, and of medium height. I interviewed him in November 2014 at the school. Only twenty years old, he struck me, in his fortitude and his clearly articulated speech, as someone who had survived multiple battles. He wore a red shirt and camouflage pants; provocatively, he set himself next to a portrait of the school's most distinguished alumnus, the teacher turned guerrilla fighter, Lucio Cabañas Barrientos. By association, Omar was projecting himself as a *guerrillero* to an audience that included Peña Nieto's intelligence services, those who considered the *normalistas* a problem of national security.

As part of their self-governance, the committee in Ayotzinapa has taken it upon themselves to construct new buildings and establish norms about uniforms and food. "The directives [of the national Normal] administrate a few things, but they don't determine anything here," explained Omar. At the time, the director of Ayotzinapa was Luis Hernández Rivera.

The call for new students is disseminated, directly by the existing ones, from community to community. I asked Omar: "When you're inviting new students, do you explain the school system?"

"Of course," he answered. "Everybody knows what this school is about, and they know what we're fighting for. They know that the state and federal governments have tried to shut it down, and yet, at the same time, it's a good option for people like me who come from the country, people who couldn't pay for private education. Here they don't charge you for anything, tuition fees, exams, report cards . . ."

He offers an example: "Lucio Cabañas, who was also from the countryside, didn't just want to be a teacher between four walls, as the government conceived the program. Cabañas and the others didn't think it was enough, because teachers shouldn't only care about what goes on in class. A teacher needed to see what the whole community was struggling with, get involved in the issues—not ignore the kid who comes to school with rags for pants, underfed, belly bloated from hunger. We need to get involved in the issues, that's the essence of the rural normal schools."

"And is that how it works for you?"

"Sure! My elementary teacher was a *normalista* from Ayotzinapa. I wanted to be like him as soon as he started teaching me. I remember the other teachers, and, really, they didn't compare. Well, you shouldn't compare people, but you could see the difference: with him I learned to read, write, add and subtract, really fast."

Initiation Week

Staying in this school is no simple matter.

Once prospective students have passed the academic entrance exam, they have to get through "initiation week," an introduction to the way of life here: first-year students have their heads shaved and must, as part of a service requirement, work in the fields under the supervision of seniors. They are put to the *chaponeo* (weeding and field work, typically performed with machetes) as well as plowing the fields belonging to the school and to neighbors in the wider community of Ayotzinapa, with whom the *normalistas* maintain tight bonds, often referring to them as uncles and aunts. The newbies are also charged with taking care of the school's livestock. All of this unpaid work is designed to teach the students the meaning of working as a community and for the community, emphasizing that after their studies they should not abandon their people. "In this Normal we don't strip people of their identity, we root their identity," Omar García explains. The students sell the crops they harvest, especially in the Costa Chica, the Costa Grande, and the center of town. Sometimes they give away corn to local families, to their aunts and uncles, who, in times of hardship, also support the school.

During the first days of the semester, the incoming class of 2014 worked under the sun from morning to night. With shovels and hoes they planted corn and, for the Day of the Dead festivals in November, Mexican marigolds and celosia flowers. The idea was to sell the blooms to raise money for the school.

Along with training in agriculture, the students are trained politically and ideologically, reinforcing their attachment to their surroundings, as well as their contentment with what they have. The idea is to help the incoming students understand what it is the *normalistas* are fighting for, to teach them what lies behind the chants they use at protests. If possible, they also participate in protests and collect money, asking for donations in the street to cover costs for food and books.

"They give us a political education so that we can pass along what we learn to those we come in contact with down the road," Fernando Marín, a second-year student who goes by *Carrillas*, told me when we spoke at the school in August 2015. Like Omar, Fernando speaks with conviction. He's tall and lanky, with light-brown skin, a thin beard, and melancholy eyes. On his right forearm he has a thick, jagged scar from the bullet that struck him on September 26, 2014. He almost lost his arm, though it was also the arm that saved his life.

In their initiation week, the incoming students are also instructed about the conflicts between the school and the government. "The Normal has always taught us that we need to pursue the fight, always, from the first until the fourth year," Fernando said.

Ayotzi isn't for everyone. I spoke with nineteen-year-old Ángel de la Cruz in 2015. He was in his second year when the *normalistas* were attacked in Iguala. Tall, light-skinned, with a round face and a strong coastal accent, he is a survivor. His father, Felipe de la Cruz, the spokesperson for the parents of the forty-three disappeared students, also studied here and is now a schoolteacher in Acapulco. According to Ángel: "There are kids who, with enough money to study, say, 'Well, I'm not staying here. I'm not going to work in the fields if I can do something else.' They leave and study elsewhere. Those who really don't have another option for school, we stay here. Which is why most of us stay, and why the initiation week is such a really important filter."

I know of at least one student who was filtered out. Just days before the events of September 26, Francisco Javier Sebastián and his wife María Luminosa, from Apango, came to Ayotzinapa to withdraw their son, Eduardo Sebastián; they didn't like the teaching methods or the activities the students were getting involved with. Somehow, however, the name of Eduardo was put on the first list of the disappeared, which initially had over fifty students on it, and his father had to go to the prosecutor's office at the beginning of October to clarify that Eduardo hadn't been disappeared, nor was he even present during the events in Iguala. "They just made them do exercise, which aggravated my son's injured knee. They shaved their heads and took them on trips without telling the parents. And so we decided to pull him out of school," he said.

The majority of the students who, on the afternoon of September 26, went to commandeer the buses in Iguala, were first-years who had just made it through initiation week. The marigolds and celosia flowers were starting to sprout in the beds of Ayotzinapa, but some of the youths who planted them would never see the blooms.

The Mentor

Lucio Cabañas was once a first-year student himself at Ayotzinapa. Born in 1938, he began his training in 1953, when he was only fifteen years old.

According to his contemporaries, Cabañas never was a typical student: he believed strongly that the job of a schoolteacher wasn't only to impart academic knowledge, but also to raise the political consciousness of surrounding communities. What is certain is that, like the Ayotzinapa *normalistas* of today, he was viewed by the government as a security risk: a series of massacres in Guerrero perpetrated by the Army convinced him to take up arms in 1967, one year before the murder of the students in Tlatelolco.

In her illuminating investigative work, *Armed Mexico* (2011), journalist Laura Castellanos explains the significance of the Raúl Isidro Burgos Normal School of Ayotzinapa to the guerrilla movements in Mexico. The seminal moment was the brutal assassination of Rubén Jaramillo, the leader of the Agrarian Labor Party of Morelos, along with his pregnant wife, Epifanía, and their three children who were forced out of their house at gunpoint and then executed by military and federal troops on May 23, 1962, in Xochicalco. The perpetrators of that crime, committed more than five decades ago, enjoyed the same impunity as that which has prevailed in more recent massacres.

Jaramillo was a forceful young man, already battle-hardened when, at the age of fourteen, he joined the Southern Liberation Army led by Emiliano Zapata. He would become friends with ex-president Lázaro Cárdenas and come to know the leader of the Cuban revolution, Fidel Castro.

46

Cárdenas was an exceptionally progressive member of the Institutional Revolutionary Party (PRI) that governed Mexico without interruption from 1929 to 2000. It was during the term of President Adolfo López Mateos that a force of commando soldiers and police, dressed in civilian clothing, came to Jaramillo's house in Tlaquiltenango to liquidate him and his family. One of his sons, Filemón, had his mouth stuffed with dirt before he was killed. Army captain José Martínez (no relation to the captain of the same name involved on the night in Iguala) led the operation.

Following the murder, news outlets aligned with the PRI described how the "lamentably famous rebel" tried to hide behind his family when a group of "unidentified individuals" accidentally fired in their direction. Despite the hard government line, there were critics of the barbaric act. Writer Fernando Benítez wrote in the magazine *¡Siempre!* (as quoted by Castellanos in her book): "This wasn't the law of flight [a Mexican law that permitted police to shoot fleeing suspects], but an orgy of blood. It wasn't even a crime of passion, but a terrorist massacre resembling something from the Nazis or the secret Argentine army."

Though the murder of the agrarian leader was met with impunity, it inspired young activist alumni of the Raúl Isidro Burgos Normal School of Ayotzinapa, such as Genaro Vázquez Rojas, who worked alongside Jaramillo towards the end of his fight, and Lucio Cabañas. By 1960, when he was elected director of the Mexican Federation of Socialist Peasant Students—an organization that still exists in rural normal schools, including Ayotzinapa—Cabañas had become a national figure.

The Jaramillo family's murder was preceded by another killing that influenced the rebellion led by Cabañas. In 1959, the bodies of *campesinos* Roberto Bello and Isabel Durán were found on the side of the Acapulco–Zihuatanejo highway: they had been assassinated by state police acting on the orders of relatives of the then governor of Guerrero, General Raúl Caballero Aburto. A few days earlier, the Guerrero Civic Association (ACG) had been founded by Genaro Vázquez, with the purpose of denouncing abuses by the state government; Lucio Cabañas was a member, and the murder of Roberto and Isabel acted as another detonator of resistance.

Attempting to shut down the burgeoning social movements, on the morning of November 25, 1960, military officers and police besieged the University of Guerrero in Chilpancingo, where members of the ACG were conducting a sit-in. When the officers entered the grounds, they beat the protesters, leaving three of them injured and arresting another 200.

Such attacks only served to radicalize the ACG. Genaro Vázquez met with members of the Zapatista Front, along with *normalistas* led by Cabañas, in Chilpancingo: in peasant clothing, the group posed with shotguns for a photograph that was published in *La Prensa*. The armed movement, at the time, amounted to little more than that photograph, but—there being no precedents for a guerrilla movement in Mexico—the government was extremely worried.

On December 30, as the sit-in at the university continued, troops opened fire on another crowd protesting the Army's murder of a local electrician. At least thirteen people were killed, including three women and three minors. The mounting public outrage led to a shakeup of state authorities a few days later.

The year 1967 was pivotal in the life of Lucio Cabañas, hitherto reluctant to use violence in the social struggle. On

May 18, another deadly crackdown was sparked after Cabañas and his organization forced out the director of the Modesto G. Alarcón School, leaving five dead and twenty-seven wounded. According to Castellanos in *Armed Mexico*, those who were closest to Cabañas explained that until then his only weapon, kept to protect himself, was a small rock tied into his belt. Though he had been angling for a pacifist solution, in line with the Mexican Communist Party, the attack in Atoyac convinced him of the need to resort to violence to combat the violence of the state.

Consequently, Cabañas founded the political organization Party of the Poor (PDLP) and its armed wing, the Peasant Justice Brigade. With the goal of encouraging discontent towards the government, as well as raising funds, the guerrillas began conducting high-profile kidnappings, in emulation of Genaro Vázquez.

In 1968 Vázquez traveled to Mexico City to join in the student movement marches, distributing flyers calling for an armed uprising. As most of the Mexico City student movement believed in open political struggle, Castellanos explains, he found few supporters. The October 2 Tlatelolco massacre, in which between 300 and 400 students were gunned down by military and police officers, did nothing to discourage either Vázquez or Cabañas.

Red Guerrero

The federal government began conducting intense military operations in various drives to capture the two insurrectionist leaders and decimate their armed movements. In December 1970, during the presidential term of Luis Echeverría, Vázquez kidnapped businessman Donaciano Luna, a member of one of the most affluent families in Guerrero, and exchanged him for a ransom of 500,000 pesos.

The so-called Dirty War, one of the darkest periods in twentieth-century Mexico, began in 1971. The military officers charged with dismantling the two movements were Captain Mario Arturo Acosta Chaparro, Lieutenant Colonel Francisco Quirós Hermosillo, and Major General Salvador Rangel. After Vázquez died on February 2, 1972, in an apparent car accident, Cabañas continued with the uprising.

The PDLP successfully built an extensive network of urban support, especially among students, teachers, and members of popular worker movements. But the more followers they attracted, the more aggressively the government hunted them down. In August 1972, Cabañas and his group launched one of the most deadly attacks against the government, leaving eighteen soldiers dead and sixteen more wounded. Two years later they brought off their highest-profile political kidnapping—one which would alter the course of Guerrero's history—when they captured the PRI senator Rubén Figueroa Figueroa, who was campaigning to become state governor.

Figueroa was a political pragmatist. Knowing he needed the support of Cabañas to win the governorship, he invited him to dinner with promises of cash, land, and amnesty for him and his family. In Laura Castellanos's account, Cabañas emphatically rejected the offer. Nevertheless, hoping to negotiate the release of certain political prisoners and members of the Party of the Poor, he agreed to meet with the senator.

On June 2, 1974, Figueroa was scheduled to formally accept to be the PRI's candidate for governor of Guerrero. The ceremony would have taken place in Iguala, but Figueroa didn't show up. A few days earlier, on May 30, he had met with

Cabañas, who kidnapped him, along with his secretary and his nephew. The guerrilla fighter told Figueroa that he would be let go in exchange for the release of all political prisoners, as well as a package of weapons and 50 million pesos.

Three months later, on August 28, the ex-governor of Jalisco, José Guadalupe Zuno, who was also the nephew of President Echeverría, was kidnapped by the Armed Revolutionary Forces of the People (based in Jalisco state). The next day, hotel owner Margarita Saad was snatched in Acapulco. The three kidnappings hardened Echeverría's posture.

The president's nephew was released on September 7, and the following day Rubén Figueroa was rescued in a military raid. The fury of the Guerrero politician, as well as family fear of the social and political milieu that nurtured the armed uprising, would last for decades. Later Figueroas, who occupied the posts of governor, mayor, and member of congress, would continue to oppose rural radical movements. As for the government's revenge, days after Figueroa's release, Cabaña's wife, Isabel Ayala, was arrested along with other family members. They were taken to Military Camp No. 1 in Mexico City, where Ayala was tortured by Captain Acosta Chaparro.

On October 1, 250 soldiers searching for Cabañas occupied the community of El Rincón de las Parotas, bursting into homes and beating, detaining, and disappearing some of the men.

Despite the opposition's calls not to vote for Figueroa Figueroa, he won the December 1, 1974 election. The following day Lucio Cabañas was hunted down and killed in a military operation conducted by plainclothes officers. The execution of the guerrilla leader was justified by the Secretariat of National Defense (SEDENA) with reference to the kidnappings and deadly skirmishes he had been a part of. "Hidden in the mountains, [Cabañas], in cahoots with local political bosses, speculators, loggers, and drug traffickers, committed criminal acts," the official communiqué explained, intending to undermine the social rebellion.

Figueroa entered the governor's office in April 1975. His pick for director of police and transit of Acapulco was Lieutenant Colonel Acosta Chaparro, who immediately launched a brutal military crackdown against social movements in the state.

Getting rid of Cabañas, however, wasn't vengeance enough for Figueroa. In a 2003 interview published in *Proceso*, Isabel Ayala claimed that in 1976 the governor interceded to have her released from prison and then raped her.

The Dirty War lasted a decade in Guerrero, from 1971 to 1981. The fighting was waged primarily by the military, whose officers raped, sent to secret prisons, disappeared, summarily executed, and threw out of planes into the sea men, women, senior citizens, boys, and girls from *campesino* families around the state.

The Heirs

In 1993, the son of Figueroa Figueroa, Rubén Figueroa Alcocer, was elected as governor of Guerrero. His term in office, however, was cut short after yet another act of bloodshed. On June 28, 1995, state police attacked members of the Peasant Organization of the Southern Sierra as they were passing Aguas Blancas on their way to a rally to demand proof of life of a colleague, Gilberto Romero, who had been disappeared that May. Seventeen people were killed and twenty-one wounded. According to the National Commission on

Human Rights (CNDH), the governor had ordered them to be stopped from attending the political rally.

The Aguas Blancas massacre inspired the emergence of a new guerrilla movement: the Popular Revolutionary Army (EPR) which remains active today. Figueroa wasn't charged, but he was removed from office by President Zedillo. Ángel Heladio Aguirre Rivero, also from the PRI, was named as interim governor. The new administration quickly perpetrated a slaughter of its own. In June 1998, a military deployment led by General Juan Manuel Oropeza cornered and killed eleven people, including some members of the Revolutionary Army of the Insurgent People (an arm of the EPR), as well as unarmed peasants. Nobody was charged with what amounted to a summary execution.

As he wasn't elected into office, Aguirre Rivero was able to run for governor in 2010. Despite his friendship with President Peña Nieto and the secretary of the interior, Miguel Ángel Osorio Chong, he didn't run for the PRI but switched to the Party of the Democratic Revolution (PRD), and, given his political alliances, he won.

He would not, however, serve his full term. Twenty-seven days after the attacks against the students of Ayotzinapa and the disappearance of the forty-three, amid widespread protests throughout Mexico and across the world, Aguirre Rivero stepped down—to "ease social tensions," as he put it.

Decades of massacres in the name of eradicating any and all social movements in Guerrero have left the state drenched in blood. Neither victims nor victimizers forget or forgive. Isabel, the widow of Lucio Cabañas, was shot and killed in the village of Xaltianguis, near Acapulco, in 2011 as she was leaving church. Newspapers described the assassins as men dressed in civilian clothes driving a blue car.

The histories of many of the students at the Raúl Isidro Burgos Normal School of Ayotzinapa feature family members who were persecuted, imprisoned, or disappeared during or after the decade of the Dirty War. Given the current situation, as well as past conflicts, it's common for local activists, including the Ayotzinapa students, to use false names as well as nicknames. Many times they themselves don't know the real names of their classmates, but they do know that their movement is being infiltrated by intelligence and military agents. The use of false names is one reason for the initial difficulty in identifying which students were disappeared on September 26, 2014. For example, Fernando Marín, known as *Carrillas*, gave a false name when he was admitted to the emergency room in the General Hospital of Iguala after he was shot in the arm.

On the rainy early morning of September 27, when the Public Ministry's José Manuel Cuenca Salmerón arrived on the scene of the attacks against the Ayotzinapa students, he didn't pay much mind to the rocks that he found in and around the buses. Those rocks had been collected by the students who, like Lucio Cabañas before them, liked to keep them at hand in case they needed to throw something at the Goliath of the government. Indeed, among the forty-three lost students were two family members of the legendary guerrilla fighter: Cutberto Ortiz Ramos, twenty-two years old, known as *Komander*, and Bernardo Flores, or *Cochiloco*, who led the effort to commandeer the buses and had been of concern to the state and federal police, as well as to the Army, for at least six days before the attacks.

Just as the government of Echeverría did with Cabañas in the years of the Dirty War, the Peña Nieto administration attempted to blacken the character of Bernardo Flores as a

54

way of hiding the political motivations for the crimes committed on September 26. Using testimonies obtained under
torture, the PGR attempted to establish a version of events in
which Flores's poverty inspired him, along with the rest of the
students, to link up with drug traffickers and go to work for
Los Rojos (a faction of the Gulf Cartel). The tale of an attack
by the criminal organization Guerreros Unidos—enemies of
Los Rojos—against the students as the Rojos's presumed
allies, was a fabrication of the PGR. As will become apparent,
the Aguirre Rivero administration was key to constructing
this lie.

4

The First Cover-Up

The sun had broken out in Iguala. It was just after nine in the morning on September 27 when officers of the 27th Infantry Battalion, under the command of Lieutenant Jorge Ortiz Canales, reported to the Public Ministry office on Industria Petrolera Street—the same street as the Iguala C4—the discovery of a male cadaver, dressed in a red polo shirt, black jeans, and black and white tennis shoes.

The victim was lying on his back. According to the ministry report, his face was partially skinned, and an eye was found thirty-five centimeters from the body. The pants were pulled down past the buttocks, and there were clear signs that the victim had been beaten in the chest and ribs. The forensic team quickly recognized that the murder did not take place at the scene and that the body had been moved after the time of death.

The victim was recognized as being a student, and relatives identified him as Julio César Mondragón. He hadn't been taken from the Estrella de Oro bus on Juan N. Álvarez Street, nor from the other Estrella de Oro in front of the state courthouse, but had fled from the attack on the students that had occurred, after midnight, on the corner of Juan N. Álvarez and Periférico Norte.

In the autopsy it emerged that the cuts to Julio César's neck and face were made by a knife, and the bruises on the torso were inflicted with a flat, rectangular object, probably a club of some sort; but what killed him were the blows that fractured his skull. According to forensic expert Carlos Alatorre, the time of death was between 00:45 and 02:45, which meant that he was killed when the Army, the federal police, and the state police already had the city of Iguala under their control.

That same morning, Governor Aguirre Rivero, close to both President Peña Nieto and Secretary of the Interior Osorio Chong, proclaimed that he would work with all the power of the law to find the perpetrators of the attacks: "I energetically condemn the events that occurred in Iguala," he said, adding that he had already sent his officers to investigate. His true intentions, however, were different.

Later that day, in a hastily organized press conference, the state prosecutor general, Iñaki Blanco Cabrera, along with the state secretary of the interior, Jesús Martínez Garnelo, relayed their preliminary information about the case. Also present were the assistant attorney of legal affairs and human rights, Ricardo Martínez Chávez, Guerrero's health secretary, Lázaro Mazón, and the secretary of state for public security, Leonardo Vázquez Pérez. After restating the number of wounded and dead, as well as describing the steps taken so far by the government, Blanco Cabrera made the disappearances and shootings of the previous night sound like an open-and-shut case. "What we have ascertained is that there was a takeover of various buses, that the municipal police worked to stop the people involved, and they engaged in an excessive use of force," he stated. This first official declaration after the attacks relied on the conjecture that the local Iguala officers bore ultimate responsibility.

Blanco Cabrera added that, in line with the initial reports, the students took two passenger buses from the station, and were followed by Iguala police who proceeded to open fire and kill six individuals: three students, one woman who had been riding in a taxi, a member of the Avispones soccer team, and the driver of the team's bus.

He confirmed that at the Santa Teresa intersection they collected .223 caliber bullet casings, corresponding to R-15 rifles, "of the kind used by the municipal police." He deliberately omitted mentioning the other types of shells found at the scenes, making sure to place all blame for the attacks squarely on the Iguala police.

To demonstrate the efficiency of his Prosecutor's Office, Blanco Cabrera boasted that 200 municipal police officers had been disarmed that morning and, from that moment onwards, the Army and the state police would assume control of the city's security operations.

He then informed the public that fifty-seven students from the Raúl Isidro Burgos Normal School of Ayotzinapa remained missing, and that they had already begun helicopter flyovers and foot-searches to look for them. He closed with the statement that the Secretariat of Public Security, the Prosecutor's Office, the federal police, and the PGR were in Iguala to "protect its citizens."

The news quickly went viral on social networks and international news agencies. The barbarity of the murder and the face-skinning of Julio César Mondragón incited shocked protests. The *normalistas* mobilized almost immediately—a crucial factor in preventing this massacre from being just another everyday story of Mexican violence or of bloodstained Guerrero. It became instead a turning point that would mark the history of the country and reveal the true face of the Peña Nieto administration, which had already been marred by another tragedy three months previously.

In the Shadow of Tlatlaya

In the early morning of June 30, 2014, in a warehouse of the small village of San Pedro Limón, part of the municipality of Tlatlaya, in the State of Mexico, twenty-two people were extrajudicially executed: one adolescent girl and twenty-one men. The incident occurred at around 05:30, according to the Secretariat of National Defense (SEDENA). The official story was that twenty-two people were killed in a military operation conducted by the 102nd Infantry Battalion of the 22nd Military Zone, in an effort to dismantle a supposed clandestine drug laboratory. According to SEDENA, when the soldiers arrived at the location they were confronted by "a group of heavily-armed men," and, in the resulting firefight, twenty-two civilians were killed and one soldier was wounded. The Army confiscated thirty-eight weapons and 112 cartridges, and liberated three women that the armed group had "kidnapped." Confusingly, these women were subsequently detained by the Army. One week after the incident, when one of the allegedly kidnapped women was set free, the case took a different turn.

The first wave of articles repeated the claim that the attackers belonged to the criminal organization Guerreros Unidos, of which little or nothing was known. The mortuary and crime-scene analysis of the "confrontation" was conducted by Eruviel Ávila, successor of Peña Nieto as governor of the State of Mexico. Hastily, by July 1, Ávila told the press that "the Army, acting in legitimate self-defense, took care of the criminals," who he described as a band of kidnappers.

In light of the information coming out of SEDENA, the case seemed closed. Almost at once, however, a different version started to come to light. In an article published on July 3, the Associated Press questioned whether all of the alleged criminals were killed during a confrontation with the troops, noting that the facade of the warehouse displayed only six bullet holes. "The bloodstains and the bullet holes in the concrete wall, as seen by AP journalists three days after the events, call into question whether all the suspects were killed in a shootout or afterwards." The AP story reported that inside, on the warehouse walls, there were five bullet markings that followed a pattern: one or two close-together holes surrounded by blood spatter, "suggesting that some of the victims were standing against the wall and received one or two shots at about chest height."

The government responded by affirming that there were no "signs whatsoever of a possible execution": on the contrary, the "ballistic evidence" pointed conclusively to a firefight. Notwithstanding, the Ávila administration classified the twenty-two autopsies as a state secret.

On September 17, AP published the testimony of a woman who witnessed the state's execution of twenty-one people. The next day, reporter Pablo Ferri published an article in *Esquire* that confirmed the AP story; the headline was "Witness Reveals Executions in the State of Mexico."

The woman's story turned out to be very different from the official state version: only one person died in the shootout with the soldiers, while the remaining twenty-one surrendered and were then executed against the warehouse wall. The woman described the events to Ferri as follows:

"[The soldiers] told them to give themselves up, and [the men] told them not to kill them. Then [the soldiers] said, 'Not so tough anymore, you sons of bitches?' That's what the soldiers were saying when they were coming out [of the warehouse]. They all came out. They gave themselves up . . . And then they asked them their names, and they started beating them, not killing them. I told them not to do it, don't do it, and they said, 'These dogs don't deserve to live.' . . . Later they lined them up in a row and killed them . . . There was terrible wailing in the warehouse, you could hear them crying out."

Contrary to the state's version, the witness denied ever being kidnapped by the men. She specified that the soldiers shot Érika, the only minor, first in the leg, and then twice more in the chest. The soldiers used gloves to rearrange the bodies and put a few who hadn't died back up against the wall to finish them off. It was an extermination, and the state had come prepared.

Seven days before the massacre in Iguala, SEDENA issued a statement insisting that the Army had "reacted to an armed attack" in Tlatlaya. "The state is committed to seeing this incident investigated in depth, as elements of the Army and Air Force are obligated to act with total respect for the rights of the people."

Soon, however, pressure from the United Nations, Amnesty International, and the National Human Rights Center (CNDH), among other human rights organizations, forced the Peña Nieto administration to conduct a more detailed investigation. José Vivanco, director of the Human Rights Watch Americas division, confirmed the versions as told by AP and *Esquire*, stating, "We're looking at one of the worst massacres in Mexico."

"The Attorney General's Office is delving deeper into this investigation, and will provide answers on the matter," Peña Nieto evasively commented to AP on September 22. Three days later, to put a halt to press inquiries, SEDENA issued a statement: eight officers had been charged with committing the atrocity. Peña Nieto and his administration were paying the price not only for the military's abuses, but for the state's attempts to cover up the truth of what occurred in Tlatlaya.

Once the government's actions had been exposed, Secretary of the Interior Miguel Ángel Osorio Chong, on September 26, attempted to minimize the issue before Congress: "If anything did happen with regards to the conduct of officers of the Army, it would be the exception, as we have a great Army." His words would be tested only a few hours later: that same evening there would be another massacre, this time in Iguala.

Purposeful Evasion

On September 29, Prosecutor General Iñaki Blanco Cabrera offered an update to the press about the night in Iguala. He focused, once again, on the local authorities: "According to all the evidence, the municipal police fired upon three buses that were in the hands of the students, subsequently killing three of them. It's undeniable, I believe, that they employed excessive force."

However, in line with rumors that paramilitary groups attacked the students and the soccer players, Blanco Cabrera ventured that the culprits also could have been members of organized gangs. He said that some witnesses described the shooters as "people dressed in black, with hoods, riding in black trucks . . . given the calibers, we can't rule out that it could have been organized crime."

He confirmed that his staff had searched for the missing students in the 27th Infantry Battalion's base, as well as at the headquarters of the Iguala police, and found nothing.

On the same day, September 29, after two days of silence, Osorio Chong supported the state's findings: "It's hard to believe . . . the actions taken by some police officers working under the orders of the local mayor." The state and federal government had begun their campaign of attributing all responsibility for the attacks to the jeweler and mayor, José Luis Abarca, and his ambitious wife, María de los Ángeles Pineda Villa, both in the PRD opposition party

Osorio Chong reiterated that the federal government, having had no knowledge of the events while they occurred, now needed to determine "how and whence came the order, if there was an order, to meet a civil demonstration with bullets." Echoing SEDENA after the Tlatlaya massacre, he vowed that the entity most committed to finding the truth was the government.

In charge of collecting the evidence and conducting inter-views—key elements of any criminal investigation—were three men with murky pasts: Guerrero's prosecutor general, Iñaki Blanco Cabrera; the deputy prosecutor for control and procedures, Víctor León Maldonado; and the deputy prose-cutor for victim assistance, Ricardo Martínez Chávez. These three men arrived in Iguala on the night of September 26 to lead the investigation.

Dark Histories

Víctor León Maldonado has been working for various sectors of the government's justice department for more than twen-ty-seven years, all the while gaining a reputation for fabricating testimonies. Those who know him describe him as a typical bureaucrat, with little initiative of his own but always willing to obey his superiors, with whom, thanks to his subservience, he was able to develop good relations. From 1987 to 2008 he worked in the Deputy Prosecutor's Office of Preliminary Investigations, part of the Attorney General's Office of the Federal District (Mexico City). In 2008 he worked as an advisor to the PGR and, on November 1 of the same year, was named coordinator general for Marisela Morales, the head of the Specialized Investigations on Organized Crime (SIEDO; after 2012, SEIDO) unit of the Attorney General's Office. According to information from the Secretariat of Public Affairs, León Maldonado and Morales had worked together for four years in the Mexico City department until, in 1997, Morales transferred to the Attorney General's Office, where she rose quickly and somewhat controversially through the ranks.

"The *maestra* brought me in, and I'm indebted to her for that," León Maldonado would often say about his time in SIEDO, making clear where his loyalties lay. He would also speak openly about the generous salary and perks that came with working in government.

Two of the most scandalous cases of fabrication and case manipulation during the Calderón administration took place in 2008 and 2009, when Morales was the director and León Maldonado the coordinator of SIEDO. In 2008, in concert with other colleague, Maldonado mounted a case ("Operation Cleanup") against federal public servants, including former SIEDO Director Noé Ramírez Mandujano and Federal Police Commissioner Javier Herrera Valles, both accused of working for the Beltrán-Leyva cartel. After four years in prison, Ramírez Mandujano and Herrera Valles, among other prisoners, were released when it was discovered that protected witnesses had been used to bring false charges against them.

The following year León Maldonado, now SIEDO coordinator, repeated the same formula he used in Operation Cleanup. Two months before federal midterm elections, in an elaborate police sweep, the PGR arrested more than thirty officials in the state of Michoacan, whose governor, Leonel Godoy, belonged to the PRD. The arrest of eleven mayors, several police chiefs, a judge, and other state officials including the deputy attorney general, Ignacio Mendoza (all of whom were accused of having ties to drug cartels, principally the Knights Templar) was widely hailed in the press. The case became known as the "Michoacanazo" and was meant to damage the image of the PRD and boost Calderón's rightist National Action Party. However, the results backfired, both electorally and legally. Just one year later all of the detainees had been set free, and the accusations of links to organized crime were proved false. Moreover, the witnesses used by Maldonado to bring charges against the PRD officials were found to have received money or other benefits from SIEDO in exchange for testifying. "Victor León Maldonado interrogated me himself when I was brought in and arrested. He was directly in charge of the investigation," Ignacio Mendoza told me. The deputy attorney general of Michoacan was released in September 2010, and his conviction was rescinded.

In January 2010, Iñaki Blanco Cabrera, who had worked in the PGR in 2001, was offered a job in its SIEDO organized crime unit by Marisela Morales. He entered the agency (where he also got to know León Maldonado) as coordinator general and later came to specialize in kidnappings. Those who knew Blanco Cabrera during his time at SIEDO described him as a neutral official who tolerated significant abuses of power. He readily endorsed sentences handed down to manufactured suspects before his time, meaning that he kept innocent people in jail. Such was the case of Florence Cassez, the French citizen who, in 2005, was falsely accused of kidnapping; the testimonies of her supposed victims had been fabricated. Blanco Cabrera was working in the PGR when he confirmed that he had "evidence and proof" of Cassez's crimes. In 2013, the Mexican Supreme Court ordered Cassez's immediate release for violations of her due process rights.

In his position as anti-kidnapping prosecutor, Blanco Cabrera served the interests of a so-called human rights campaigner, María Isabel Miranda Torres, to bolster the case of the alleged kidnapping and murder of her son, Hugo Alberto, with false evidence and forged documents, as well as testimonies obtained under torture. The prosecutor even planted evidence at the crime scene and forged a birth certificate for Hugo Alberto that registered him as the biological son of José Enrique Wallace, when his actual father was Jacinto Miranda Jaimez, a crucial fact for the solving of the case.

In December 2010, Juan Jacobo Tagle was arrested in the State of Mexico, accused of homicide, and forced to testify against himself and his accomplices. During his arrest and torture, as Tagle later told a judge and the National Commission on Human Rights, María Isabel Miranda Torres, who currently heads the Stop the Kidnappings NGO, was present.

By concocting evidence and false testimonies, the anti-kidnapping prosecutor also arrested and imprisoned Brenda Quevedo Cruz, Juana Hilda Lomelín, and César Freyre, as well as Alberto and Tony Castillo.

On January 1, 2011, a new official joined the Assistant Attorney General's Office: Ricardo Martínez Chávez, who had worked as a personal attorney for Miranda Torres. He had also worked for the Mexico City justice department between 2000 and 2001, a period overlapping León Maldonado's tenure. His stint in the PGR was brief, but he was able to form a relationship with Blanco Cabrera when the latter was representing Miranda Torres in the case concerning her child.

Marisela Morales and her accomplices left a legacy of corruption and abuses at SIEDO, though neither she nor members of her team were ever sanctioned. On the contrary, President Calderón named her attorney general of the republic in 2011. Four months later she tapped Blanco Cabrera as PGR delegate in Guerrero—a position he held at the time of the first attacks against the Ayotzinapa *normalistas* on the Mexico–Acapulco highway on December 12, 2011, when Gabriel Echeverría and Jorge Alexis Herrera were murdered. Blanco Cabrera, along with his boss Morales, were cognizant of all the abuses committed by Guerrero officials and federal police against the *normalistas*: so much is evident from the March 2012 document, "Current Special Topics," delivered to the National Security Council. Those officials and police, however, remained untouched.

The favor would be returned. In June 2012, Blanco Cabrera was invited by Aguirre Rivero to form part of his administration, first as undersecretary of government for legal affairs and human rights, then as deputy attorney of regional control and legal proceedings, and finally, in June 2013, as state attorney general. In his new post, he would invite his old pals from SIEDO, Víctor León Maldonado and Ricardo Martínez Chávez, to complete the trio that would turn out to be so disastrous for the state's administration of justice.

In 2013 Martínez Chávez left his job at the Attorney General's Office to work as a lawyer for Alejandro Iglesias Rebollo, businessman and owner of a chain of strip clubs, as well as the discotheque Lobohombo, the site in 2000 of a fire that left twenty-two people dead. In July 2013, as ordered by the capital city's attorney general, Mexico City police and federal police raided Iglesias Rebollo's strip club, Cadillac, where they discovered a network of sex trafficking and exploitation of Mexican and foreign women, including minors. As reported by the journalist Sanjuana Martínez, writing for the online *SinEmbargo*, horrors went on in this club: gang rapes (occasionally perpetrated by politicians, police, or business owners), forced sex with other employees, even murder.

As Iglesias Rebollo's attorney, Martínez Chávez was accused of threatening forty-six women who had been forced to work at the bar, so they would retract their testimonies about the abuse they had suffered (*Excélsior*, July 9, 2013). Of these forty-six women rescued, only seventeen testified that they were sexually exploited, and they would later retract their statements after receiving his threats. The city prosecutor, Rodolfo Ríos Garza, later even confirmed the threats, but, as none of the victims dared to denounce them, neither Martínez Chávez nor the owner of the Cadillac club were ever charged.

First Responders

The first officials to arrive at the scene of the crime on September 26, 2014, were Blanco Cabrera, León Maldonado, and Martínez Chávez. From the beginning, the trio would skew the investigation, hiding key information, and, as in their old days, tampering with evidence. One month later, on October 29, each one would make a statement to the Attorney General's Office, to form part of criminal case file 1/2015-II.

Víctor León Maldonado claimed that he was the first official from the State Prosecutor's Office to arrive in Iguala. Between 23:00 and 23:30 he was informed that "there were a few injured people, likely students from the Raúl Isidro Burgos Normal School of Ayotzinapa." He added that "given the magnitude of the events, and as we didn't yet know what had happened, we followed instructions from the attorney general and went to Iguala."

When he reached the Santa Teresa turn-off, he saw a bus crashed into a tree in a ditch, with nobody around and all the lights off. "As I was traveling with only two other officials, I did not think it prudent to stop in that location." According to his timeline, that bus had just come under attack.

Some twenty meters further on, the statement continued, he saw two federal police vehicles and a taxi with its doors open. After identifying himself, he asked the federals what had happened, and their response, according to him, was vague: "They informed me that they didn't know, but that it appeared as if various persons had shot at the taxi and killed a woman." As he was talking to the officers, two Army vehicles drove up, and he directed them to the bus in the ditch.

Some people now emerged from the bus, explaining that they were a soccer team and that there were some casualties still on board. They said that "a big group of masked men had stopped them and started shooting . . . I remember they said [the shooters] desisted after they yelled that they were soccer players." León Maldonado then called 066 for an ambulance.

"The federal police and soldiers explained to us," Maldonado testified, "that there had been shootouts on a number of different streets in Iguala." Coming into the city he searched the streets and, on Periférico Norte, encountered two dead bodies and three passenger buses riddled with bullet holes. A group who said they were students at the Raúl Isidro Burgos school told him that "they had been assaulted by local police officers, and some of their classmates, trying to protect themselves, had run away and hidden." Only then, according to his testimony, "the area was cordoned off and the necessary steps were taken to preserve the scene of the attack, evidence was collected, and the bodies were taken away." Which is to say, León Maldonado was present when the Public Ministry investigator, Cuenca Salmerón, conducted his flawed initial investigation.

According to León Maldonado, it was ministerial police officers who looked for the hidden students, finding thirty of them.

While Blanco Cabrera ordered Martínez Chávez to go to the Iguala police station, León Maldonado coordinated the interviewing of the Avispones team and the wounded who had been taken to the General Hospital. "I realized that some of the local police officers, the same ones who had been disarmed, had been taken to the state police station." He confirmed that a few of the students identified a number of policemen in photographs: "If I remember correctly, there were six *normalistas* who recognized nineteen officers." According to León Maldonado, Blanco Cabrera then ordered him: "Start making arrests immediately, Víctor. I don't want any mistakes."

The situation was getting tense in the state-run Regional

Police Training Center (CRAPOL): "The police were very aggressive," Maldonado reported, and there were people outside calling loudly for the detained local police officers to be released.

The person responsible for opening the preliminary inquiry was the ministry official, who along with Jesús Villalobos, an advisor from the Prosecutor's Office, filled out the charge sheet.

"In the course of doing my job," Villalobos stated, "I began to realize that there were criminal elements, including Los Rojos and the Guerreros Unidos, working inside state territory."

For his part, as Deputy Prosecutor Ricardo Martínez Chávez stated in his official statement to the PGR, Blanco Cabrera called him at 23:00 to report "disturbances in Iguala, [but] that the details were unclear." In reality, however, Blanco Cabrera already knew, courtesy of the Center for Investigation and National Security (CISEN), a great deal more about what was happening.

Martínez Chávez called the regional prosecutor, Marco Antonio Vázquez Flores, who told him that he'd heard "that some of the Ayotzinapa students had shot at the police, and the police had returned fire, but so far it was a rumor, as no formal denunciation had been received, nor did he know of any casualties in the hospitals." But either Martínez Chávez or Vázquez Flores was lying, as the Regional Prosecutor's Office had in fact opened a preliminary inquiry at 23:00, after getting reports of casualties at the Jorge Soberón Acevedo General Hospital.

"I remember that there was a downpour that night," Martínez Chávez recalled. "About two kilometers before Iguala we saw a lot of flashing lights from federal police vehicles, and one of my guards told me that the other deputy prosecutor was there, and a bus."

They stopped in the same place where León Maldonado had called for the ambulances. "I saw Army troops and a bunch of kids getting soaked, some of them crying. I remember one of them started to go towards the bus, which was about five meters away, but a soldier yelled at him, 'Don't move!'"

"And I think," Martínez Chávez declared, "because I saw the buses, that they had been mistaken for the *ayotzinapos*."

A witness helping the Public Ministry who was with Martínez Chávez on that night confirmed that when they arrived at the Santa Teresa turn-off, at 00:40, they saw the crashed Avispones bus and a few minors standing in the road, along with some soldiers, federal police officers, and Deputy Prosecutor León Maldonado. "It was raining and neither the soldiers nor the federal police had offered any help [to the victims]," the witness declared to the PGR, on the same day that the three prosecutors also filed their testimony to the Attorney General's Office.

Martínez Chávez described how he took almost all of the Avispones players to the Iguala Prosecutor's Office in his and his guards' vehicles. Since only one ministry staff member and two police officers were there, they put out a call for further personnel to help take statements from the players and their families.

Blanco Cabrera later phoned Martínez Chávez to give instructions: "They're telling me that municipal police were involved. If we don't collect evidence quickly, we're not going to be able to charge the likely culprits. Figure out how to do the Harrison tests [for gunpowder residue on clothing], ballistic comparison, and get them to hand in their weapons."

"You want me to disarm them?" Martínez Chávez asked.

"This is no joke," Blanco Cabrera responded.

Next, regional prosecutor Vázquez Flores called the Iguala secretary of public security—or local chief of police—Felipe Flores Velázquez, and asked him to present himself within five minutes. Flores Velázquez, far from running away, immediately went to see the prosecutor.

Asked why he didn't arrest Flores, Martínez explained: "There were no denunciations, no direct witnesses to the crime . . . he wasn't caught in the act, and there was no expert evidence to tell us what had happened. Let me be clear, we didn't have it then and didn't have it for the next few hours."

"What happened?" Martínez Chávez asked the chief.

"I know that some *ayotzinapos* came, there was an incident in the town center, according to a report from the mayor's wife, there were shots fired, and I know that there was a chase but I'm not aware of exactly what occurred, and at the moment I don't have any official reports nor have I gotten on the radio to find out what exactly happened," Flores responded.

"There are two kids from the Avispones team dead in the road and I think, by what you're telling me, that it could have been the local police [who killed them]," Martínez Chávez said.

"Which officers?"

"Maybe you know them. I don't."

"What do you suggest?" Flores Velázquez asked, sounding eager to cooperate.

"That all of them, including you, voluntarily present yourselves for ballistic tests of your weapons, for the Harrison test, and everything else necessary to figure out who is responsible."

Flores Velázquez said: "Allow me to submit my weapon as the first piece of evidence."

Martínez Chávez refused, saying that all the weapons should be given up at the same time. Nonetheless, Flores took out his pistol, removed the cartridge, and handed it over to one of the prosecutor's guards.

As the majority of the weapons of the Iguala police were at their station, that's where they headed next. It was well past midnight when they arrived and called in the local officers, about ten of them.

"Please," Flores instructed his officers, "obey the deputy prosecutor."

As Martínez Chávez later stated, "Their chief asked them to voluntarily hand over their weapons as evidence and [informed them] that they will be taking tests to determine responsibility."

The policemen removed their cartridges and placed their weapons on a table before the deputy, his five bodyguards and a Ministry official. Given that they outnumbered the officials, they could have refused the request or even challenged Martínez Chávez, but they didn't, showing themselves willing to be investigated. Remarking that the local police station didn't have space for all the officers to come at once to hand over their arms, it was Flores himself who suggested they do so at the federal police base, located in the center of Iguala.

Martínez Chávez left to check on a report of injured parties arriving at the Security and Social Services Institute for State Workers Hospital. Meanwhile, state ministerial police officers remained at the police station with Flores Velázquez, who was busy collecting his officers' files noting their respective vehicles and weapons.

When Martínez Chávez was in the hospital, he received a call from Vázquez Flores: "He told me there were reports of gunfire fatalities on Periférico Norte and had me move to that location, where I saw soldiers and journalists standing around a bus, a passenger bus if I remember right, and I saw that some people were talking to the journalists and I could see, from a distance, Mr. Víctor León, who is the other deputy prosecutor." Student David Flores Maldonado approached him, saying he was one of the organizers of the Committee for Struggle of the Ayotzinapa Normal School. "I later found out they called him *La Parka*, weird nickname for a student leader," Martínez Chávez said. (*La Parka* is the name of a popular Mexican wrestler; spelled La Parca, it's a name for the figure of Death.) "He told me there were two fatalities on the left side of the road and his van and some other vehicles, and that there were three buses that had been the target of two outbreaks of violence in that location . . . He wasn't involved in the first, but was in the second, and wanted to see if the bodies belonged to his friends. I told him that this was a crime scene, that he couldn't get closer because he might disturb the evidence, but that he could look from a distance, which he did and told me at first that he didn't know them. Then he went straight to the press and started telling them that those were Ayotzinapa students and that they had been killed by local police."

Martínez Chávez added: "*La Parka* told me at that time that he had audio recordings of what had happened, and video, and that he had the numbers of the police vehicles that were involved, they were written on his hand, and he told them to me, I might be forgetting, but they were 17, 18, 20, I think, 26, 28, and 302. But he told me that some of his classmates had been taken to the police station . . . I told him that I had just come from there and I hadn't seen anyone."

The student leader said that he intended to give a statement and asked for help finding his classmates who had hidden themselves after the shooting. Martínez Chávez let him go with one other student and a woman to conduct the search. "The three of them, in the rain, were calling out for their classmates. We found a few of them on the roof of a house." Other survivors were found at two other private residences and in an Oxxo convenience store.

La Parka then asked to go to "the battalion," and the deputy prosecutor took him to Iguala's municipal police station. Outside were officers of the Special Immediate Reaction Team (similar to a SWAT team). "I asked what they were doing and they told me they had been sent to guard me. I asked if anybody had come in or out of the station since they had been there, and they said that nobody had," Martínez Chávez explained.

Felipe Flores Velázquez, the police chief, told him that they weren't letting any local officers into the federal police base, so Blanco Cabrera ordered him to take the officers to CRAPOL and run the tests there, Martínez Chávez said, "to avoid a fight with the victims of the crime, who are notoriously aggressive." Along with *La Parka* and another classmate, he checked the jail cells. "We didn't see anybody."

The jail magistrate, Ulises Bernabé García, "told us that nobody had come in, and so I asked *La Parka* if he was sure [that there were students who were detained] and he told me one of his friends was [sure]. I asked the Public Ministry officer and the regional delegate of the ministerial police if they had seen anyone enter or leave, and they said they hadn't."

By the time Martínez Chávez returned to the regional prosecutor's headquarters, family members of the Avispones and the *normalistas* had arrived, along with some of their teachers, investigators, Public Ministry officials, and State Prosecutor General Blanco Cabrera. When Martínez Chávez tried to convince some of the students to make statements, "they started chanting slogans as if it were a demonstration, saying that they were venting their anger. One of them, I don't know who it was, said that they had been preparing themselves for this for years."

Blanco Cabrera then went to the state police base and ordered the deputy prosecutor to come as well. All this time, the Iguala police chief, Felipe Flores, was waiting for orders in front of the prosecutor's office. He asked Martínez Chávez if, since he didn't have a vehicle, he would give him a lift so he could ask his officers for their weapons for testing by the Public Ministry. Flores suggested getting the officers of both shifts to convene at the police training center, CRAPOL.

When they got to CRAPOL there were already some local police officers standing outside. Flores proceeded to take their weapons. "They were all lining up to give up their weapons to the chief who would put them at the disposal of the Public Ministry," Martínez Chávez stated. The investigators took photographs and fingerprints, and conducted Harrison tests on the officers, who voluntarily obeyed all orders.

The photographs were sent to the state prosecutor's office and, that afternoon, a number of them were identified as participants in the attacks against the *normalistas*. "That's to say, of the approximately 150 photos, nineteen officers were identified, and there were [student] declarations that they had been involved . . . By the afternoon of September 27, we already had twenty-two people identified as probable suspects." They began interviewing the officers, including their chief of police.

Outside of the CRAPOL offices, microbus drivers were congregating, as well as nearly 300 people yelling that they weren't going to let them take away the police officers. The officers, according to Martínez Chávez, joined in the chorus. This was his justification for detaining twenty-two officers— nineteen of them supposedly identified by students, and three more who had allegedly occupied vehicles present during the attacks.

According to Martínez Chávez, Felipe Flores Velázquez and other officers went running out of the building and were "welcomed like heroes by the 300 people who had gathered . . . and these officers started surrounding us outside the center, and I even saw some of them try to get in the helicopter that the secretary of public security [Leonardo Vázquez Pérez] was departing in." In light of these supposed threats, the state police transferred the first twenty-two suspects, suspected of killing two students, to Acapulco.

Flores Velázquez, the Iguala police chief, was summoned to give another ministerial statement the following day. "At the moment of his [initial] declaration there was no evidence against him for these events," Martínez Chávez stated. "Up until that moment I thought we'd done what we needed to do, but then the mess of the disappeared fifty-seven people started coming out, and [people saying] that the Army, the federal and local police had taken them, and that was when the formal charges were filed with the names of those who had allegedly been disappeared, [a number] which came down to forty-three." For Martínez Chávez, from the beginning, the attacks were committed by the Guerreros Unidos gang.

Iñaki Blanco Cabrera, meanwhile, was quite terse in his own statement of the events of September 26 and 27. The state prosecutor general confirmed that after 23:00 on the 26th, as he was arriving at his home in Mexico City, he was notified of a shootout in Iguala, in which it seemed that Ayotzinapa students were involved. It's worth pointing out that this is not what he told his two deputies when he ordered them to go to Iguala. According to his statement, the information came to him from his personal secretary, Cándido Joel Zamudio, then from the state secretary of Public Security, Leonardo Vázquez Pérez, and finally from Ernesto Aguirre Gutiérrez, assistant to Governor Aguirre, who passed along the governor's order to go to Iguala. "I communicated with the CISEN delegate in Guerrero, José Miguel Espinosa Pérez, who informed me that he had evidence that was pointing to the fact that there had been a confrontation in Iguala." Blanco Cabrera ordered his secretary to find out more about the incident and to get in touch with the regional prosecutor and the director of the investigative ministerial police. He also personally ordered León Maldonado and Martínez Chávez to go to Iguala.

Blanco Cabrera said that he arrived at the city between 01:30 and 02:00 on the morning of September 27. In the state prosecutor's office he spoke with the two deputy prosecutors and the state prosecutor, who informed him that students from Ayotzinapa had come to Iguala to ask for donations and commandeer passenger buses, with the intention of traveling to the October 2 memorial demonstration. He ordered them to follow investigative procedures, collect the evidence, and conduct all the necessary tests. Later that morning he ordered as many local Iguala police as possible to be taken to the state police headquarters.

Between 07:00 and 08:00 Ernesto Aguirre Gutiérrez, the governor's external counsel (to whom Blanco Cabrera had given a report, and who then passed it on to the governor), showed up. Later, along with the secretary general of government, Jesús Martínez Garnelo, and other officials, they would hold a press conference describing the attacks and placing all the blame on the local Iguala police.

The secretary of public security in Guerrero, Leonardo Vázquez Pérez, would later tell a different story, however, undermining the version offered by the deputy prosecutors and their boss, Blanco Cabrera. In his first declaration to the Attorney General's Office, on October 21, 2014, he affirmed that at 22:00 he received a call from his man in charge of state police, undersecretary Juan José Gatica Martínez, who informed him that there were reports of shootings in Iguala.

In sum, Vázquez Pérez told the PGR, the undersecretary "was informed by C4 that . . . there were civilians wounded, and that the coordinator [of the state police's north base, José Adame Bautista] had gone to the General Hospital in Iguala, where he found that the wounded were civilians, apparently students from the Ayotzinapa Normal Rural School, who informed him that their attackers were . . . from the local Iguala police."

Vázquez Pérez said that he ordered "the injured in the hospital to be protected and watched over." He later spoke directly to Adame, who corroborated the information and told him that he was at the hospital, where security was already being provided to the injured students.

The chief of public security in Guerrero added that he reached Iguala at two in the morning on September 27 and met with Blanco Cabrera at the regional prosecutor's office. Soon afterwards, Ayotzinapa students and members of the Avispones arrived. "Given the circumstances," he said, "we ordered immediate coordination with the Mexican Army with the intention of securing the entrances and exits of the city and taking control of Iguala's security."

According to Vázquez Pérez, State Prosecutor General Blanco Cabrera first ordered the local police officers to gather at the base of the 27th and 41st Infantry Battalions, but the army refused to have them, and they were redirected to the CRAPOL training facility in the Tuxpan neighborhood. Vázquez Pérez claimed that he, and not Vázquez Flores, called police chief Flores Velázquez, ordering him to bring all of his officers, vehicles, and weapons to CRAPOL. He also said that it was he who accompanied the students in the search for their *compañeros* who had fled and hidden after the attack. "The result of the patrol and search," he specified, "was the discovery of around thirty students who had dispersed. From that moment we focused on patrols in collaboration with the Mexican Army, watching over the entrances and exits to the city."

He confirmed that as of September 27, Iguala was divided into six security areas—four controlled by SEDENA and SEMAR, and two more by state police.

In his second testimony, on October 29, Vázquez Pérez reported some of these events differently: he claimed that local police officers came to CRAPOL at four in the morning and that state prosecutor staff took control of their weapons and vehicles. "Our state-level department had no contact with the local police, but I saw Felipe Flores there with people from the Prosecutor's Office."

According to Vázquez Pérez, all of this happened while he was coordinating "the operations searching for the disappeared students" with the commanding officer of the 35th Military Zone, Brigadier General Alejandro Saavedra Hernández. In reality, however, at that time no reports of missing students even existed.

Secretary Vázquez Pérez then left CRAPOL to coordinate with other security agencies. His testimony contains nothing about the alleged threatening behavior of the municipal police and their families or the alleged attempt to board the departing helicopter. None of it had happened.

Speaking to the PGR, Vázquez distanced himself from all the denunciations received through emergency numbers 066 and 089: "I had no direct knowledge of [them]. I only was generally aware of their existence." He confirmed that the agency responsible was the State Security Council, whose director, Porfirio Fabián Hernández Catalán, "is the person with access to that information." He also ducked any responsibility for the C4 security cameras, indicating that the Telecommunications Directorate maintains the technical aspects, while the State Security Council decides if the video content is to be handed over to other agencies: "In regards to videos from the C4 security cameras, from September 26, 2014 in the cities of Iguala and Cocula, I don't have access to or knowledge of such videos. I am not aware if they were handed over or not to the state prosecutor of Guerrero or to another agency, as this is not within my purview, but in that of the State Security Council."

This footage from the Iguala C4, showing that officers from all the security agencies at the local, state, and federal level were present, is evidence that would be crucial to uncovering the truth of what took place during the attacks and, above all, to determining who disappeared the forty-three students and in what direction they were taken.

On the morning of September 27, the state of Guerrero's ministerial police coordinator, José Luis Vega Nájera, went to the Iguala C4, which is located only a few blocks from the double crime scene in Juan N. Álvarez Street. On the premises were state police officers, telephone operators handling emergency calls, and officers from the 27th Infantry Battalion, in charge of CCTV the previous night.

Vega Nájera took possession of five videos that had been recorded from four security cameras in different locations. He copied the videos onto CDs, packed the CDs, and took them to the Guerrero Public Security base in Iguala. This is according to the chain of custody document, part of file HID/SC/02/0993/2014 of the preliminary investigation.

Vega Nájera joined the Guerrero ministerial (investigative) police a few days before the attacks. For fifteen years he had been deputy commander of the State of Mexico's corrupt Judicial Police, where, between February and early September 2014, he ran the Special Prosecutor's Office on Kidnappings. And though many other police chiefs left their positions after the events in Iguala, he remains in Guerrero's Prosecutor's Office.

One of the five videos he copied was particularly important: a recording from a camera located on Periférico Poniente, in the Esmeralda neighborhood. Though the cameras record twenty-four hours a day, there is a suspicious gap of just over one minute edited out from this footage. The rest of the footage from that night was permanently deleted, a critical lacuna that serves to both hide the truth and allow the government to fabricate a false version of events.

The video, labeled "26-09-2014 11-9-32 p.m., police officers transferring detainees," has been buried by the governor of Guerrero and the Attorney General's Office. Only the segments that happened to correspond to the state and federal versions of events, taking up mere seconds of tape, have been released. In the course of my investigation, however, I gained access to five videos, which, taken together, show a different chain of events.

The Convoy of Death

At 23:19 on September 26 in Iguala, at least thirteen vehicles drove rapidly down the empty West Benito Juárez Avenue, also known as Periférico Poniente. They drove through the neighborhoods of Emiliano Zapata, Esmeralda, Bugambilias, and Villa de Guadalupe, passing in front of the camera in fifty-one seconds. A few blocks later, on Juan N. Álvarez Street, one of the attacks had just occurred: at 23:15, at least twenty of the forty-three *normalistas* were disappeared.

Three of the vehicles in the convoy, from what you can make out in the video, resemble Iguala local police vehicles. In one of them, in the rear bed, are at least six civilians who are, according to the state and federal governments, among the disappeared forty-three.

And yet, contrary to claims made by the federal and Guerrero state officials, officers of the local Iguala police weren't acting alone in the attack against the students; they were part of a larger operation. The vehicles in this convoy look similar to the trucks that, according to survivors' testimonies, were used in the attacks.

The vehicles come from the direction of the scene of the attacks, on Juan N. Álvarez and Periférico Norte, not far from the C4 offices, and are heading towards Ciudad Altamirano, Teloloapan, and Cocula.

In the shorter video you can see that a dark SUV leads the convoy and another dark SUV makes up the tail. The first SUV contains at least two people in similarly colored clothing, resembling a uniform. You can't tell if there is anybody else in the vehicle.

I talked to witnesses who described seeing men in similar SUVs who seemed to be part of the military and who were present while the first shots were fired against the students. These same men, in these same trucks, were later seen after midnight, pursuing students after the second attack.

Directly following the first dark SUV are three trucks similar to those used by the Iguala police: in the first, three uniformed men are riding in the bed of the truck; in the second, there are at least six civilians in postures of submission, guarded by two or three uniformed men; and in the third, uniformed men can be seen riding in the back. The first and third truck bear the same markings and symbols, while the second—where the civilians are riding—though similar in model to the other two, has a different paint job on the roof and could be a vehicle made to look like a police vehicle.

Next comes a white pickup truck, followed closely by a motorcycle. Though markings and shields can't be seen in the video, the pickup looks like an Iguala ministerial police vehicle. Student survivors said that as they fled their attackers, four men in civilian clothing got out of a white ministerial police truck and shot at them.

Another vehicle in the convoy, a dark sedan with a mounted machine gun and a shield on the trunk, seems to be guarding a white tow truck, without visible markings, towing another dark sedan. Following the tow truck is another dark sedan with no markings. Last in the convoy is a motorcycle riding close to the second dark SUV. After the convoy passes, the street is deserted. Seconds later, the video ends.

Surviving student witnesses said that they saw men on motorcycles watching them throughout the night. One of the students said that the motorcyclists were armed.

At one moment in the video, the C4-controlled camera suddenly moves: while the convoy is still passing, the camera points to the sky. When it points back down to the street the images have changed from color to black-and-white, which makes it more difficult to distinguish both the trucks and their drivers, now lost in the darkness. Nothing is known of any students who were in the bed of the pickup that was part of the convoy.

After Vega Nájera recovered the videos from the C4, that same morning of September 27, ministry prosecutor Ángel Cuevas Aparicio asked investigator Adriana Salas Domínguez to analyze only one segment of video, "to extract the sequence of images where you see the three trucks with roof lights driving down the street at 11:19:34 p.m." Following orders, Salas Domínguez edited out a section of video in which you could see three presumed local police trucks.

Salas Domínguez took eight stills from the video, which the prosecutor's office used to support their investigation and incriminate the local officers and the mayor of Iguala, José Luis Abarca. At the same time, the presence of the SUVs and other vehicles used to disappear the students was concealed—even though, in their first declarations on the morning of September 27, surviving students described the vehicles that had taken part in the attack against them as having identical characteristics to those that can be seen in the uncut video of the convoy.

Reviewing the ministerial declarations made by the twenty-two policemen detained in the CRAPOL training facility, it's clear that they were shown a few seconds of the video in which the three police vehicles appeared, but, tendentiously, were never shown the whole minute-long sequence of the full convoy.

As part of preliminary investigation PGR/SEIDO/UEDI MS/87/2014, the SEIDO (previously SIEDO, the PGR's organized crime unit) sent the Guerrero prosecutor an official letter, dated October 29, 2014, requesting a "copy of the public street security camera recordings [from C4] for the days 26 and 27 of September of the year 2014 in the city of Iguala de la Independencia, concerning the events related to the disappearance of [the students of] Ayotzinapa." Almost a month after the events, the SEIDO had barely begun collecting information on the case.

On October 31 the Prosecutor's Office delivered the five videos, on a USB memory stick, to the SEIDO, but the PGR never conducted an analysis or investigated the convoy. The parts of the case file that were released to the public only contained reference to the expert opinion of the governor's office on the five videos, with the federal prosecutor censoring the images.

Not until November 12 did SEIDO send experts in computer science and forensic video to the Iguala C4 to review the recordings taken on September 26 and 27—and yet the C4 had been under control of the Gendarmerie Division of the federal police since September 29. When the experts arrived at C4 headquarters, they were told that all the videos recorded on that night had been erased.

On November 13, SEIDO again asked the governor's office for the C4 videos. The following day, the director general of the State System of Police Information (SEIPOL) responded that the videos from those dates had been erased because the system is set up to delete the recordings after seven days. "And yet I must inform you that the recordings from the 26th and 27th of September were handed over to the official from the Federal Public Ministry," according to a letter made public by SEIPOL.

According to the testimony provided to the PGR by troops of the 27th Infantry Battalion, which I was able to obtain, on the night of the attacks in Iguala it was military personnel who were in charge of the C4 security cameras—even though the secretary of public security of Guerrero (Leonardo Vázquez Pérez at the time) is directly responsible for the C4. Therefore, these military personnel were the only ones who could have changed the camera angle, pointing up to the sky as the convoy passed. And that wasn't all they did that night.

The Version of the Twenty-Two Detained Police Officers

On September 26, there were 142 police officers on the clock in Iguala, according to the guard log I was able to review. Nineteen of them were administrators working in the station and six of them were in training, which left 117 working officers, including the police chief, Felipe Flores Velázquez.

Iguala's municipal police station is at 109 Ignacio López Rayón, a small street in the downtown neighborhood. The modest station is surrounded by homes, small buildings, and stores. There is only one small entrance gate, not high enough to let pickup trucks with roll bars through to enter the lot, which means that if one of these trucks is transporting an arrested suspect, officers need to park in the street and walk into the station. The station has only one story and is built in the form of a set square, with a triangular central patio over-looked by neighboring houses.

Between 22:30 and 23:00 on September 26, Flores Velázquez ordered his on-duty officers to convene outside the federal police base. According to these men, nobody told them why they were meeting at the base, though they remained there for hours until they received new orders to go to the state police training headquarters, CRAPOL, on the outskirts of the city.

That morning, as fresh officers arrived for work, they too were ordered to go to CRAPOL.

At the training headquarters the police officers, if they hadn't already done so at their own station, handed in their weapons. In total, ninety-seven weapons were handed in, including semi-automatic Berettas, G36 .223 (5.56 × 45mm) caliber, 9mm pistols, ammunition, and cartridges, as well as the nineteen vehicles that were being used. Sodium rhodizonate tests—to ascertain whether or not someone had recently fired a gun—were only conducted on 105 officers. It is unknown why the tests weren't conducted on all the officers. One commanding officer who was not tested was Francisco Salgado Valladares.

The police officers lined up on the patio stepped forwards one at a time, as people wearing masks indicated those they recognized. According to the state prosecutor's record, the students Cornelio Copeño, Alejandro Torres Pérez, Brayan Baltazar Medina, Luis Pérez Martínez, Yonifer Pedro Barrera, and Miguel Ángel Espino recognized nineteen of their attackers. The state prosecutor's staff singled out another three, for a total of twenty-two municipal officers, of whom sixteen tested positive for traces of gunpowder.

The officers recognized by the students were the following: Fausto Bruno Heredia (testing negative for gunpowder), Margarita Contreras Castillo (testing positive), Juan Luis Hidalgo Pérez (positive), Baltazar Martínez Casarrubias (positive), Mario Cervantes Contreras (positive), Arturo Calvario Villalba (positive), Emilio Torres Quezada (positive), Abraham Julián Acevedo Popoca (positive), Raúl Cisneros García (positive), Miguel Ángel Hernández Morales (positive), Rubén Alday Marín (positive), José Vicencio Flores (positive), Iván Armando Hurtado Hernández (positive), Zulaid Marino Rodríguez (positive), Salvador Herrera Román (positive), Hugo Hernández Arias (negative), Fernando Delgado Sánchez (negative), Marco Antonio Ramírez Urban (positive), and Osvaldo Arturo Vázquez Castillo (positive). The prosecutor also decided to detain Alejandro Andrade de la Cruz, Hugo Salgado Wences, and Nicolás Delgado Arellano, all three of whom allegedly tested positive for traces of gunpowder.

Also testing positive was Captain Alejandro Tenescalco, who was riding in patrol car 018. Attached to the Secretariat of Public Security of Iguala, Tenescalco coordinated part of the operation on the night of the attacks, according to testimony offered on September 27 by detained officers who claimed he was present during the attack in front of the state courthouse. Despite this, both he and Captain Luis Francisco Martínez (who was working directly under Tenescalco, tested positive, and was riding in patrol vehicle 011 with Hurtado Hernández) were protected by the Prosecutor's Office and remain free to this day.

In the ministerial statements taken by the Prosecutor's Office on September 27 and 28, ten of the officers admitted to having had access to information about the *normalistas'* commandeering of the buses and to having been present on Juan N. Álvarez Street or in front of the state courthouse. They also mentioned the presence of federal police and state ministerial police vehicles. Subsequent medical examinations of the twenty-two suspects found no signs of torture or physical abuse. Officers from the National Human Rights Commission were present during some of the testimony.

Ten officers admitted their presence during the attacks: Alejandro Andrade de la Cruz and Hugo Salgado Wences, occupying patrol vehicle 028; Juan Luis Hidalgo, 026; Raúl

Cisneros, 023; Fausto Bruno Heredia, 020; Mario Cervantes Contreras, 027 (riding with Alejandro Mota Román and Edgar Vieira); Miguel Ángel Hernández Morales, 022; Rubén Alday Marín, 019; Emilio Torres Quezada, 024, and Iván Armando Hurtado Hernández, 011. Three of them, Andrade de la Cruz, Cisneros, and Hurtado Hernández, admitted to having fired "into the air." During this first interview, all suspects denied arresting the *normalistas* or loading them into their vehicles. They voluntarily submitted to gunpowder tests on both hands, gave their fingerprints, and let their photos be taken.

As well as taking statements from the twenty-two officers, the investigators conducted ballistic tests on their weapons. Despite having collected more than 190 shells during the night of the attacks and into the next morning from both crime scenes, only twenty of those shells made it to the CRAPOL offices to be tested. And only two, according to the forensic analysis, were found to have been fired by police weapons, specifically Winchester Model 54s, carried by Salvador Herrera Román and Raúl Cisneros García. "The other eighteen shells, though of the same caliber, were fired by other rifles," according to the case file: that is, by people other than local Iguala police officers.

At 07:30 on September 27, only a few hours after the disappearance of the forty-three students, investigators proceeded to search for traces of blood and count bullets in the city's nineteen police vehicles. The interior, exterior, and trunk or bed of each vehicle was searched, according to the report written by Dulce María Elías Bustamante and María Guadalupe Moctezuma Díaz.

According to this search, vehicle 028 had a broken back left window, and two .223 shells were found in the interior. In vehicle 002, assigned to Raúl Javier Crespo, and which was used as a roadblock to stop the three buses on Juan N. Álvarez Street, there were two bullet holes in the passenger side of the windshield, and the rear driver's-side door displayed a stain that "seemed hematic"—a spray of blood. In the back seat there was also a black backpack with a bloodstain measuring 10×17cm. Inside vehicle 022 there were three .223 bullets. In vehicle 026, a .223 shell was found under the driver's seat. In vehicle 020, assigned to Fausto Bruno Heredia—working that night under the command of Alejandro Tenescalco—there was a .223 bullet. In vehicle 024, on a raincoat in the back seat lay a nine-millimeter shell. In vehicle 011 were two 9mm shells, one between the windshield and the hood and the other underneath the windshield wiper, both on the exterior of the car. The discovery of shells and blood seems to indicate that the vehicles were not altered or cleaned before their inspection. However, none of the truck beds of any of the nineteen vehicles that were examined were found to bear any traces of blood, hair, or other clues.

Andrade de la Cruz, one of the ten officers who admitted being present, said that he fired his weapon into the air in downtown Iguala as the three buses were driving through the streets. He explained that some time after 21:00, after the magistrate judge had ordered two drunks to be locked up, he heard on his radio that help was needed on Galeana Street, "saying that there were some aggressive subjects on a bus. Hearing this my fellow officers and I went to the location previously mentioned on the radio where help was requested, and after arriving at Galeana Street almost at the intersection with Bandera Nacional [in the center of Iguala] we saw a bus that was parked and a few male subjects next to it with rocks in their hands . . . On seeing the situation I told the driver,

'Pull out of here,' but the subjects then threw the rocks at us, damaging the police vehicle I was in charge of, breaking the left window, and forcing us to leave the location."

De la Cruz admitted to having fired his gun "only once, and I fired into the air while on Bandera [Nacional] corner with Galeana, right by the Monument to the Flag in the center of Iguala . . . I did it because they, this group of people right by the bus, attacked me with rocks, and I did it while riding in vehicle number 028 in front of my fellow officers, Hugo Salgado Wences . . . and patrolman Nicolás Delgado Arellano. After I fired the weapon we left the scene."

He also detailed a second encounter with the *normalistas*. Leaving Periférico Norte, he realized that on Juan N. Álvarez Street "there were other police vehicles with their lights flashing," and he parked his car to help with perimeter security, remaining parked for a few minutes until he heard a radio call for reinforcements under the [foot] bridge in front of the state courthouse. "And so I indicated to my colleagues to get back in the vehicle to go and offer assistance . . . arriving at the location I did the same, parking sideways in rearguard security, and I noticed that there were a number of police vehicles, five or six . . . I didn't see their [vehicle] numbers nor did I count the exact number of vehicles, though there were a bunch of them, and among the officers present were captains Hidalgo and Álvaro Ramírez Márquez, covering their faces, and I saw two federal police vehicles and one from the ministerial police."

Torres Quezada, another patrol officer on duty that night, recalled that "around nine o'clock I heard on the radio a fellow officer report he was following a bus on Aldama Street in the center of town and that the driver wasn't stopping. Just then my partners and I were at the El Naranjo neighborhood checkpoint, about five minutes away from the center, heading towards Taxco, Guerrero. I'd been at that location since five or six in the afternoon ever since my captain, Alejandro Mota Román, had sent me there. I didn't make much of the call [on the radio]. About five or six minutes after hearing the call I heard various officers talking on the radio about following a bus, naming the streets they were driving through, and that dialogue lasted about ten minutes . . . it was intense, and I assumed that several patrol vehicles were engaged since I heard a lot of different voices, though I couldn't identify them, it's an open channel . . . About fifteen minutes later I heard that they had been able to pull over the bus they were pursuing and it had come to a stop underneath the bridge on the Mexico–Acapulco highway [in front of the state court-house], and so I told my partners, *Huri* [Ernesto Castro Bautista] and Abraham [Acevedo Popoca] that we needed to get to the city to help our fellow officers."

Quezada said that on arrival he saw another Iguala police vehicle and two colleagues who had stopped a passenger bus, the Estrella de Oro 1531. He blocked the highway by parking his vehicle sideways. Fifteen minutes later, "I saw a state ministerial police vehicle arrive, a white double-cabin Dodge Ram pickup truck, though I didn't see the plate number, but two officers were riding in the truck, who I couldn't identify because they pulled off at a turnout and they were too far away, and I'm not sure if the other officers arriving at the scene were from our unit or some other unit." He confirmed that he remained on the spot for one hour, and then received an order to go to the Iguala police station: "At that moment I saw the ministerial police pull away along with the other municipal police officers with them, but I didn't see where they went."

Another local Iguala officer, Hurtado Hernández, admitted to firing his weapon. Arriving in his patrol car at the corner of Juan N. Álvarez and Periférico, he explained, "I heard various gunshots and they . . . were coming from automatic weapons, in bursts. The driver parked the vehicle and we walked about forty or fifty meters. While we were approaching I was able to observe three buses. I also saw a group of people, though I couldn't say how many, but a lot, all men, and they were covering their faces with their t-shirts, leaving their torsos bare. I also saw another group of men with t-shirts up over their faces who were damaging other police vehicles that were parked there . . . That exact moment I saw that people were exiting one of the buses and were running towards us, and they also had their faces covered and were carrying sticks or rocks, acting as if they were going to hit us, and so my fellow officers and I ran back to where we had parked the vehicle we had arrived in. As I ride guard [in the back] it was easy to jump in, and the captain opened the driver's door and got behind the wheel, started the engine and began to reverse, but . . . the subjects were very close. As there were more of them than of us I had to shoot into the air to frighten them, and it worked and they went back toward the bus they had gotten off."

Officer Cisneros García described hearing a report over the radio of a possible robbery on Galeana Street, close to where he happened to be. "We arrived with our lights flashing and the siren on, to see a bus about twenty meters away stopped in the street. I couldn't make out any details of the bus because there weren't many streetlights and it was dark, so I got out of the vehicle, leaving my partner, Eleazar, waiting in the truck and I walked up to the bus gripping my rifle, which I already mentioned, and I got up to about one and a half meters from the front door of the bus. I saw that the interior lights of the bus were on and then I could see that there were two people inside with some sort of cloth over their faces, but I can't remember what kind of clothes they were wearing . . . and since there weren't any other patrol cars around from any of the forces I immediately called in on my radio letting the operator know that there were basically two individuals with their faces covered inside of the bus . . . When three minutes later [vehicle] 018 arrived with supervisor [Alejandro] Tenescalco and his driver, who is also a municipal police officer, though I don't remember his first or last name but he's an officer who works regularly with [Tenescalco] . . . [they came from] Galeana Street, parking behind our vehicle 023, and supervisor Tenescalco, carrying his rifle, came towards where I was standing . . . Before he got to me two individuals grabbed me by the neck from behind . . . and I struggled, trying to get away and . . . supervisor Tenescalco fired a couple shots, I think with his sidearm, not sure how many times [he fired] and then I was able to cock my rifle and I fired two rounds into the air, and the subjects released me and ran back into another bus." According to Cisneros, those were the only shots he fired.

Zulaid Marino Rodríguez described arriving at the federal police base a little after 22:30. "Outside of the federal police buildings there were already a number of other officers and their vehicles. When we showed up, my superior officer talked to the other officers and came back and told me to await instructions."

Hugo Hernández Arias testified on September 28 that on the night of the attacks he received an order at 18:30 to provide security at the place where María de los Ángeles Pineda Villa, the mayor's wife, was speaking. Before that event was finished he was sent to work security at the Iguala sports complex, where a soccer game was taking place between the Chilpancingo Avispones and the local team, and where he remained until 21:30. The game ended with the Avispones winning 3–1. He went on:

"It was about ten-thirty when we went over to the exit gate, and maybe ten minutes [later] the second-in-command, Tomás Martínez Beltrán, told us to take vehicle 16 and head towards the Municipal Police station, which is at number 1 Rayón Street, in downtown. When we arrived, he gave instructions over the radio to all officers, telling me that the three other policemen I had come from the sports complex with and I were in charge of security at that location. Later he asked me for my rifle, though I was only carrying a pistol, a Pietro Beretta PX4 Storm, license number PX60575, 9 × 19mm . . . and from the weapons locker of the Iguala police, my Beretta rifle, model SC-70/90, license A24966g, 5.56 × 45mm [.223], as I show here on my original police license, of third rank, and then [he requested the weapons of] the three other officers, Fernando Delgado Sánchez, Gilberto Jiménez Pérez, and Juan Carlos Rodríguez Montes. . . . By around eleven on that night, the 26th, we were already on the roof of the municipal police offices, on alert, providing building security. To clarify, only the undersigned was armed. From there, through the radio operator, officer Natividad Elías told us there was a red [maximum] alert and I told my fellow officers to keep their eyes peeled . . . Cutting in on the radio we could hear 'ten' and 'eleven,' which are code for 'wounded' and 'dead,' but I didn't know the locations, I could just hear the sirens, I never heard gunshots. We stayed there until around two-thirty in the morning on September 27 . . . when some trucks arrived with the deputy attorney of justice, I don't know his name, and a few officers of the ministerial police. I'll clarify that no more of our own officers came to the station where we were, as they'd already been ordered to meet at the federal police headquarters."

This was the only official declaration that Hernández Arias would make. During these interview sessions, the Public Ministry posed forty-one questions about the series of attacks, none of which referred to the presence of students in the Iguala police stations. Later, however, the Prosecutor's Office altered the official statement made by Hernández Arias, by adding two further questions.

The additional questions, intended to incriminate the local Iguala authorities, were as follows:

Forty-second: What was the name of the magistrate judge on duty on September 26 of this year?

Answer: I only know they call him *Licenciado* [the title for graduates] Ulises.

Forty-third: How many cells are there in the security area?

Answer: There are three cells, one for miscellaneous crimes, one for administrative crimes, and one for women. When I came to work at eleven at night I saw that there were ten young men detained in the patio of the Iguala police station, and that *Licenciado* Ulises, I don't know his last name, was talking to them . . . I just saw them for a second and they were about ten or fifteen meters away. The cells are in the back, but they weren't in the cells, they were in the patio. There was a light on and it lit up the area perfectly. After picking up my rifle, a Beretta 5.56 × 45mm, stocked with twenty-seven rounds, I went to follow my orders, received earlier via radio from the commander in charge, second officer Alejandro Tenescalco Mejía, to work security for the building, the armaments, and the officers, in case of a possible attack by individuals looking to target the station with the intent of stealing our weapons. I saw officers arrive in two patrol vehicles and saw them loading up the young men I had seen earlier, crammed in and talking to Ulises, the magistrate judge, but I don't know where they took them. I just caught a glimpse of all this, and I don't know what happened next. I saw more civilians arriving in nonofficial vehicles.

The alteration of Hernández Arias's official declaration turned out to be an essential element in the construction of the "historical truth" that the PGR presented in January 2016 to exonerate the national and Guerrero state governments. The parents of the forty-three *normalistas* refer to the statement as the "historical falsehood."

The Army and PGR Impede the Search

By the morning of September 27, 2014, the public prosecutor's office had heard the declarations of the surviving *normalistas* and had access to videos recorded during the attacks, which pointed to the participation of the local Iguala police, as well as the presence of the federal police and the Army.

Luis Pérez Martínez, a first-year student whose testimony was used in the arrest of the nineteen local police officers, declared that he arrived in Iguala between 22:00 and 23:00 with a group of others, after getting a call for help from *compañeros* who said they were being attacked. On Juan N. Álvarez Street, he saw about thirty fellow *normalistas*. "I asked them what had happened, and they told me that they had been shot at, I mean, they were shot at and one of our classmates was killed, I don't know his name, but he's a first-year and goes to the school, and some others were wounded, I don't know how many, and so I asked who'd shot at them, and the ones who had been there when it happened explained that first it was the local police who intercepted them in their patrol truck, and some students got out to get the truck to move so they could pass . . . and then the federal police showed up and they were the ones who shot at them, wounding some, and killing one, but they didn't know his name, and then the rest scrambled out of the buses and ran to protect themselves from the *federales'* bullets, and some took cover behind the buses and others hit the ground . . . One of the *federales* lit up a cigarette on the corner, and gestured for the other officers to come over, and then the *federales* started picking up the shells so they wouldn't leave evidence at the crime scene, and then they left."

Francisco Trinidad Chalma described what he lived through on that night, corroborating the story of local Iguala officer Cisneros García that there was a struggle between him and one of the students. "We got off the bus and got around the police because they were surrounding the third bus, the Estrella de Oro," he said.

"I got behind a local officer who had already cocked his gun and was aiming and ready to shoot at my *compañeros*, and more students came up, and the other officers, seeing that I was behind him, pointed their weapons at me and my classmates . . . and to stop the police I pushed the cop a little and grabbed the butt of his rifle and he threatened me, saying that if I didn't let go he was going to shoot us, and we struggled . . . and as I was grabbing his gun he shot off a burst of fire, first at the ground, and then he raised [his weapon] and fired towards my *compañeros* from about a meter away, but when he had raised his gun to shoot at them, my *compañeros* had already split. . . . The other police, when they saw him start to shoot, they also . . . shot at my *compañeros*."

Francisco Chalma also mentioned the actions of the Army after the third attack on Juan N. Álvarez, after 23:00, when the students took his classmate who had been shot in the face to a private clinic, the Hospital Cristina, on the same street: "We were there [at the clinic] about a half an hour because they didn't have any doctors. When we were there two army vehicles arrived and when the soldiers got out we could hear them cocking their guns and asking us to open the door, which we did, and the person in charge asked if we were *ayotzinapos* [to which we responded that we were] looking for help for our classmate who was bleeding, and they told us that we should have the balls to face up to the mess that we started. They searched the whole clinic and made us sit in the waiting room, and had us lift up our shirts and they searched through all our stuff looking for guns, but we weren't armed. . . . We asked them again for help, to call an ambulance to take our *compañero* [to a hospital] but they told us they were going to send the local cops, that they had to go because there were two bodies in the road."

"Actions Taken by the State Governor in the Events of September 26 and 27, 2014, in the City of Iguala de la Independencia" is the title of a secret report I discovered during my investigation of October 2014. I shared it with the GIEI on 2015, when they arrived in Mexico to begin their own inquiry. According to this text, during the hours following the first attacks of September 26, the Public Prosecutor's Office received anonymous reports stating that some of the disappeared *normalistas* were in the local Iguala police station, others in the 27th Infantry Battalion barracks, and a few more in the state police station. Given this information, as well as taking into account the testimonies given by the *normalistas* and the local police on September 28, 2014, two officials of the local Public Ministry of the Hidalgo Judicial District in Iguala decided to do their job. The first officer, Maribel Morales García, sent an official letter to Commander Luis Antonio Dorantes, the director of the federal police base in Iguala, urgently requesting information about the vehicle numbers of the federal police, copies of the weapon licenses and their allocation to officers on the base, the log book showing which federal officers entered and exited the base, and "a weapons' registry from September 24." The letter finally urged him "to immediately answer this ministerial agency if police officers under his command actively participated in the events that took place on September 26."

She requested the same information of José Adame Bautista, coordinator of the state police's North Base which was active in Iguala on that night, as well as asking Leonardo Octavio Vázquez Pérez, secretary of public security in Guerrero, for immediate delivery of video recordings taken by C4 between 18:00 and midnight of the same night. And yet, by the time the Public Ministry official made these requests, the ministerial police of Guerrero had already taken those videos. The federal police never responded. On October 4, 2014, the preliminary inquiry and entire case was taken over by the PGR, the Attorney General's Office at national level.

For his part, Elmer Rosas Asunción, another Public Ministry official, ordered Wagner González, "coordinator of Iguala investigations," to conduct an inspection of the 27th and 41st Infantry Battalions' base on Periférico Norte; the PGR's Center for Strategic Operations, on Nicolás Bravo in the Centro neighborhood; the federal police base and the local police station, to determine if anybody was being held in those places. Rosas Asunción also ordered a forensic field report and a photographic analysis.

The state police, the local police, and the federal police allowed the inspection of their facilities, according to a report I was able to review, but the Army and the PGR refused. At 15:00 on September 28, 2014, experts showed up at the Center for Strategic Operations, where they were denied entrance to search for signs of the students. The guard on duty, Fidel Jiménez Morales, admitted that there were detention facilities on the premises but for "reasons of security" he couldn't allow access; they would need to submit a written request.

Earlier the same day, when investigators arrived at the Army base of the 27th and 41st Battalion Infantries, Colonel José Rodríguez Pérez denied them access to conduct an inspection, for supposed reasons of "national security." Here too they needed to file a formal request, with the 35th Military Zone based in Acapulco—a process which would take days. Colonel Rodríguez Pérez did allow them to view a secure area for storing decommissioned drugs, but they were not allowed to inspect the base for evidence of the forty-three disappeared students.

Since then, the Army has continued to resist any inspection of its base. Secretary of National Defense Salvador Cienfuegos has also refused permission to independent investigators from the Inter-American Commission of Human Rights to interrogate soldiers who may have been present on that night in Iguala.

5

The Story of the Abarcas

José Luis Abarca Velázquez, the former mayor of Iguala, seems to inspire as much admiration as he does hate. Those who know him either love him or despise him, with almost no middle ground. It's been that way since the late 1980s, when he started selling gold in a small shop close to Iguala's central market. Riding the region's precious-metal boom, he made himself into a prominent businessman, forging ties with jewelers in both the United States and Italy.

The PGR publicly pointed to Abarca Velázquez and his wife, María de los Ángeles Pineda Villa, as the prime instigators—in collaboration with the criminal organization, Guerreros Unidos—of the attacks on the forty-three *normalistas*, as well as of their disappearance and presumed death.

To understand the one-time former mayor, you have to understand his past history. Short, reserved, and slightly haughty, he is neither charismatic nor very friendly. His associates describe a man who is diligent and obsessed with work. First on the job and last to leave at the end of the day, he spared no effort to put his competitors out of business.

Inflexible and persevering, Abarca had a good head for business and invested the money he made from selling gold in real estate. But his success also brought him criticism: despite his willingness to invest, long before he became mayor he was considered stingy, even towards his family.

Nor did his second marriage—to María de los Ángeles Pineda Villa, daughter of a seamstress who sold dresses to his father's shop—do much to boost his reputation. Attractive, with a strong character, jealous, and demanding, María worked alongside her husband in all of his business ventures. In 2009 she was publicly associated with her two brothers, Mario and Alberto Pineda Villa, both lieutenants in the Beltrán Leyva cartel, causing many to suspect that the mayor himself had links to the criminal organization.

The population of Iguala remains divided on their ex-mayor. Some would like him to return to office, citing his role in the recent economic success and improved safety of the city, while others hold him responsible for the resurgence of organized crime. What is certain is that ever since he was officially indicted, three days after the attacks against the *normalistas*, local business owners and workers began reporting an increase in incidents of extortion and kidnapping.

The Future Doctor

José Luis Abarca was born in 1961 in the town of Arcelia, Guerrero. He was the youngest child of Nicolás Abarca and Esther Velázquez, with two half-brothers and a full sister and brother, Roselia and Javier. When they were kids, their father left for the United States as a bracero worker, and the older siblings went to work: Roselia sold gum and Javier, newspapers. Their maternal grandfather, Isidro Velázquez, who died aged 110 in 2014, owned a hat shop. Abarca's mother worked at a clothes stall in the Iguala market and sold bedding to nearby ranches. She slowly expanded her clothing business, opening other market stalls—where her children would work—and finally renting a storefront, Novedades Roselia, where she sold wedding dresses. Thanks to the father's savings, the family built a house on Joaquín Baranda Street, a few blocks from the central plaza of Arcelia, where Abarca's mother still lives. An important figure in his life, and a source of economic support for the family, was his aunt María Velázquez, who made a living selling gold for more than forty years.

When he was fifteen, Abarca moved to Mexico City with a group of other children, including cousins, to begin his studies at the National Autonomous University of Mexico. He entered a pre-medicine program. During his time at the university, however, he began selling gold and found what he really wanted to do. Without telling his family, he dropped out of his last year of med school to concentrate on his budding jewelry career. He traveled to McAllen, Texas, where he bought gold for resale in Mexico. Carrying suitcases full of the precious metal, he began selling in towns and villages close to Iguala, and then expanded to Acapulco and the states of Puebla, Oaxaca, Tabasco, and Chiapas.

Despite admonishment from his mother—she found out that he'd left school—José Luis stuck with the gold trade. He began working in the Iguala market every day, showing up at eight in the morning. He mostly sold on credit and also to middlemen. He also helped his brothers establish their own gold business.

José Luis's first marriage was to a young woman named Rosalinda, with whom he had his first child, José David, but the relationship didn't last. He later met María de los Ángeles, the oldest child of Salomón Pineda Bermúdez and María Leonor Villa, and followed by Guadalupe, Mario, Alberto, and Salomón.

"This is the most beautiful day of our lives. And I want to tell you that today and forever I will love you endlessly," María de los Ángeles wrote when she married Abarca on February 14, 1988. She was twenty years old; he was twenty-six. From that moment on the couple became inseparable—sometimes even wearing matching outfits.

Abarca soon began investing in real estate. He bought a plot of swampy land on the outskirts of Iguala from his brother and started buying up other nearby properties. Operating the excavator himself, he filled in and leveled the ground where one day he would build a shopping mall; there he would throw a party for his oldest daughter, Yazareth, on her fifteenth birthday, to save money from renting a hall.

He later detailed to the PGR the sources of his wealth, offering to give proof of receipts, tax records, and even the results of the audits he passed—all before he had any political aspirations.

In 2008, Abarca began work on an ambitious project: Galerías Tamarindos, a small shopping mall. Lacking capital and seeking investors, he traveled to Mexico City, and, on February 21, 2008, through his Asociación Yozy's, he sold part of the land to Inmobiliaria Gleznova for 20.2 million pesos, on which the superstore chain Comercial Mexicana would construct its section of the shopping center. Inmobiliaria Gleznova is a subsidiary of Controladora Comercial Mexicana, part of Costco Mexico.

Galerías Tamarindos, which launched at the end of 2008, was also partially funded by three loans from BBVA Bancomer, totaling another 22 million pesos. Two years later, in 2010, the couple had not yet cleared the bank debt.

Abarca didn't own all of the stores in Galerías Tamarindos. The communications director of McDonald's Mexico, Félix Ramírez, explains that the stores were rented rather than owned by the companies who occupy them. McDonald's invested some of its own money in the mall and, since they began operating there in December 2008, they hadn't had any trouble with Abarca or with Asociación Yozy's.

Ten percent of the mall is occupied by Coppel—a small electronics and department store—and the rest by fast food chains or small stores, which are owned outright by Abarca and his family. They charge rent for each locale based on surface area.

The Troublesome Brothers

The PGR has divergent explanations as to when and how Mario and Alberto Pineda Villa, Abarca's brothers-in-law, entered the world of organized crime. According to their father's supposed ministerial testimony, it was in 2000. However, official court documents from 2008 and 2009 maintain that it was in June 2002. That was when Richard Arroyo Guízar, stepson of Jesús Reynaldo Zambada *El Rey* (The King)—himself the brother of Ismael Zambada García, then leader of the Sinaloa cartel along with Joaquín Guzmán Loera, *El Chapo*—received a call from Mario Pineda Villa, known as *el MP*.

Thanks to his proximity to *El Rey*, Arroyo Guízar became a Mexico City plaza boss (running operations in a specific drug market) in 1992, reporting to Ismael Zambada. He was in charge of receiving drug shipments in Mexico City, either by plane or by truck, and awaiting instructions before sending them off on the next leg of the journey. He operated at leisure until his arrest in October 2008, in the Lindavista neighborhood of the capital. He then joined the witness protection program operated by the PGR and given the codename of "María Fernanda."

Mario Pineda had kidnapped some Colombian drug traffickers in Mexico City after they had kidnapped his brother, Alberto Pineda, alias *El Borrado*, in Colombia. Alberto owed the Colombians $5 million for a drug shipment the pair had purchased, as Arroyo Guízar explained to the PGR in his May 28, 2009 testimony.

The Colombians contacted Arroyo Guízar to ask him to intercede with Mario. A settlement was reached: both parties would release their hostages, and the Pinedas would pay up. That is how the Pineda Villa brothers entered the Sinaloa Cartel, working closely with Arroyo Guízar. Under the direct command of Arturo Beltrán Leyva, the brothers oversaw operations in Ixtapa-Zihuatanejo. They quickly proved reliable in receiving drug shipments from Colombia and Venezuela, which arrived on speedboats on Guerrero's coast or by airplane at the Acapulco airport. In 2008, when Beltrán Leyva broke with the Sinaloa Cartel and waged a bloody war against Zambada García and *El Chapo*, the Pineda Villa brothers chose Beltrán Leyva's side.

Since 2009, the PGR had struggled to get drug trafficking charges to stick against family members of Mario and Alberto. Salomón Pineda Villa was arrested, on charges of organized crime, with his parents in Cuernavaca. The parents were let go almost immediately. On April 5, 2013, the Second District

Court of Federal Criminal Proceedings, in Nayarit, acquitted Salomón and issued an immediate order of release.

I did an exhaustive search through PGR records on Mario, Alberto, and Salomón to see if they contained some mention or investigation of their sister, María de los Ángeles, or their brother-in-law, José Luis Abarca; I came up with nothing.

In December 2009 the federal Secretariat of Public Security announced the deaths of Alberto and Mario, whose bodies, it said, were found alongside the Mexico–Cuernavaca highway. The murders were attributed to Arturo Beltrán Leyva, supposedly in retaliation for a betrayal.

The double homicide of the brothers-in-law of Iguala's prosperous jeweler was the talk of the town. "When news broke that they were involved in drug trafficking, María was really embarrassed in front of all the people at the Centro Joyero [another retail project of the Abarcas]. It was a really tough, scary time," Roselia Abarca said in an interview. As for María, "It's not my fault," she would say. Abarca was unmistakably affected by the news, though he couldn't have imagined the consequences that were still to come of this family connection.

Abarca and his wife kept living and working in Iguala, but the murmurs and questions never stopped. Suspicion had been cast. Nevertheless, this wouldn't deter more than one political party, a few years later, from seeing Abarca as a potential mayoral candidate.

Exonerated in 2010 of Illicit Use of Resources

The first formal accusation against the couple, for supposed criminal activity, came by way of an anonymous phone call to the PGR on June 1, 2010.

According to file PGR/GRO/IGU/M-I/64/2010, the caller said: "The economic legacy of the Pineda Villa brothers is flourishing in the city of Iguala de la Independencia, Guerrero, through their sister, María de los Ángeles Pineda Villa and her husband, José Luis Abarca, who recently made substantial investments of more than fifty million pesos . . . in plots of land, apartment buildings, houses, and the commercial center, Galerías Tamarindos, in the city of Iguala. They travel in armored cars and are followed by an entourage of bodyguards surrounding them twenty-four hours a day." The case was entrusted to Humberto Martínez Martínez of the Public Ministry.

The accusation sparked an investigation into an alleged crime of conducting business with resources of illicit origin, and both husband and wife were cited by the attorney general. On July 23, 2010, the couple voluntarily presented themselves, along with their lawyer, José Luis Argüelles, before the PGR. Though they didn't make a statement at that time, they returned on August 31 to submit a formal declaration. The couple requested a "professional, extensive, and detailed investigation into the civilian complaint," according to the record. Abarca argued that since his youth, "following the tradition of the family business," he had devoted himself to jewelry, buying and selling gold and other precious metals, traveling the region to sell his products door-to-door. Since 1988, the year he married Pineda Villa, he had worked alongside his wife and daughters. By 2010 he had earned enough to invest in the Tamarindos shopping center. He declared that he was the owner of fifteen properties in Iguala, and he presented deeds and paperwork tracing the origin of the funds used to purchase them. His properties consisted of six premises in the Centro Joyero shopping center, downtown Iguala, as well as in other neighborhoods. He owned houses at 4 Roble Street (purchased in 1987) and 8 Roble Street, where he lived with his wife and children. Three more properties had been purchased between 1987 and 2005, and the remainder after 2006.

He reported that between 2006 and 2009, his income from rent and the jewelry business amounted to 19.5 million pesos, and he clarified that he did not own the Centro Joyero de Iguala but was one of the 145 businesses that collectively owned it.

Abarca also reported owning five plots of undeveloped land on Boulevard H. Colegio Militar, where he had built a part of his Galerías Tamarindos. In May 2003 he founded the company Asociación Yozy's, Inc., owned by his wife, his oldest daughter, and himself. It was registered in the federal taxpayer registry as AYSO 39522UV2, certifying the five land plots, which he had acquired between September and October of the same year. "Asociación Yozy's, Inc. has provided tax papers, in which its income is clearly explained and accounted for. You can see clearly the licit origin of all my income and my investments, which were made without breaking any law. It follows that the investments made and the links between them are clear . . . and therefore I deny what is stated in the anonymous letter of complaint that gave rise to this investigation," Abarca concluded in his declaration to the PGR.

For her part, María de los Ángeles Pineda Villa submitted a written request that "my testimony given to the federal ministerial police that interrogated me" should be included in this case file. She confirmed that she had been working with her husband in the Centro Joyero since 1988, where she was "earning money with my husband in the work of purchase, sales, and distribution of jewelry" and later in the administration of Galerías Tamarindos.

She explained that she registered her income with the Tax Administration Service on May 6, 1991, and paid all taxes due. Between 2005 and 2009, she specified, she earned 5.2 million pesos. She owned a property in the Tlatel neighborhood of Iguala, purchased on September 17, 1996, and a store in the Centro Joyero, which she acquired on April 18, 2006.

I was able to obtain access to records of the federal ministerial police's own investigation into the couple. On December 31, 2010, they issued a ruling, included in case file 1138/169/2010, that "no criminal charges" should be brought against Abarca and his wife for illicit gains. According to the PGR statement: "In reviewing each and all of the inquiries of the present investigation, no verifiable elements have been found of the crime of operating with resources of illicit origin." In conclusion: "For this reason the determination is reached, due to the elements reviewed by this investigation, that no criminal prosecution is in order."

Political Ambitions

Lázaro Mazón—two-time mayor of Iguala, founder of the Party of the Democratic Revolution (PRD) and Guerrero's secretary of health under the Aguirre administration—has been friends with José Luis Abarca since they were children. It was through Mazón that Abarca entered politics. By 2011, he was known as a prominent businessman and was courted by both the PRI and the PAN as a potential mayoral candidate. The PRD was also interested, but he rejected them out of hand.

That's when Governor Ángel Aguirre Rivero, a long-time PRI member who had defected to the PRD, sought to install a mayoral candidate, Oscar Díaz Bello, who would act as his pawn. Other groups—concerned that if Abarca didn't get tapped soon, he would be snapped up by the PAN—were eager to push him into the race. He was seen as the people's candidate, and polls showed he had a chance. Aguirre made Abarca an offer to run as local deputy, letting Díaz Bello go for mayor, and then they would switch; but Abarca wanted it the other way around. They finally reached an agreement, in which Abarca promised to support Díaz Bello for mayor in the next race, in 2015.

When Abarca consulted his brothers, they advised him not to enter politics, which they saw as a less than honorable profession. In 2012, however, to the consternation of some local party members, he was named PRD candidate for mayor of Iguala. He won the election and was sworn in in September of the same year. His wife soon took on an integral role in his work as mayor, while using her position as first lady to launch her own political platform.

The Secretary of Municipal Public Security: A Key Factor

Felipe Flores Velázquez, stoutly built, with gray mustache and gray hair, was the secretary of public security (or chief of police) in Iguala at the time of the disappearance of the *normalistas* and became a key factor in the PGR's accounting of the events. For two years after the attacks, nobody knew where he had gone. In October 2016, he was found and arrested—he had been hiding out in Iguala.

Before becoming police chief, Flores Velázquez had had a long military career working in intelligence for the Mexican Army. In the 1980s he was commander of the Intelligence Squad of the 27th Infantry Battalion in Iguala, a crucial component in the surveillance of guerrilla groups, social movements, and even the Normal Rural School of Ayotzinapa, which was seen by the government as a breeding ground for guerrilla fighters. From 1990 to 1994, General Juan Heriberto Salinas Altés commanded the 9th Military Region, with headquarters in Acapulco, where he brought Flores Velázquez to collaborate with him on intelligence matters. Contrary to some media reports, Flores had no family relation to Abarca.

Flores Velázquez returned to Iguala when Lázaro Mazón, the mayor-elect, named him the city's secretary of public security, chief of police. He would hold the position without attracting particular attention until 2005, when he became coordinator of State Public Security (SSP) for the Acapulco Region, which was the most important region of the state in terms of economics and tourism. This new position revealed the trust General Salinas placed in Flores. In 2009 he was named SSP coordinator in the Costa Grande region, with headquarters in Zihuatanejo, a challenging region both politically and in terms of criminal activity.

When Abarca became mayor of Iguala, he was advised— presumably by Mazón—to appoint Flores Velázquez once more as chief of police.

However, as part of the internal investigation conducted by the PRD into Abarca's role in the Iguala attacks, Mazón claimed it was a colonel in the 27th Infantry Battalion who recommended Flores. Abarca, for his part, explained that he had to ask permission from Governor Aguirre, since Flores Velázquez had been working in the state rather than municipal police.

Superior army officers describe Flores Velázquez as an "intelligent" and "honest" man. His knowledge of guerrilla movements and the Popular Revolutionary Army, which accused the Mexican Army of having a hand in the events in Iguala, was profound enough that SEDENA officials often consulted him.

On the night of September 26, 2014, Flores Velázquez was working in his office in city hall, very close to where María de los Ángeles Pineda Villa's speaking event was being held, and also to where the first shots of the night were fired. Later that night, as we have seen, Flores Velázquez would hand over his weapon, call in his officers to disarm them, and then order them to present themselves to the state police training center on the outskirts of Iguala, where twenty-two of them would be arrested. He would also turn over the entire armament, as well as all of their equipment and vehicles, to state authorities.

The ex-military officer submitted his declaration in two parts, on September 27 and 28, to the PGR, claiming that he kept both the federal police and the mayor updated as the events unfolded. And then he disappeared. His side of the story is vital to understanding the events of that night, not only to clarify comments he made in his statement, but for what he would say later to people he trusted. One of his confidants told me that Flores Velázquez explained to her that, just after 22:30, when he was first learning of the ongoing attacks, he was accompanied by officers from the 27th Battalion, and that for the rest of the night, even as he was ordered to call in all of his officers, he was acting only in assistance to the military, which had taken control of the several crime scenes, and were conducting patrols in the city.

The Dispute with *El Tigre de Huitzuco*

The first challenge Abarca faced as mayor was from the social and political groups of his own party, regarding the state's Fertilizing and Transfer of Technology Program. Each year the state of Guerrero launches a farmer support program with local governments; for years they bought fertilizer for farmers from the company Agrogen.

One of the owners of Agrogen was the former governor, Rubén Figueroa Alcocer, better known as *El Tigre de Huitzuco*; his father, Rubén Figueroa Figueroa, had been the nemesis of guerrilla leader Lucio Cabañas—Ayotzinapa's most celebrated alumnus. Huitzuco is a town adjacent to Iguala, where the Figueroa family wields so much influence that the official name of the place is actually Huitzuco de los Figueroa. Its local police force, too, was implicated in the disappearance of the forty-three *normalistas*.

Although his name doesn't appear in the incorporation filings of Agrogen—one of the largest producers of fertilizer in the country—Guerrero's ex-governor has been publicly identified on more than one occasion as one of its owners. In 1999, members of congress accused then-Governor René Juárez of enriching Figueroa Alcocer through contracts made with Agrogen. René Juárez claimed not to know whether his predecessor was indeed one of the owners. In 2005, *El Sur* newspaper made multiple accusations of governmental favoritism toward the company. And in 2010, a former mayor of Arcelia, Nicanor Adame, as well as ex-congressman Martín Mora, confirmed that "Armando Sotelo Sotelo" was a pseudonym for Figueroa Alcocer. In the incorporation filings, Sotelo Sotelo appears as one of the six owners and the general director of Agrogen.

During his first months as mayor, Abarca decided to change fertilizer suppliers and have the city government distribute directly to farmers, instead of working through the social organizations. Some of his officials had found that they could buy fertilizer at lower prices in Veracruz. This move won him the enmity of the ex-governor, who wasn't used to people standing up to him.

Three days before September 26, 2014, Congressman Salomón Majul, who was part of Figueroa Alcocer's clique, staged a press conference in Iguala to issue an unexpected warning. "Iguala is a very dangerous place," he told reporters, "where you can't even go out at night." At the time, Iguala was still a typically calm small city.

An official who worked in Abarca's administration contended: "Figueroa didn't like Abarca because he couldn't control him."

Abarca ordered the fertilizer to be distributed according to a registry that had been approved in March 2013, but the leader of the Popular Union and the Emiliano Zapata Farmers' Union, Arturo Hernández Cardona, complained that some farmers were getting more fertilizer than others. Hernández Cardona's partner, Sofía Mendoza, a Rural Development councilor from the PRD, backed him up in laying political pressure on Abarca.

That same month, Hernández Cardona and the city finance officer, Justino Carvajal Salgado, began an unrelated dispute. On the radio, Carvajal accused Cardona of receiving and then reselling government-provided fertilizer for profit. In response, Cardona accused Carvajal of being a kidnapper.

In an interview given the day after the accusation, Hernández Cardona said: "They started it. It wasn't us. And there are other things, I didn't say everything . . . I know of some very bad things that have happened, sure, and I'll say it again. With all the risks and possible consequences . . . You said it, sir, I have the date, the place, and the witnesses: 'I am a kidnapper.' The thread is being stretched to breaking point. There are issues in state politics with Rubén Figueroa Alcocer."

Hernández Cardona went on, allegedly repeating words said to him in confidence by Carvajal Salgado: "I admit to being a kidnapper . . . I admit to having kidnapped under the orders of Héctor Vicario. I never kidnapped anybody because I wanted to. What I've done, I've been ordered to do." Hernández Cardona then insisted, "I know where, when, why, who, all of it . . . and I've got a lot more information, just as bad as this."

Abarca found himself in the middle of his own party's fertilizer-sparked political dispute. Days later, on March 8, Carvajal Salgado was found dead inside his home. He had been shot five times. Abarca was welcomed at the funeral. When Hernández Cardona showed up, he was chased out, wreath and all, according to a May 10 article in *El Sur* newspaper. He was, unsurprisingly, the prime suspect. Days later, Abarca made a public statement that, at the request of the city council, the PGR had begun to assist the police in the murder investigation. He didn't disclose any leads.

On May 29, Hernández Cardona and ten members of the Popular Union presented a written statement to the Guerrero State Prosecutor's Office, laying out their clashes with Abarca around the fertilizer affair. Among other issues, the statement referred to an April 1 council meeting in which Hernández Cardona called out Abarca for wanting to imprison him for the murder of Carvajal Salgado. "A man, Justino Carvajal Salgado, is dead, and we who lead the different organizations that make up the Popular Union now have a well-founded fear that we may in turn perish. And though it may seem unfair, we hereby inform you that we will hold you responsible if any of us loses his life to a murderous bullet."

Abarca allegedly responded by standing up and retorting, "You're a crazy idiot. Now you expect us to protect you, so you don't get killed for all the mischief you're causing, you bastard." Abarca's wife also waded in, apparently screaming at Hernández Cardona: "You're scum! A criminal! A parasite!"

Leaders of the Popular Union told the prosecutor that they were scared that Abarca, his wife, or Felipe Flores Velázquez, the police chief, could have them killed, "because, as far as we are aware, we don't have any other enemies."

The Murder of Hernández Cardona

On May 30, 2013, Hernández Cardona and seven other people disappeared after taking over a toll booth on the Iguala–Cuernavaca highway, in a bid to demand 200 tons of fertilizer.

Two days later, on June 1, family members reported them missing. Pablo Mendoza Angulo, son of Nicolás Mendoza Villa, reported to the Prosecutor's Office that his father had no enemies and he couldn't think of any potential suspects. María Soledad Hernández Mena, daughter of Hernández Cardona, said, "I take for granted that the disappearance of these men involves all three levels of government."

Judith Ávila Pineda, the wife of Héctor Arroyo Delgado, reported that before the disappearance, "the engineer Arturo Hernández Cardona, during their demonstration, had an altercation with a federal highway police officer by the name of Roberto Castillo Villa." On June 3, the bodies of Hernández Cardona, Ángel Román Ramírez, and Félix Rafael Bandera were discovered. On June 26, PRD councilor Sofía Mendoza requested that the Guerrero state congress remove Abarca from office "for grave and systematic violations to individual rights." Alluding to Castillo Villa, the federal highway police officer, and his altercation with the demonstrators, she said: "After the aforementioned discussion, they were disappeared."

In one of the six criminal prosecutions brought against Abarca after the disappearance of the forty-three *normalistas*, the PGR recycled these earlier denunciations and charged him with the kidnapping and homicide of Hernández Cardona. According to the case files, the only accusation linking him to the death of Carvajal Salgado was a statement taken one year after the murder, on March 12, 2014, from Nicolás Mendoza Villa, Hernández Cardona's driver. In it he claimed that during the kidnapping of the union boss, on May 30, 2013, he heard one of the abductors saying "That damn finance officer, he was pretty strong," and recalling how Carvajal Salgado had got away from them at first.

The testimony of Ernesto Pineda Vega, taken on May 1, 2014, was also used in the case against Abarca. Pineda Vega, who had collaborated with Hernández Cardona, said he had once received an aggressive call from Abarca saying, "'Alright, you son of a bitch, I've had enough, either you stop working with Cardona or you got the same thing coming.' I also know he ordered the killing of Justino Carvajal."

With regard to the kidnapping of the Popular Union members, the victims' testimonies differ substantially. Mendoza Villa, Cardona's driver, said in a declaration to a notary public on June 25, 2014 (divulged in November of the same year by the Solidarity Network Decade Against Impunity): "Mayor José Luis Abarca Velázquez shot him [Hernández Cardona] with a shotgun in the face and again in the chest and left him slumped in the grave." But according to the autopsy report, included in the indictment against Abarca and of which I have seen a copy, the union leader was shot three times: in the face, the back of the head, and the right leg—not in the chest, as his driver claimed. The size of the wounds and the ballistic evidence also cast doubt on the weapon being a shotgun.

On May 31, 2015, in a statement to the PGR, Mendoza Villa changed his story. Now he claimed that, from a distance of ten meters, he witnessed Abarca, in the presence of Felipe Flores, shoot Hernández Cardona point-blank in the left of his face and then shoot him again.

Héctor Arroyo Delgado, another of the kidnapping victims, told a different story again. On October 14, 2014, he claimed he saw both Flores and Mauro Valdés, the city council's legal director, but never mentioned the presence of Abarca. "They made our colleague Arturo walk right up to the grave that had been dug the day before. Then we heard two shots, and we assumed that they had taken the life of Hernández Cardona."

Efraín Amates Luna, who was also kidnapped, stated: "I'd like to express that I witnessed them beating Arturo Hernández Cardona and [because] he was screaming they took him away . . . where they started beating him even more, until I didn't hear him calling out any more and then I heard two shots. I'd like to add that I heard this from about ten meters away from where I was, and I didn't hear Mr. Arturo Hernández Cardona again, so I figured they'd killed him."

Abarca and Aguirre Rivero

The relationship between the mayor of Iguala and the PRD governor, Ángel Aguirre Rivero, was, according to mutual acquaintances, more than just political. The two were close friends. The governor frequently visited the mayor's office, allegedly even sometimes sleeping at Abarca's house, though not in the few months leading up to September 26, 2014.

On becoming the PRD's mayoral candidate, Abarca had made an agreement with Ángel Aguirre that next time he would cede the candidacy to Oscar Díaz Bello. But once in office, he and his wife found that they liked their new position, with María becoming popular for the social programs she initiated: offering prosthetics, medicines, wheelchairs, and sports equipment; helping patients to access treatment options abroad; and holding free breakfasts. She also offered gifts to journalists, attended graduation ceremonies, and lost no opportunity to be seen in public. María Pineda Villa's political profile grew, and, in some instances, seemed even to over-shadow that of her husband.

The couple decided to break their pact with the governor and planned for María Pineda Villa to run as Abarca's successor. For many, the event on September 26, 2014, during which Pineda Villa would present her record as local president of the DIF (a federal social services program for families), was the starting gun for her political race. "The whole world knew that this was really a campaign launch," a city official observed in an interview, adding that almost 150 DIF employees were part of the pre-campaign team. Plenty of people urged the couple to honor their agreement and launch Pineda Villa as the candidate after Díaz Bello's term. They refused, reckoning she had enough popularity to stiff-arm her way past the agreement, with Abarca eyeing a potential congressional seat.

Governor Aguirre had known for weeks what their intentions were, and the change of heart cooled their relationship. Not even Lázaro Mazón, a friend and political advisor to Abarca, as well as health secretary under Aguirre, liked the couple's plan. After picking a fight with *El Tigre de Huitzuco*, Abarca and his wife were making yet more enemies.

Among those who received invitations to the DIF event on the night of September 26 were the governor and a host of other state officials, but owing to the tension in the air, only Silvia Romero, Guerrero's secretary of education, accepted.

The evening began at 19:00 on the esplanade next to city hall, with about 4,000 people in attendance, and was scheduled to last two hours. Organizers were hoping to project a lengthy video celebrating the first lady's projects, but there was a technical glitch, the video failed to play, and the event ended early. If the video had worked, the couple would still have been there when the first attack against the *normalistas* occurred in the main square. Belying the official version of events, of course, the *normalistas* had no intention of disrupting the event of First Lady Pineda Villa; in any case, as they passed close to city hall it was already long over, and the mayor and his family had left.

When the event ended, shortly after 20:00, the couple remained for the photographs, until around 21:00 when they went for tacos with their children and extended family to the Taquería Lili, on the corner of Agustín Melgar and 13 de Septiembre, close to their Galerías Tamarindos, fifteen minutes from the center. In a later interview, Lili herself confirmed that the family ate there that night, along with their usual three bodyguards.

According to other witnesses, the mayor and about eight family members, including his brother and wife, remained at Lili's until 22:00, which was when the first attacks were unleashed against the students in the center of Iguala.

Felipe Flores, Iguala's police chief, first heard about the attacks not from the C4 command center, which had been monitoring the students for at least three-and-a-half hours, but from a local resident, who told him that she was in the bus station and a group of students from Ayotzinapa were seizing buses. "I told her to keep calm, it was no problem, they were just taking the buses and weren't going to harm the passengers," according to the ministerial declaration Felipe Flores submitted on September 27. Two minutes after that call, the police chief phoned Luis Antonio Dorantes, chief of Iguala's federal police base, to notify him "in compliance with the collaboration we have with these police agencies. He told me he had taken note and would keep alert." In reality, however, Dorantes had already been informed of the events by the C4. "Later, at nine-forty-five," Felipe Flores continued, "I heard screaming and people running, the noise coming from the entrance to city hall . . . They were yelling that there had been shooting, and I immediately left my office and told my guard to open the gate so people could get into the building and out of harm's way."

Abarca's family members who ate with him that night later explained that after they had already ordered their tacos, at approximately 21:30, one of his sisters-in-law received a phone call about a skirmish in the center of town involving a "group of people in masks." According to this version of events, this was the first that Abarca had heard about the attacks.

For his part, Flores Velázquez declared to the State Prosecutor's Office that around ten o'clock he informed the mayor of what was happening and was asked to investigate more thoroughly. While they were eating, more of Abarca's family members started receiving calls from friends who were close to the attacks. After they had eaten, Abarca, his wife, and their children went to their home on Roble Street in the Jacarandas neighborhood, in the center of Iguala. According to his relatives, he called the federal police, the Army, and the governor's office, but nobody explained to him what was happening.

Months previously, Abarca had signed the "Single Command" directive, in which the local police would function under the command of the state of Guerrero. "Nobody's telling me anything, nobody's telling me anything," he repeatedly cried, according to family members' testimonies.

Members of PRD Ask for
Three Million Pesos for "Media Protection"

Saturday, September 27, was the day of what would have been Abarca's second mayoral address. He asked his lawyer José Luis Argüelles if he should go ahead with the event (the city council wanted to cancel it); Argüelles advised him to submit the report in writing but suspend the political ceremony. He followed the advice. On Monday, September 29, he traveled to Mexico City to meet with PRD members, specifically Jesús Zambrano, the national party leader, and Congressman Sebastián de la Rosa, according to a press conference given by de la Rosa that November (*El Universal*, November 6, 2014). What de la Rosa did not mention during his press conference was that in the course of the meeting he asked Abarca for 3 million pesos, "to pay media outlets and control the press coverage," according to sources directly connected with the ex-mayor. The sources maintain that Abarca paid the money.

The PRD demanded he immediately step down as mayor, which he refused. They settled on him taking a thirty-day leave while Guerrero's prosecutor's office crossed off potential suspects. Before the city council, on September 30, and flanked by his wife and family, he temporarily stepped down as mayor, with a defiant speech:

"On Friday, September 26, our city suffered a violent attack in which people, apparently from outside our community, lost their lives. Others were wounded. The social peace we so desire and that I worked for so hard was damaged. I offer in deep solidarity my feelings of brotherhood, my sincerest condolences to the family and friends of the people who died in this painful event. The acts were not committed in isolation, and the state and federal authorities, in conjunction with local officers, have permanently rolled out an effort to stem this violence, not only in the city of which I am the mayor, but in all of Guerrero. They will investigate and, for the sake of justice, punish the perpetrators, not leaving to impunity those who were either intellectual or material agents of these horrible events. The reestablishment of the rule of law requires a thorough investigation that matches the severity of the situation and strictly follows all legal and constitutional frameworks.

"As a citizen of Guerrero, as an *Igualteco*, and as a member of the Party of the Democratic Revolution, I will not allow the events that occurred in our city to remain in the realm of impunity and for the guilty to go unpunished. With dignity, with head held high, I tell you that you can trust me, that you elected me as your mayor, and that my conviction and dedication would never let me commit such an atrocity . . . Confirming that I had no part in any act that would tarnish me in front of the community, and with the goal of assisting in an exhaustive investigation, transparent and impartial, an investigation whose results will leave nobody in doubt, I have made the decision to legally step down from my position, asking an official to temporarily take over for me for thirty days."

Various council members spoke up during the session. Valentín Amador Matal complained that the state and federal authorities didn't reestablish order that night—the official version of events was still that they took no part. "The *federales* didn't hear the gunshots? The state forces, why didn't they intervene? It's the obligation of federal and state authorities to maintain order, and they should have helped to stop these lamentable acts from occurring. I think the fact that they didn't respond to the call for help comes down to competition between the federal and state governments."

Councilwoman Soledad Mastache, ex-leader of the Iguala PRD, commented: "My stance is only this, backing and supporting our city's mayor." Councilwoman Sofía Lorena Mendoza, former partner of the murdered Hernández Cardona, said she was in favor of the investigation, though without seeming to point the finger at Abarca: "After demanding justice for a year and a half for what happened to the social leaders of this community, I am asking, once again, for justice."

Immediately after the mayor left city hall, PGR and state officials surrounded the mayor's offices, calling for Abarca, claiming they had a subpoena for him. The officials next went to his home, searched it top to bottom and arrested his domestic workers, Elvia Salgado and Adriana Figueroa. According to lawyer Argüelles, this search "was one hundred percent illegal." Argüelles added: "In defense of his personal liberty and that of his family, he removed himself from further injustice." The mayor and his wife vanished from Iguala.

The Escape

Soon to turn fifty-three, enjoying a position of relative wealth and political importance, by October 2014 José Luis Abarca was suddenly plunged into disgrace. Though he was on the run for almost twenty days before an official arrest warrant was issued, the public smearing had already begun to destroy him both psychologically and physically. He barely ate. He contemplated suicide. One of his family members recalled, "Seeing no end in sight, he felt horrible and didn't know what he was being accused of." Only the company of his wife was able to keep him from ending his life.

As soon as they learned that their house had been searched, on the advice of their lawyers Abarca and his wife immediately left Iguala for Mexico City. They took their passports in case they decided to go abroad. His official leave of absence would have ended on November 5, and, according to family members, the couple was planning to return to Iguala then.

Starting on October 1, the media, along with Guerrero's government officials, began talking about Abarca as if he were a fugitive from justice for having left Iguala, though no legal summons for him to appear or arrest warrant had actually been issued. On October 8, Víctor León Maldonado, in his role as deputy state prosecutor, presented before the state congress an application for criminal liability and a petition to revoke Abarca's position as mayor. It was the second such petition that had been issued for Abarca: the first, as we have seen, came on June 26, 2013, from Sofía Lorena Mendoza, Arturo Hernández Cardona's partner, on grounds of "serious and systematic violations of individual rights," and was rejected. This second petition against Abarca was for "serious and systematic violations of individual rights," "conduct contrary to public order and public peace," and "repeated omission of civic obligations." He was not accused of ordering the killing or disappearance of the *normalistas*.

Abarca and his wife, along with their four children, went to their unfurnished Mexico City apartment, located in the Tepepan neighborhood, in the south of the city. According to family members, their "anguish, fear, and confusion grew." Abarca didn't have a television and made few phone calls. Scared of being assassinated or extrajudicially detained, the family soon moved to the apartment of their eldest daughter, Yazareth, which she was renting from some Anáhuac University school friends in the Olivar del Conde neighborhood. A few days later, the three youngest children all returned to Iguala to go back to school.

On October 10, after a press conference held by Prosecutor General Iñaki Blanco Cabrera, Abarca read in the papers that he had been personally accused of the attacks of September 26 and 27. The public lynching led administrators at Anáhuac University to request that Yazareth Abarca leave the school in mid-semester, which she did. The family's situation grew more precarious by the day. Even those who worked for the Abarca family were scared to walk the streets in Iguala, for fear of being swept up in the accusations.

Abarca called his four children together at the apartment in Olivar del Conde and reassured them that everything would be sorted out. It was the last time the whole family would be together. Knowing that the federal government was

131

monitoring them, the couple sought refuge in the Unidad Independencia neighborhood, in an apartment lent to them by friends. The plan was to stay there until Abarca's leave was up and he could return to his position in Iguala. The couple was isolated in their new place, hardly communicating with the outside world so as not to reveal themselves. One day, Yazareth received an unexpected message from her father: "Go to Anáhuac." He was asking her to meet at the old university apartment. Things were bad: the previous night their friends, grown scared of harboring them, had turned them out of their apartment. They had nowhere left to go. Even their driver had left them. Day by day, their fear increased, and they were also running out of food. Their daughter brought water and some basic provisions.

José Luis Abarca was desperate. He wanted to come out of hiding and make a public statement in his own defense, but his lawyer advised him to sit tight, because "it wasn't the right moment." Yazareth came to see the couple every two or three days. Almost completely isolated, Abarca celebrated his fifty-third birthday on October 17 with a Jell-O, a loaf of wheat bread, and a bottle of Old Parr Silver whisky, remembering better times. On that same day the Guerrero Prosecutor's Office applied to the Second District Criminal Court of the Higher Court of Justice in the State of Guerrero for an arrest warrant for Abarca, on suspicion of "first-degree murder" as well as "attempted murder" of those who had been injured. A few days later, even before the arrest warrant was granted, the family's apartment in Tepepan was searched, and, according to family members, extensively damaged. It was just after his birthday that the mayor began to contemplate suicide.

When an arrest warrant was issued on December 21 by Guerrero's Higher Court of Justice, Abarca legally became a fugitive. In case file 217/2014, he stands accused of first-degree murder of six people (three of them students) on the night of September 26 and the attempted homicide of another seventy. The disappearance of the forty-three is not mentioned in the warrant.

The State Prosecutor's Office claimed that Abarca gave the order to detain the students "by all means necessary, to stop them from interrupting the events in which the president of DIF [his wife] would present her work." The ceremony at city hall had already ended, however, and Abarca and Pineda Villa had left, before the students had even initially commandeered the buses from the station. The prosecutor told the judge that police chief Felipe Flores had said that Abarca gave this order; but in his only statements, given on September 27 and 28, Flores never mentions receiving such an order.

Although the PGR did not charge Abarca and his wife with maintaining a relationship to the Guerreros Unidos, Attorney General Jesús Murillo Karam accused Pineda Villa on October 22 of being one of the "principal organizers of criminal activity acting [on behalf of the Guerreros Unidos] in city hall, working in complicity with her husband, Mr. José Luis Abarca, and the chief of police, Felipe Flores Velázquez." Nothing of the sort is mentioned in the criminal case file itself. The attorney general also repeated the erroneous statement made by the state prosecutor, that the attack against the students was carried out to stop them from interrupting Pineda Villa's presentation.

Two days later, a federal judge at the First District Court for federal criminal proceedings in Tamaulipas granted an arrest warrant for Abarca for his alleged involvement in the killing of Hernández Cardona, though the same warrant was denied for Pineda Villa.

Yazareth Abarca decided to move her parents out of her apartment when Abarca's official leave was up. The couple moved to a small room offered by a friend of hers, Noemí Berumen, in the Iztapalapa borough of Mexico City. To keep busy, Abarca washed the apartment's walls. He had lost a lot of weight and wasn't hungry. The couple slept in their clothes and with their shoes on. Their daughter, knowing that the federal police were watching, brought them food. She lived between the two apartments.

On October 29, Secretary of the Interior Miguel Ángel Osorio Chong rekindled the public's fury against Abarca when, in a radio interview, he claimed that after the attacks in Iguala he had immediately asked Governor Aguirre to monitor Abarca.

On Saturday, November 1, Abarca told Yazareth to go to Iguala. He was preparing his return. "I'm almost back already," he said, referring to the end of his leave. Abarca would not make it back, however. Three days later he and his wife were arrested.

On the night of November 3, 2014, federal police officers searched the house where Yazareth and her friend Noemí were staying. The officers pointed their weapons at the two women and took photos and video, which were then distributed to the media. The next morning, November 4, Abarca and his wife were arrested. The mayor, along with his wife, daughter, and his daughter's friend, were separated and taken to the SEIDO offices, where Attorney General Murillo Karam was waiting for them.

Abarca was first interrogated by Murillo Karam himself.

"I'm just going to ask you one question," the attorney general contemptuously said. "Where are the students?"

"I don't know, sir," Abarca responded meekly.

"I'm going to leave you in the street, I'm going to strip you of everything."

"Sir, if that's your decision."

"It would have been better if you'd killed yourself," Murillo Karam said.

"You have a weapon, sir," Abarca said to one of the officers in the room. "If you care to give me your pistol I could get rid of a problem."

"You're shameless," Murillo Karam said and left the room.

Tomás Zerón, the shady head of the Criminal Investigations Agency, took over the interrogation. When Abarca didn't give up any information, they began with the threats. "We have your daughter and we're going to rape her!" they told Abarca, pressuring him to admit that he was guilty. He remained firm, refusing to make any admission. "If you do that," Abarca told them, "what can I do about it?" This made Murillo Karam, who had returned, even more angry.

Meanwhile, Pineda Villa told the official who was interrogating her, "It's not my fault if those people [her drug-trafficking brothers] are my relatives." Neither Pineda Villa nor Abarca would make a confession.

Officials took Yazareth into the basement, the dungeon of the building, trying to intimidate her, until finally, unable to come up with any charges, they released her. Noemí Berumen was released on bond.

The government made public the video of the moment Abarca and his wife were arrested in the Iztapalapa apartment. PGR files, however, contain two distinct accounts of how the arrest had taken place, neither of which correspond to the version fed to the public.

According to file PF/DI/COE/2625/2014, signed by federal police officers Daigoro Xiuhtecuhtli Herrera, José Hugo Espejel, Agustina Calvo, and María Lucerito López, on November 4, at 02:30, a taxi arrived at 50 Cedro Street in Mexico City and "a couple was observed leaving the building," prompting the officers to approach and confirm that it was Abarca and his wife. Allegedly, these then offered the officers half a million pesos to let them go. When they refused, Pineda Villa took 23,000 pesos out of her bag and additionally promised a Mercedes-Benz complete with purchase receipt. At that moment, the officers detained the individuals for attempted bribery.

Alternatively, according to court records of case 100/2014, in the file PGR/AIC/PFM/UA IOR/DF/ATPI/1246/2014 (signed by federal ministerial police officers Javier Herrera Barrios, Elpidio Hernández Nájera, Aurelio Álvarez García, and Juan Manuel Santiago García), Abarca was arrested on November 5, 2014, "in the vicinity of 75 Paseo de la Reforma, close to the corner of Violeta Street, in the Guerrero neighborhood [of Mexico City]." This is close to the SEIDO offices and not in Iztapalapa, as the federal police had claimed.

In June 2015 the PGR was forced to open a case against the officers who claimed to have been offered a bribe by Abarca and his wife. In September of the same year they determined that the officers had engaged in "unlawful conduct," but, as of October 2016, none of them had been sanctioned.

According to José Luis Argüelles, the attorney representing Abarca and Pineda Villa, their constitutional rights were violated by the arbitrary method of their arrest. Argüelles claims that his clients were arrested inside of the apartment where they were residing. They were asleep when the officers burst in, and they were allowed to collect their belongings before being filmed. As the authorities didn't have a warrant to enter the building, or even an actual arrest warrant for Pineda Villa, the arrest was illegal. "The only way to have her arrested was to invent an attempted bribe," Argüelles explained. "They are innocent. They have not committed the crime the PGR is accusing them of, let alone the crime the media and public opinion imputes to them."

For Argüelles, the motive for the scapegoating of Abarca and his wife is "one hundred percent political." He reiterates that two years on from the attacks in Iguala, the PGR has not produced a single piece of evidence against him for the killing of Hernández Cardona or the other union leaders, nor anything connecting him to the Guerreros Unidos. So much so, he points out, that none of Abarca's properties have been embargoed, and his businesses remain open and functioning though he himself is in jail.

At 17:10 on November 5 Abarca was committed in the Federal Center for Social Rehabilitation (Cefereso) #1, known as El Altiplano, where he has remained ever since. His state of health was found to be poor: he had an inflamed liver, a tumor in his thyroid, and neurocysticercosis (a parasitic disease of the nervous system) in his brain. Pineda Villa, meanwhile, was held for sixty days while the PGR looked for a reason to keep her inside with an official arrest warrant. Before the maximum time they could hold her was up, they resorted to a discredited witness, Sergio Villarreal Barragán, alias *Mateo*, who had been extradited to the US in 2012.

I was able to review dozens of witness reports provided by *Mateo*, from 2010 to 2014, discussing the Beltrán Leyva cartel and the brothers Mario and Alberto Pineda Villa. Nowhere did he name María de los Ángeles Pineda Villa as forming part of the criminal network. He named her for the first time only at the prompting of the PGR: on December 11, 2015, in the Mexican Consulate in the United States, when his testimony against her sufficed to justify an arrest warrant for the offense of working with organized crime "with the intent of committing acts against public health with resources from illicit origins." Suddenly, *Mateo* remembered seeing Pineda Villa in a safe house in Cuernavaca, sometime in 2006. She had greeted her brothers and was present during a discussion of the arrival of boats loaded with five tons of cocaine. The discredited witness claimed that he saw her get into a Volkswagen Bora containing large egg-boxes stuffed with cash.

Mateo claimed that during another alleged visit by María, "she told her brothers that they'd bought a few properties and impounded a few others . . . passing along information about the properties, jewelry stores, and the shopping mall." However, at the time that the witness was claiming María made these statements, the mall hadn't even been built yet. On the same day, the witness claimed, he saw her leave in a maroon BMW X5 that held five egg-boxes filled with dollar bills. He added that on another occasion, without specifying the year, María paid another visit to her brothers in a light-colored sedan with two or three egg-boxes of cash, "noticing that the vehicle was weighed down by the weight of the boxes." *Mateo* even hinted at a romance between Arturo Beltrán Leyva and Pineda Villa, who he described as a "babe."

False testimonies previously supplied by *Mateo* caused serious problems for the PGR during Felipe Calderón's presidential term, when they relied on him as a witness during "Operation Cleanup." He made accusations against six Army officers, including the deputy secretary of SEDENA, Tomás

Ángeles Dauahare, though all the prosecutions collapsed when, at the beginning of the Peña Nieto presidency, Murillo Karam publicly stated that he was investigating the use of false witnesses. Even so, the PGR relied on *Mateo* as a witness to bring charges against Abarca's wife.

"There was never evidence against abarca": Blanco Cabrera to the PGR

Despite the dark rumors surrounding the couple since at least 2010, the Guerrero Prosecutor's Office had no hard evidence against either of them. In his declaration to the PGR on October 29, 2014, Prosecutor General Iñaki Blanco Cabrera—who had himself made various public accusations against the couple—admitted that the testimonies surrounding the killing of Arturo Hernández Cardona contained certain "contradictions and inconsistencies," in terms of the number of people involved, the type of weapon used, and the method of injury. He also granted that the testimony given to a notary by Cardona's driver, Nicolás Mendoza Villa, and since picked up by various media, was a lie.

In his own declaration, Deputy Prosecutor Ricardo Martínez, who was present in Iguala on September 26 and 27, testified before the PGR on October 29 that during a previous investigation into the Guerreros Unidos, conducted in May 2014 on one of the properties belonging to Hernández Cardona, they discovered nineteen bodies buried in clandestine graves. They arrested two people in the act of digging graves who were, they claimed, following the orders of one of Hernández Cardona's daughters.

Martínez explained that he worked with the PGR for months investigating the accusations against Abarca, regarding both the Hernández Cardona killing and his involvement with the Guerreros Unidos, but the evidence against the ex-mayor remained weak: "It would be hard for any judge to lend it credibility." Martínez added that on September 10, 2014, just weeks before the attacks in Iguala, Jesús Villalobos, of the SEIDO, told him that what evidence they had "was insufficient to prove that José Luis Abarca was part of the Guerreros Unidos."

The Night of Iguala, According to Abarca

Inside the Altiplano maximum security prison, José Luis Abarca maintains his innocence. I spoke with him by phone in June 2015, from the home of one of his relatives in Iguala, and we talked for the ten minutes he was permitted. It was the first interview he'd given since his arrest on November 4, 2014. Since that day he hasn't even given a declaration to the PGR or a judge. Throughout our brief call, Abarca's voice sounded calm and clear.

As he described it, on the night of September 26 he requested the assistance of the army and the federal police, but they didn't come.

"How did you become aware, sir, of what was happening on September 26, 2014?"

"I realized from the media, and that night by talking to my police chief, right, that there were disturbances underway."

"Who did you call when the chief of police told you of the disturbances?"

"First, the first person to report to me was the secretary of government [Jesús Martínez Garnelo], he was the one who told me, from state government."

"And who else kept you informed?"

"He updated me throughout the night about . . . about what was happening. He was the one who knew first, right, about what was going on in the city, since, well, I don't know where he was getting it from, but he told me 'There's a problem here,' 'There are gunshots in this part of town,' or 'There are dead and wounded in this other part of town,' and so on."

"Did he tell you that it was students from Ayotzinapa who were being attacked and killed?"

"No, not at first. At first he just told me that there had been shooting and then later I understood, from the police chief, that it was students who had kidnapped the, uh, buses. But not that they were being killed."

"Sir, do you remember more or less what time you received the call from the interior secretary?"

"Between nine-thirty and nine-forty-five . . . The attacks were just beginning, nine-forty, ten at the latest, because that was when I got home . . . I was taking a shower when I got . . . the call, from him, and from then until two or three in the morning we kept talking."

"Sir, at what time did Guerrero attorney general's officials arrive in Iguala? I understand that the prosecutor general and the deputy prosecutor came. Do you know what time they arrived?"

"Yes, with, uh, the chief of police they had a meeting at one, one-thirty in the morning, when they were rounding up all the police. They didn't invite me, and it was the deputy prosecutor who was running the meeting."

"What did you do when you came to understand everything you were being told, bit by bit?"

"What did I do? Well, you know, I started talking to the media, the media started interviewing me and I was talking to the secretary of the interior, asking him to tell me what was going on since I wasn't getting any official reports, and I wasn't invited to any of the meetings they were having. It was Friday night, then Saturday, Sunday, Monday, not until Tuesday that I took my leave, and still I hadn't gotten an official report."

"That night did you also call the federal police and the Army, did you try to get in touch with them?"

"Yes, well the only ones I phoned were the federal highway police [federal police], since I didn't have any of the other numbers. The other people my secretary always called. They [the numbers] were in my office so the first thing that came to mind at that moment was to call the federal police. But, anyway, I told the chief that if he hadn't already gotten in touch with all the forces, that he better do it, right? I told him 'Call all the police and the Army,' and he said to me, 'I already did, sir, and they told me they didn't have any men prepared to engage.' I said, 'What?' 'Well they're not hearing any gunfire,' he said. 'That's what they told me. But I already notified them all, the ministerial police, the state police, and the Army.'"

"How did the federal police respond when you spoke with them?"

"They didn't pick up, and I called twice. They didn't answer, so, in my desperation, the only thing I could do was keep talking to my chief of police to know what they were doing, and he was the one keeping me informed, of how officers could be seen coming in, and they were taking action to provide security to the city and keep it calm and tend to the wounded, you know, take them where they needed to go, right, to various hospitals."

"Sir, the Mexican public needs to know, and I'll ask you directly: did you order the Iguala police to attack and detain the students?"

"No, because I didn't even know. I didn't even have a radio, you know, to be in contact with them. Not for one second was I in contact with them. I was only and exclusively ever in contact with the chief of police."

"Did you order the killing of the students?"

"Not at all. That would be horrible. No, no, no."

"Do you belong or have links to the criminal organization, Guerreros Unidos?"

"Not at all. No way. We are hardworking people and we never had anything to do with criminal groups. We've always worked, that's it, and this was the first time I got involved in politics. I was always in business and, well, I'd never before even been at a political meeting, even for five minutes."

"Why didn't you go out that night? You were the mayor, those things were happening in your city. Your people were in the streets, the people you work for, they were scared. Why didn't you go out?"

"I did not go out. Right, well, the fear of . . . like a lot of people were calling me, telling me there was all this shooting everywhere. Yeah, those who supposedly had the guns didn't go, right? Well I stayed on the sidelines to be able to see what was happening, because really there are a lot, a lot of police in Iguala, Guerrero, and I think that it's their job, not the mayor's."

This was the first time José Luis Abarca had admitted to being scared to leave his house to see what was happening in the city he worked for.

"You have children. You have children that you raised and cared for. What do you think of the disappearance of those forty-three students, that were the same age as some of your kids?"

143

"Sure. First, well, I'm horrified about what happened. Absolutely none of that should have taken place. I was the first one to [to put myself] in the hands of the authorities so they could investigate, as this was a criminal act, right? By people with totally criminal minds, who, well, how can I put it? I completely denounce all this and I feel, as I said from the beginning, the pain that the families are carrying right now. Really, I reject this type of action."

"What happened that night, on September 26, do you think it was planned? Was it an attack on you? What do you think happened?"

"No, no. No, not at all. No, it was . . . something that just happened, because they [the students] didn't come straight at us. They went straight to the bus station, and not once did they come towards where we were."

"I meant the disappearance, the attacks in the streets, the shootings. Who planned that?"

"I couldn't tell you. I was in my house and I had no official information. I repeat, all the police were keeping guard and they're the only ones who know what happened. To this day no one has told me, not even, from what I hear [have they explained in] the testimonies they've given. Right? Or in the news reports that have come out by now."

"But now that time has passed, what do you think actually happened? Were the Iguala police capable of organizing all this?"

"No, no. No. Obviously not."

"Who had the ability to pull something like that off?"

"Well, honestly, I'm in the same place as you, I couldn't tell you who put all that together. What to me seems unjust is that they arrested me, right? Here for something that I didn't have anything to do with, nothing, didn't even know about it . . ."

The version offered to the PGR by the state government secretary, Martínez Garnelo, days after the attacks, was that he couldn't find Abarca until the morning of the 27th, and that Abarca told him he had been asleep and didn't know a thing. Abarca's lawyer, Luis Argüelles, however, confirmed in an interview that Abarca did speak with Martínez Garnelo on the night of the 26th and that the PGR has recordings of those calls.

The former prosecutor general of Guerrero, Iñaki Blanco Cabrera, as well as the former governor, Ángel Aguirre Rivero, both testified, first to the PGR and then to the special congressional commission created to investigate the crimes, that on the night of the 26th and the morning of the 27th they requested assistance from the Army but were refused. On October 21, 2015, in a meeting with the special congressional commission, Secretary of the Interior Osorio Chong and the then commissioner of the federal police, Enrique Galindo, both denied receiving any such request.

"We don't deserve this"

I was also able to speak by phone with María de los Ángeles Pineda Villa, who was in Cefereso #4 in Tepic, Nayarit. It was the first interview she'd given since the attacks in Iguala. Unlike her husband, she seemed at moments depressed, even desperate.

"The government accuses you of having ties to drug trafficking through your brothers Mario and Alberto Pineda Villa. Are they part of your family?"

"They are part of my family, but I am innocent of everything I'm accused of. I have never committed the least offense."

"Were you involved with them?"

"Of course not. No one will ever be able to connect me to anything they did."

"Have you ever conducted any business with, or used any money from, your brothers?"

"Never. Each peso that my husband and I earned was from putting in the work. We've always been transparent, and we can prove it. For almost thirty years, almost every day, we've worked hard, and we have witnesses among the people in our city, that not only know us, but love us."

"Is Mr. Abarca related at all to the chief of police, Felipe Flores Velázquez?"

"Of course not. They're not related. They have the same last name, but they're not related."

"Why do you think that the PGR is accusing you of disappearing the students and of everything else that happened that night?"

"They're not accusing us of that. I was arrested in an illegal manner, with a lot of violations, without any warrant, and they charged me with crimes I don't know anything about . . . They threatened to arrest my kids as well if I don't confess to what they're saying I did, and I'm really worried," she said, becoming tearful.

"And what did you say to the officials when they threatened you like that, ma'am?"

"I defended myself. I told them I was innocent, I've always said so and I'll go on saying so. I'm innocent of those accusations. And they're never going to prove anything against me because I never committed a crime, nor has my husband, we are responsible people. Society judged us, and that hurts a lot, because we're innocent, we're innocent of those accusations, we don't belong in this place," she said despairingly, beginning to cry again. "We don't belong here! It's a miserable place, you can't live here! I'm so sad, I feel so sick, we don't deserve this treatment, we were responsible officials and did our jobs, we were responsible business owners as well, model parents, and they are discriminating against my family."

"What would you say to the parents of the forty-three disappeared students?"

"I'm a mother, just like many parents of young kids and teenagers. I take care of my kids every day, and so I need to be with them, and I'm really sad. I haven't spoken with anyone since September 30, so I don't know what happened, or what supposedly happened, and, as a mother, I feel so awful about it. Just like I want to be with my kids, I know they want to be with their kids . . ."

"Did you use illegal funds?"

"Never, not at all. I worked every day from sunup to sundown and I never earned a peso that you couldn't trace or that I didn't earn from my work and effort. My husband gave me and my kids all we needed. My husband is a working man. I want you to understand, want someone to listen to me!" She was sobbing. "You must listen to me! I beg you all, as neutral observers, all of you, please listen to me, let us go home, please."

"The PGR accuses you of being the 'boss' of Iguala, of being part of the Guerreros Unidos. How do you respond?"

"I'm incapable of doing something like that! I'm innocent of all of it."

The Abarca Pineda Bunker

A few weeks after they were detained, I took a tour of the Abarca Pineda home, at 8 Roble Street in the Jacarandas neighborhood of central Iguala. The Mexican government accuses José Luis Abarca and his wife, María de los Ángeles Pineda Villa, of directing the Guerreros Unidos, which, according to Guerrero's security services, is a drug cartel. But the house that the couple lived in up until the day that Abarca took a period of leave looks nothing like a cartel boss's home, a mansion fit for narcos or corrupt politicians. Anybody entering the house that was described in the media as an impenetrable bunker would be up for a big surprise.

The property, consisting of two plots with one house on each, is large. The exterior wall is imposing, and inside the enclosure there's a good-sized pool, but the buildings themselves are run-down, dated, and devoid of expensive furniture or decoration. The furniture is varied, often shabby or in poor condition. One house contains the master bedroom, a spare room, and the dining room. The bedroom has a large closet and a small bathroom. The couple had a weakness for clothes, which dangle from hangers on all the walls. Abarca has a large quantity of close-fitting t-shirts and dress shirts in bright colors, as well as dozens of ties and shoes. Pineda Villa has more than a hundred brand-name dresses, dozens of colorful high heels, a few expensive purses, and boxes of imitation jewelry.

The four children slept in the other house on the property, which also boasts a living room and a kitchen with old, shabby furniture. The dining table where the Abarcas ate breakfast every morning is made of white plastic. The only hobby Abarca was known to have was exercising, but the only exercise equipment, in the garage "gym," were makeshift iron free-weights.

Despite the lack of evidence, some people still insist that Abarca and his wife were involved in organized crime. In an off-the-record conversation, one official directly involved in the investigation told me there was no chance that the ex-mayor and his wife could have orchestrated the attacks against the *normalistas*.

Abarca and Pineda Villa were indicted as the masterminds behind, and the highest authorities involved in, the attacks that occurred on September 26 and 27 in Iguala. That is not the case.

6

Manufacturing Guilty Parties

"The first thing we want to say is, we don't trust you," the parents of the forty-three disappeared *normalistas* warned Miguel Ángel Osorio Chong. On October 10, 2014, the parents were in Osorio Chong's offices in Mexico City for their first meeting with the secretary of the interior, during which Osorio Chong sat quietly and listened to a barrage of complaints.

Until that day, the government's official stance had been one of indifference, but now alarm bells were ringing in President Peña Nieto's administration, keenly aware of the public's negative view of their handling of the case. Indeed, the whole world had heard the story of the attacks and disappearance in Iguala. After the Army's recent massacre in Tlatlaya, the federal government didn't want to be tainted with yet another scandal. As their first order of business, without yet resorting to violence, they sought to drown out the intuitive and spontaneous slogan that echoed through the streets of Mexico in marches and demonstrations: "*¡Fue el Estado!*" "It was the state!"

The government's priority was to minimize the impact of the crimes and protect the image of the president in the international media. The near-total confusion surrounding the events, even among the surviving students, and the first actions taken by Ángel Aguirre Rivero, the governor of Guerrero, gave the federal government time to plan their cover-up. Despite the surveillance conducted, for decades, by the Center for Investigation and National Security (CISEN) and the Army on the Ayotzinapa Normal Rural School, government officials underestimated the *normalistas*, the families of the victims, and their ally organizations, such as Tlachinollan and the Prodh Center.

For his part, Ángel Aguirre—a personal friend of both Peña Nieto and Osorio Chong—had his own stake in making sure the truth didn't come out about his administration's role in the events of that night. To succeed in his cover-up he had to steer the investigation, entrusted to Guerrero state officials Iñaki Blanco Cabrera, Víctor León Maldonado, Ricardo Martínez Chávez, and Leonardo Vázquez Pérez.

In Los Pinos, Mexico's White House, it was decided that the best men for the job were Luis Enrique Miranda Nava, Humberto Castillejos Cervantes, and Tomás Zerón de Lucio (deputy secretary of the interior, legal advisor, and head of the Criminal Investigations Agency [AIC], respectively). The three men brought a wealth of experience in conducting cover-ups and had the imprimatur and unconditional support of the president.

In the meeting with the parents of the disappeared students, on October 10, Nava, Castillejos, and Attorney General Murillo Karam were also present. The parents, accompanied by their legal representatives, accused the 27th Infantry Battalion of participating in the attack against the students. They also criticized the federal government for letting so much time elapse before taking over the investigation: it wasn't until October 5, nine days after the attacks, that the PGR announced it would be stepping in. In contrast, when Alfredo Guzmán Salazar, the son of *El Chapo* Guzmán, was kidnapped on August 15, 2016, in Puerto Vallarta, the PGR took over the case within three days and was able to quickly find and rescue him. The Mexican government, clearly, has its priorities.

"We were not aware of what was happening. It wasn't until the next day that we found out and took action," Osorio Chong told the parents, justifying the government's procedure. "We are as upset as you are, we condemn the actions as much as you do." And yet the secretary of the interior was lying. One year later, in October 2015, Osorio Chong admitted before Congress that he was kept up to date by CISEN, in real time, about the attacks happening in Iguala.

At the end of a tense and futile meeting, the parents felt that talking to Murillo Karam was not enough, and they demanded to speak with Enrique Peña Nieto. Frowning, Deputy Interior Secretary Miranda Nava claimed that the meeting with Murillo Karam was all that could be arranged: he did not wish to appear incapable of keeping the problem from bubbling up to the presidency.

On October 29, 2014, the parents met with Peña Nieto for more than five hours. According to information I was able to obtain, by that point CISEN had notified the president that the forty-three students hadn't been disappeared but were hidden away in the mountains.

The Cover-Up Men

Luis Enrique Miranda Nava

For nine years he was part of Peña Nieto's team in the State of Mexico, and the two remain very close. They share a love of golf and play together on the Valle de Bravo and the Ixtapan de la Sal courses. When Miranda Nava speaks of the president he refers to him as Enrique.

Miranda Nava is one of those people who, just like Peña Nieto, no matter what, even in dreadful circumstances, is always neatly dressed and keeps his hair perfectly combed. His political position is untouchable. Those who have glimpsed the inner circles of government affirm that it is Miranda Nava, and not Osorio Chong, who actually wields the power in the Ministry of the Interior. Astutely, however, he prefers to be deputy secretary, to shield himself from the blows of the media and have more latitude in exerting control.

He's also considered an intelligence expert and is believed to be the effective head of CISEN, though the ostensible director is Eugenio Ímaz (an official connected to Osorio Chong, who worked for him when he was governor of Hidalgo). Ímaz's fight with cancer has rather hindered him from fulfilling his duties.

In September 2016, Peña Nieto commended Miranda Nava by naming him director of social development.

CISEN's mission is to gather intelligence, conduct operations, raise alerts, and implement the agenda set by national security directives. Significantly, one of these directives was focused on the Raúl Isidro Burgos Normal Rural School of Ayotzinapa.

Among Miranda Nava's most trusted acolytes is Gerardo García Benavente, also a close friend of "Enrique." In 2005,

García Benavente was a CISEN delegate in the State of Mexico and, during Peña Nieto's time as governor, worked in the State Security Agency.

When the attacks in Iguala took place on September 26 and 27, García Benavente was the coordinator general of intelligence for CISEN, which was monitoring the students hours before the attacks. At the beginning of 2015 he became coordinator general of counterintelligence, replacing Daniel Santos Gutiérrez Córdova. According to CISEN, García Benavente is in charge of both intelligence and counterintelligence, and reports directly to Miranda. Benavente was also exclusively in charge of the eight offices tasked with monitoring Joaquín Guzmán Loera, *El Chapo*, when he escaped from the Altiplano prison in July 2015.

Humberto Castillejos Cervantes

One of the most powerful and influential of Peña Nieto's cabinet ministers, those who know Humberto Castillejos Cervantes emphasize both his abilities as an attorney and his lack of scruples. He has influenced major policy decisions that have turned out to be serious mistakes.

When he came into the president's inner circle he already had a bad reputation, not only for being brother-in-law and friend to the polemical police chief Luis Cárdenas Palomino—accused by narcotraffickers of accepting bribes—but also for being involved in the alleged extortion by Federal Investigation Agency (AFI) officials of Enrique Salinas de Gortari, the brother of ex-president Carlos Salinas de Gortari, culminating with Enrique's murder in 2004.

When Castillejos Cervantes arrived in Los Pinos, he became the principal protector of Cárdenas Palomino, who was criminally prosecuted for abuse of authority in the case of the falsely accused and imprisoned Florence Cassez. Cárdenas Palomino also enjoyed protection from the nefarious ex-secretary of public security, Genaro García Luna.

In 2001 Castillejos Cervantes was appointed as an advisor to former Attorney General Rafael Macedo de la Concha; it was said he got the post because of his father's good relations with Macedo (which did not prevent his father from being murdered by the mafia in 2008).

At the beginning of Felipe Calderón's presidential term, Attorney General Eduardo Medina Mora named Castillejos as coordinator of counsel to the PGR. Here he met Yessica de Lamadrid, the deputy director general who had an affair with Peña Nieto when he was governor of the State of Mexico. In April 2008, he left his post.

Humberto Castillejos Cervantes has been an advisor to Peña Nieto since the latter first became governor, and has been influential in deciding Peña Nieto's judicial appointees. It was he who recommended Alberto Bazbaz as attorney general of the State of Mexico, who resigned after the failed investigation into the disappearance of little Paulette Guevara, in 2010. When Bazbaz left, Castillejos Cervantes also recommended the new attorney general—his own first cousin, Alfredo Castillo Cervantes, who, as deputy attorney general, had been chiefly responsible for the same debacle.

In the State of Mexico, Castillejos Cervantes, Castillo Cervantes, and Tomás Zerón de Lucio formed an inseparable trio. They became known for their sprees and extravagances, and frequently boasted of them.

In 2012, the Ecological Green Party picked him for a council seat in the State of Mexico, but he resigned that position to join Peña Nieto's transition team as an advisor and, later, as legal advisor to the president. Members of Peña Nieto's cabinet describe Castillejos Cervantes as a rising star in Peña Nieto's circle, gaining undue and perhaps dangerous influence.

Meanwhile Castillo Cervantes, his cousin on his father's side, has become somewhat of a liability. Castillo Cervantes also worked with Cárdenas Palomino in the Secretariat of Public Security in 2007. In 2012 Castillo was named as justice coordinator in Peña Nieto's transition team and had his eye on the attorney generalship, but Jesús Murillo Karam eventually took the spot, and he had to settle for being deputy attorney general. Murillo Karam soon got rid of him, however, for overstepping his legal authority in hiring and firing police chiefs and officials. After that, Humberto Castillejos Cervantes endorsed his cousin to work in security in the state of Michoacan and later named him as director of the National Sports Commission. Despite Castillejos's checkered history in public office, Peña Nieto has kept him as part of his cabinet. The tight crew that has stuck together since their State of Mexico days seems indissoluble, and other cabinet members can only speculate as to why.

Tomás Zerón de Lucio

Zerón de Lucio completes the trio of federal officials in charge of the investigation into the disappearance of the *normalistas*. Zerón's career has been relatively short and atypical: until 2007 he had no experience in either public service or policing. He graduated from the National Polytechnic Institute, one of the largest public universities in Mexico, where he studied Industrial Administration. In 1993 he was a financier at the Compañía Industrial de Parras, a denim manufacturer; in 2002 he became the financial director of the consulting firm Control Risks Group, and in 2006 he worked for two months, also as financial director, of Construsistem, a sheet metal manufacturer.

Those close to him described how, as part of Genaro García Luna's team that was gaining power in the AFI, Zerón forged strong ties to two of García Luna's principal henchmen: Francisco Javier Garza Palacios, the director of special operations, and Luis Cárdenas Palomino, both of whom shared Zerón's love of ostentation and bombast.

When García Luna and his team transferred to the Secretariat of Public Security in 2006, Garza Palacios invited Zerón, who still had no police or political experience, to become coordinator of police operations. During his brief stint in that position, former federal police accused him of selling plum commissioner jobs to commanders in the AFI. Each post, it is said, cost $50,000, pickings that Zerón allegedly shared with Garza Palacios and other officials.

On May 18, 2007, Zerón, Garza Palacios, and four other top federal police officials were sacked for having allowed a group of fifty hit men to travel freely for more than 250 miles on a federal highway to Cananea, Sonora, where they slaughtered five policemen and a dozen civilians; the federal police ignored the calls for help during the attack. Among the officers removed from their positions were Vidal Diazleal Ochoa, the general director of surveillance operations. Diazleal would later be promoted director of the federal ministerial police, a position he still held at the time of the attacks in Iguala.

During Peña Nieto's time as governor of the State of Mexico, Zerón was the chief of intelligence services of the Justice Department there. Despite his lack of experience, he was touted as an "intelligence expert"; it's said he was propelled into the position by his two chums, the cousins

Humberto Castillejos and Alfredo Castillo. "He knows everything about the president," is one explanation for the protection Peña Nieto has afforded him. A source told me, "Zerón does the dirty work, he doesn't hesitate, and he's good at talking up and justifying" the president's actions.

In 2015, during the Infraiber scandal (in which the company questioned Peña Nieto's awarding of millions of dollars of contracts to the Spanish firm OHL), the president unleashed Zerón to contain the mess before it exploded. Zerón ordered a raid against Infraiber's lawyer, Paulo Díaz, allegedly planted an illegal weapon on him, and then had him arrested. When a video surfaced of agents planting the weapon, the PGR couldn't ignore it and charged ten federal ministerial police officers. Zerón himself remained unscathed.

On September 14, 2016, after months of the parents of the forty-three students demanding the ouster of Zerón for manipulating the investigation and tampering with evidence, he left his post at the AIC. Not because he was kicked out: the man behind the "historical truth" was rewarded for his services by Peña Nieto when he named him technical secretary of the National Security Council. Meanwhile, Vidal Diazleal Ochoa remained in the AIC.

A day after Zerón left the AIC, Vidulfo Rosales, the lawyer supporting the parents of the missing students, issued a statement: "There is an internal investigation [in the AIC] into Zerón, but given his departure we have not been informed of its progress. Today the mothers and fathers and the students of Ayotzinapa, as well as our supporters, demand a prompt resolution and the punishment of those accountable. There is clear evidence that he is responsible for the misdirected investigation, as well as for erecting obstacles to keep us from the truth. If Tomás Zerón is absolved . . . it will only confirm the message of impunity and protection that yesterday the president of the republic sent us."

The Lawyer-Warrior

Thirty-nine-year-old Vidulfo Rosales represents the students from the Raúl Isidro Burgos Normal Rural School of Ayotzinapa, as well as the parents of the forty-three disappeared. He was born in the village of Totomixtlahuaca, outside of Tlacoapa, Guerrero, along the mountainous coast where the famed guerrilla fighter Genaro Vázquez made his mark and where, decades ago, community policing was born. Rosales's father and grandfather were both part of the Vázquez movement. During the Dirty War, local *caciques* (wealthy political bosses) tried to take the Rosales's small plot of land, and they had to go to court to defend themselves. With his father's encouragement, he studied law at the Autonomous University of Guerrero.

Years later, active in the Chilapa community, Rosales realized that the law could be at the service of small towns and social organizations. "Law can also be on the side of the weak and the destitute," he told me.

The lawyer from the mountains has taken part in many of the battles of the dispossessed. Together with the organization Tlachinollan, he won two victories over the government and the Army that would mark the history of Guerrero.

Supporting the Council of Ejidos and Communities Against the La Parota Dam (a pet project of President Vicente Fox), Rosales succeeded in legally stopping the construction in 2003. About twenty miles from Acapulco, La Parota would have flooded thirteen villages, displaced 20,000 inhabitants, and indirectly affected another 75,000.

Rosales also represented a young indigenous woman,

Valentina Rosendo Cantú, before the Inter-American Commission on Human Rights. In 2002, aged seventeen, Valentina was gang-raped by eight soldiers in Acatepec, Guerrero. The Secretariat of National Defense (SEDENA) denied the allegations. The case was jointly taken up by Tlachinollan, the Indigenous Organization of the Mixtec and Tlapaneco People, and the PRODH Center. In 2010, the court issued an historic ruling against the Mexican government: "The State is to blame for the violation of the rights of personal integrity, dignity, and privacy . . . of Mrs. Rosendo Cantú."

The Construction of the "Historical Falsehood"

Albeit covertly, Tomás Zerón and the federal ministerial police were in charge of the investigation of the initial twenty-two arrested Iguala police officers.

The federal government's construction of its "historical falsehood"—spun by the PGR and the AIC, using the federal ministerial police—began on the night of September 26, 2014.

The Iguala PGR opened an investigation, based on intelligence from the C4, for "violation of the federal firearms and explosives act." According to the documents I have obtained, they immediately informed the PGR delegate in Guerrero, Miguel Amelio Gómez.

In a document drafted by the Public Ministry's César Iván Pilares, dated September 26, a "detailed and exhaustive investigation" was ordered based on a call made by the C4 which claimed, though as yet without confirmation, that students from the Ayotzinapa Normal Rural School were being shot at by the municipal police in an intensive operation unfolding in the center, on Galeana and Mina streets, where some buses in the students' power were blocked.

Federal minsterial officers Romeo Ortiz Valenciana, José Manuel Dirzo Correa, and Enrique Ramírez Hernández drove out that night, as did officers from the federal police and the Army.

According to their own reports, the patrols were on the Iguala–Chilpancingo federal highway when they saw the Estrella de Oro bus 1531—from which at least twenty of the forty-three students were disappeared—with its windows shattered and its tires punctured. One of the reports states: "For obvious reasons it is here corroborated that, on September 26 of the current year, abuses were carried out by supposed students."

The team subsequently went to Juan N. Álvarez Street, where they observed three more buses with punctured tires, "along with some young people who appeared to be students . . . and so we proceeded to depart from said location in order to avoid an altercation with the individuals in the bus." The report also states that the Prosecutor's Office had opened an investigation into people wounded by gunshots. From information given in the report, the State Prosecutor's Office must have opened this preliminary inquiry by 21:30 that night—before the forty-three students had been disappeared and before the final shootout on Juan N. Álvarez Street, during which two students were killed and others wounded. In other words, Zerón's men were already on the streets of Iguala when the worst atrocities occurred.

In my investigation I was able to obtain the uncensored testimonies that were given to the PGR by forty-seven of the people arrested, allegedly confessing to having knowledge of the events or having directly participated in the attacks. These individuals, as of this writing, are still being tried or are awaiting trial in criminal courts. After reviewing and comparing the documents, I found that each one provided a different version of how the *normalistas* were attacked and taken away, and where they ended up. Despite the fact that the Mexican government arrested more than 100 presumed suspects, to date not one of them has been able to reveal the location of the forty-three students.

For two years I interviewed dozens of family members of the allegedly guilty parties and examined unpublished material including police reports and the medical reports on those arrested. Beyond the incongruences in their testimonies, the common denominator in all of those who have confessed was their injuries.

Beginning in December 2014, I began to report for *Proceso* magazine on the federal government's coercion of confessions and its mistreatment of many of the men and women detained. The federal ministerial police, the federal police, and the marines resorted to increasing violence as the arrests went on.

Notwithstanding that the PGR doesn't have a shred of actual evidence about the destination of the students or even a demonstrably plausible lead, in October 2014 the SEIDO affirmed that the disappeared students "seem to have been incinerated completely, due to which even if some remains are discovered, it might be impossible to identify them." Irrespective of the veracity of the forced "confessions," the PGR already had come to its own conclusions.

The "Confessions"

On October 5, 2014, Guerrero's prosecutor general, Iñaki Blanco Cabrera, declared the case closed. He announced that the forty-three disappeared *normalistas* had been killed and buried in hidden graves and that the culprits were the Iguala municipal police officers, along with José Luis Abarca and the Guerreros Unidos. To back up his claim he produced the (altered) declaration of Iguala police officer Hugo Hernández Arias, who "indicated seeing ten detained [students] in the patio of the police station who were then taken away by other officers, whose names he didn't know, in two patrol cars."

Blanco Cabrera maintained that the information matched "the video recordings obtained by Iguala C4 from security cameras on Periférico Benito Juárez at the intersection with the Iguala–Taxco federal highway, in which images of vehicles appearing to belong to the police can be seen. In one of the videos, at 23:21, an official police vehicle is seen driving on the aforementioned roads, with civilians in its truck bed."

But Blanco, again manipulating his evidence, only showed a fraction of the video labeled "26-09-2014 11-19-32 p.m. Police officers transporting detained subjects." I was able to see the entirety of the video. Blanco's fragment failed to show the convoy that was escorting those vehicles; and, contrary to his claim, it came from a security camera on Periférico Oriente, on the road to Cocula, not Taxco.

"Due to investigation carried out by intelligence and cabinet" officials, according to Blanco, they proceeded to arrest Honorio Antúnez Osorio, alias *El Patachín* (an Iguala police officer), Martín Alejandro Macedo Barrera, Marco Antonio Ríos Berber, and Luis Alberto José Gaspar, alias *El Tongo*. All of them allegedly confessed to being members of the Guerreros Unidos and directly implicated José Luis Abarca and the Iguala police in the attacks.

On the previous day, October 4, Blanco went on, Macedo Barrera and Ríos Berber had confessed to capturing seventeen students and taking them to the small community of

Pueblo Viejo. When prosecutors went there, they discovered hidden graves containing twenty-eight bodies, "some complete and others in pieces, showing signs of having been burned."

That same day (October 5), in a press conference, Rodrigo Archundia Barrientos (then head of SEIDO) and Tomás Zerón vowed to work together to elucidate the facts, but important headway had already been made: the federal government, in collaboration with the state of Guerrero, had arrested the presumed killers and these had confessed their crimes.

Zerón now began to construct a version of events that would allow the federal government to foreclose the affair. Though the PGR's various versions would differ regarding the final destination of the disappeared students, strangely enough they all coincided in the claim that some or all of the students had been "burned."

On October 3 and 4, Antúnez Osorio, Macedo Barrera, Ríos Berber, and José Gaspar were arrested in Iguala in a joint operation by the AIC, the Army, and the Guerrero ministerial police led by Fidel Rosas Serrano. According to the police, the suspects were picked up after they were seen "acting suspiciously" in the street, which contradicts Blanco's statement that it was an intelligence operation. The men submitted their first declarations to the state prosecutor and were turned over to SEIDO the next day, October 5.

It was their testimonies that disclosed the nicknames of the members of Guerreros Unidos who supposedly carried out the attacks and the disappearances: *La Mole*, *El Tíner*, *Amarguras*, and someone called *El Choky*, who would become an almost constant refrain in dozens of subsequent confessions.

165

Antúnez Osorio, who had previously been a soldier in Iguala's 27th Infantry Battalion, was the first witness to give the names of various current colleagues in the Iguala police— officers he accused of working for the Guerreros Unidos, as well as taking bribes from them in return for protection. Among others, he named Ulises Bernabé García, *El Gay*, the prison magistrate who Osorio alleged was also a member of the police emergency response team, Los Bélicos. Osorio maintained that though he wasn't present, he had heard that some of the students had been taken to Iguala police station, where Bernabé García turned them over to "assassins from Cocula" and to Iguala police captain Francisco Salgado Valladares. During the course of my investigation, Bernabé García would become a key element for overturning the state's official version of events.

Macedo Barrera, another supposed member of Guerreros Unidos, claimed that it was *El Choky* who ordered the attacks against the *normalistas*. Barrera admitted to having participated and also claimed that the students had been armed and had been firing in the center of Iguala, "managing to injure various people," causing him and fellow gang members to fire back. They then loaded seventeen students in their vehicles and took them to "la Loma," where they shot some of them and beat a few others to death. Seven of the students they allegedly set on fire in a grave:

"[The students] got really violent when we were kidnapping them, and to stop them fucking around we decided to kill them. I think they used the excavator to bury them on the ranch we were at. I killed two of the *ayotzinapos*, though not the ones we burned, shooting them in the head."

Ríos Berber, meanwhile, said that *El Choky* was the chief assassin of the Guerreros Unidos, and he also mentioned some of the other members' nicknames: *La Mente*, *El Chino*, *El May*, and *El Gaby*. In his first testimony he claimed that already at 18:00, *El Chino* had ordered him to keep an eye on the *normalistas* who had entered Iguala in an Estrella de Oro bus. In fact, at that time the *normalistas* had only just left Ayotzinapa.

According to the first statement given by Ríos Berber, it was the local Iguala police, following the orders of "Valladares" (the captain), who transported twenty students to their headquarters, while *El Choky* himself carried another three students in his gray Mustang. Then, according to Ríos Berber, he and *El Choky* took thirteen *normalistas* to a hill near the Pueblo Viejo community, where, as he dug the grave into which the bodies would later be dragged, doused with diesel fuel, and burned, he saw three of the students being murdered. Later, he drove a white pickup truck transporting another ten students, six of whom were killed. "I shot two of them in the head with *La Mente*'s gun. *El Gaby* killed two more. *El Choky* killed one. *La Vero* killed another, and we left four of them alive." They then threw those six bodies into the grave and burned them with the others.

Curiously, neither Macedo Barrera nor Ríos Berber mention taking part in the attacks against the *normalistas*; their declarations are a separate account of mass murder, relating to the hidden graves that were indeed found in Pueblo Viejo, and which altogether contained twenty-eight bodies. It was at this point that the lawyers and families of the forty-three students asked the governor of Guerrero for the immediate intervention of the renowned Argentine Forensic Anthropology Team. These specialists flew in to identify the remains, effectively derailing the government's first attempt to wrap up the case. Thanks to the expertise of the prestigious forensic team, it was determined that, despite the detailed testimony claiming otherwise, none of the remains belonged to the missing students.

On October 16, in another statement to the PGR, Ríos Berber laid out another version of events. SEIDO, working behind the scenes like a director with a script in his hand, was nudging each new version towards the government's predetermined denouement. This time Ríos Berber didn't claim to have been personally involved with the murder of the students, but instead affirmed that when Guerreros Unidos captured anybody in Iguala, they delivered them over to a man known as *El Gil,* who always took them to Cocula, "so I guess they probably killed and buried them there." Thus the way was paved towards the "historical truth."

One month later, on November 24, 2014, these four members of Guerreros Unidos described to Judge Guillermo Baltazar the conditions under which they were made to confess. This explains why, despite the profuse detail of their account of the students' ultimate fate, the victims were not found in the locations they pinpointed.

The "Killing" and "Burying" of the *Normalistas* in La Parota

Even before the collapse of the Pueblo Viejo story, the PGR had built a second version of the final location of the forty-three students: mass graves in the hills of La Parota, where, they claimed, the bodies had been incinerated.

At noon on October 8, 2014, officials of the Criminal Investigations Agency (AIC), with the help of three marines, detained Carlos Pascual Cervantes Jaimes in Cuernavaca, along with Miguel Ángel and Osvaldo Ríos Sánchez, all of whom sold clothing in the market. The agents mistook one of them for Salomón Pineda Villa, the brother of Mayor Abarca's wife.

"You're *El Molón*," the officers told Osvaldo.

"No, boss, I'm just here to sell clothes," he replied.

It wasn't until October 9—a delay from supposed mechanical problems in their vehicles—that the three men were presented at SEIDO headquarters. Miguel Ángel and Osvaldo Ríos Sánchez, in their confessions, described the structure of the Guerreros Unidos, claiming that Raúl Núñez Salgado, known as *El Camperra*, along with *El Choky*, *La Mente*, and *El Gil* were the leaders of the organization, though he also named *El May* as another important actor in the attacks of September 26. It was via these new "confessions" that the PGR was first able to suggest that the forty-three students themselves had been involved in organized crime.

The Ríos brothers claimed that the Los Rojos gang picked a fight with the Guerreros Unidos by coming into Iguala on September 26 and infiltrating the *normalistas*. They also stated that *El Choky* attacked the students and took them to La Parota. According to official documents, they even marked an X on a map to show where the remains had been left.

At 06:30 on October 9, the marines helicoptered the Ríos Sánchez brothers from Mexico City to the Iguala–Teloloapan federal highway, where they proceeded in military vehicles to a deserted area of La Parota. There, the men who had allegedly confessed to killing the students pointed out what they said was the site of their remains. According to a Public Ministry certifying document, it was obvious that digging had recently taken place.

However, a medical check performed on Miguel Ángel that same day, before he directed officials to the supposed resting place of the students, found more than ten injuries on his body. On Osvaldo there were fourteen. Family members of the two men told me that the marines tortured them and even forced them to dig their own graves.

The following year, on June 10, 2015, the PGR's ombudsman, the Visitaduría or Inspector General, began looking into possible "criminal conduct" on the part of the Navy officers and federal ministerial police who participated in the apprehension of the Ríos Sánchez brothers and Cervantes Jaimes.

Even after their self-incriminating confession, the PGR, citing lack of evidence, let the Ríos Sánchez brothers and Cervantes Jaimes go free. Then, almost right away, on October 13, 2014, two federal ministerial police officers, Felipe Gutiérrez Díaz and Héctor Eduardo Estévez Girón, arrested them again outside of the SEIDO offices.

Weeks later, more clandestine graves were found in the La Parota area, along with remnants of human flesh and blood, as well as shoes, backpacks, and pens, according to various reports released to the press. Despite the "detailed" and "precise" assurances provided to officials that this was the final location of the students, none of the DNA extracted from the remains corresponded with the missing forty-three.

On the night of October 9, in the Brisas neighborhood of Iguala, marines—based on supposed anonymous tips—arrested a second group of presumed members of Guerreros Unidos, including Raymundo Salvador Bernal and brothers Luis Alberto and Juan José Estrada Montes de Oca. According to the marines, they were carrying a restricted firearm and "openly acknowledged that they belonged to the criminal organization, Guerreros Unidos."

When he was presented to make his confession, Luis Alberto appeared with a broken nose and had clearly been beaten. He claimed to have been assaulted by some taxi drivers. Jazmín Jiménez Zúñiga, of the Public Ministry, took his brief confession: all he had heard, Alberto claimed, was that members of the Guerreros Unidos had attacked the *normalistas*. Zúñiga asked him if he wanted to file a complaint against any public officials, and he said that he did not.

Juan José also appeared to have been beaten when he was presented to make his confession to another ministry official, Denisse González Sánchez. He claimed to be a nudist, who worked selling various products to the Centro Botánico Azteca. He made no statements relevant to the night of September 26.

Raymundo Salvador Bernal, who was in the worst shape of them all, claimed not to have been arrested on the street but to have been pulled out of his cell phone stand in Iguala market.

On June 10, 2015, the Special Unit of Investigations of Crimes Committed by Public Servants against the Administration of Justice opened a further investigation into crimes committed by marines, this time during their apprehension of the brothers Estrada Montes de Oca and Salvador Bernal.

In short, the precedent set by arresting alleged members of the Guerreros Unidos was repeated to the letter. The three men were eventually released. And again, following the same pattern, they were soon picked up again by ministerial police officers—the same two officers (Gutiérrez Díaz and Estévez Girón) who had picked up the Ríos brothers—and the men were "interviewed" again.

The PGR would repeat this procedure multiple times, letting individuals who confessed to knowledge or participation in the attacks believe that they were being released, only to detain them again. Again on October 9, again based on supposed anonymous tips, the marines Celso Mario Rendón Mejía and Reynel Calvo Molina detained Ramiro Ocampo Pineda and a woman named Rosario Manuel Borja on the streets of Iguala for allegedly belonging to Guerreros Unidos. The marines claimed that Ocampo Pineda was carrying a grenade in a suitcase. He later admitted, "voluntarily," to being a member of Guerreros Unidos.

Ocampo Pineda made his first confession to the PGR on October 11. According to a medical report from the same day, he appeared dizzy and bore wounds on his body, but the ministry's Luis Armando García Sánchez still made him give a statement. The first thing that Ocampo Pineda stated was that he hadn't been picked up in Iguala, but in a hotel in Taxco. He claimed to belong to the Guerreros Unidos and mentioned other supposed members, including the leader, Mario Casarrubias, and Víctor Hugo Benítez Palacio, known as *El Tilo*. He also mentioned *El Camperra* and *El Gil*. In June 2015, the same Special Unit of Investigations began investigating complaints of torture committed against Ocampo Pineda and Manuel Borja.

Ocampo Pineda claimed that, on September 26, he was working as a "hawk," or lookout, while *El Chuky*, *El Choky*, *La Mente*, and *El May* attacked the students on Juan N. Álvarez Street and (mistaking them for more students) the Avispones team on the Chilpancingo highway. He described that under the Tomatal bridge, close to the state courthouse, *El Chuky*'s men, along with local Iguala police, pulled the students off a bus.

According to the PGR, Ocampo Pineda confessed that the police, transporting them in various private and police vehicles, finally handed over the students in Pueblo Viejo, where they were doused with diesel fuel, set on fire, and buried.

In the first medical report released on Ocampo Pineda and Manuel Borja, they allegedly presented with no wounds. In a second medical report, dated the same day, however, Ocampo Pineda had dozens of injuries on his face and body, burn marks, and a burst eardrum.

Again, like the Montes de Oca brothers and Raymundo Salvador Bernal, Ocampo Pineda and Manuel Borja were released by the PGR and taken back into custody almost immediately, on October 13, 2014, outside of the SEIDO offices. The agents were once more Gutiérrez Díaz and Estévez Girón, presenting an arrest report identical to the one that they had previously used, changing only the names. On October 14, the PGR requested Ocampo Pineda make another confession, but he refused.

On October 10, federal ministerial police Jesús Omar Maciel Álvarez and Miguel Ángel Romero Hernández detained a twenty-year-old Iguala firefighter, David Hernández Cruz. Predictably, he too admitted to working for Guerreros Unidos and distributing cash to lookouts and local notables.

Cruz gave his first brief testimony the same day, at 21:00, to the Public Ministry's Antonio Suany López. He confessed to working as a lookout and maintained that *El Chuky* and *El Choky* were the same person, though others had them as separate. He alleged that certain municipal policemen, plus a figure he called Raúl Núñez Salgado, *El Camperra*, were involved in the criminal network. He also named three brothers—Víctor Hugo, Orbelín, and Salvador Benítez Palacios—as leaders of the Los Tilos gang, apparently allied with the Guerreros Unidos. He made no reference to Mayor José Luis Abarca or to the events of September 26.

Hours later, at 04:30 in the morning of October 11, Hernández Cruz delivered another, much longer statement, in which he asserted that the students in the bus outside of the state courthouse were armed. "I saw about forty people get out of the bus, civilians, some of them armed with shotguns, but I didn't hear any shots." These people, he said, boarded a white Urvan and a white Suburban and drove towards the Pajaritos neighborhood.

Hernández Cruz said that around 23:45, *El Chuky* called him on his cell to ask who was going to deliver the "packages," clarifying that he was referring to the students, and Cruz told him that he didn't know. He continued: "Going back to the moment that *El Chuky* called me, after that call I heard on the Matra radio that the [deputy] chief of municipal police [of Iguala], [Francisco Salgado] Valladares, transmitted an order from A5 to arrest the students, 'because you know how they are.' The A5 code refers to the mayor, whose name is José Luis Abarca Velázquez."

Though he directly implicates the mayor in his confession, at the hour when Hernández Cruz claims that *El Chuky* asked about the "packages," the students hadn't yet been taken.

Cruz's confession implicated, for the first time, the local Cocula police. The firefighter claimed that, after 23:45, he clearly observed on the Períferico four Cocula police vehicles and saw them pick up five or six students who were then hustled into the truck beds, "sitting or crouching down," with four officers standing guard over them. The trucks drove away from the scene towards Cocula. He said that the Cocula police commander, César Nava González, later called him to ask where they should take the "packages."

The fireman's confession, however, doesn't fit with the timeline of that night. By 23:45, the students had already been disappeared. Furthermore, while he claims that the Cocula police were in four trucks, they actually occupied only three.

And the circumstances of his confession had something else in common with the others: according to the PGR's own medical check, before making his first statement he presented as having been severely beaten. His family has no doubt that he was tortured. In June 2015, the PGR was obligated to open an internal investigation against federal ministerial police officers Jesús Omar Maciel Álvarez and Miguel Ángel Romero Hernández, who had arrested Hernández Cruz.

After his confession, he was released on October 14. He was immediately rearrested outside the SEIDO by two other federal ministerial police, Israel Jiménez Cruz and Miguel Eduardo Castañeda. They brought him before the Public Ministry to make another statement, but, according to the PGR report, he refused.

The Eleven Versions of the Cocula Police

After the confession submitted by Hernández Cruz, the PGR started looking for the Cocula and Iguala police officers he named. At this point, the person in charge of the investigation was public prosecutor Lourdes López Lucho Iturbide—notorious for the dirty work she had put in for the Calderón administration, when the PGR, under the direction of Marisela Morales, was conducting operations such as the "Michoacanazo" or "Operation Cleanup."

According to an October 13 federal ministerial police report, their agents arrested twenty-four local police officers at Cocula city hall, eleven of whom admitted to having gone to Iguala in three pickup trucks to assist the Iguala police with "the emergency" or "shootout" that was underway. Each of the eleven officers, however, provided divergent details of the same event. However, all claimed to have been following the orders of Captain Ignacio Aceves Rosales and the deputy chief of Cocula, César Nava González, both of whom would turn out to be key in understanding the Cocula force's role on the night in question.

Cocula police officers detained by federal ministerial police

1. Ignacio Aceves Rosales*+
2. Alberto Aceves Serrano+
3. Ángel Antúnez
4. Willber Barrios
5. Salvador Bravo
6. Juan de la Puente+
7. Alfredo Alonso Dorantes
8. Pedro Flores
9. José Antonio Flores Traín+
10. Ignacio Hidalgo
11. Joaquín Lagunas+
12. Jorge Luis Manjarrez
13. Julio César Mateos Rosales+
14. Antonio Morales
15. José Luis Morales
16. Ysmael Palma Mena*
17. Jesús Parra Arroyo *+
18. Roberto Pedrote Nava *+
19. Arturo Reyes Barrera+
20. Nelson Román Rodríguez+
21. Marco Antonio Segura
22. Marco Jairo Tapia
23. Óscar Veleros+
24. César Yáñez

*Officers, including César Nava González, who passed "trust-worthiness exams" conducted by Central State Control and Monitoring of Trustworthiness.
+Officers who admitted to having gone to Iguala.

Federal ministerial police officers who detained the Cocula officers

1. Ehecatl Eduardo Águila Pineda
2. Román Almazán Hernández
3. Manuel Tadeo Camarena Porras
4. Roberto Campos Cruz
5. Jonathan Grishan Chimal López
6. Julio Dagoberto Contreras Saucedo
7. Josefina de la Cruz Rosales
8. Luis Nicasio Díaz Elizalde
9. Rafael González Castelán
10. Ángel Alfredo Gutiérrez Chagoya
11. Carlos Antonio Hernández Campos
12. Sergio Hernández Carranza
13. Rafael Hernández Flores
14. José Eduardo Lavariega Pérez
15. Jesús Omar Maciel Álvarez
16. Arturo Martínez Pérez
17. Juan José Ortega Garcés
18. Miguel Ángel Pita Casco
19. Julio César Ramos Lorenzana
20. Jesús Rudimiro Rodríguez Reyes
21. Sergio Rojas Mireles
22. Miguel Ángel Romero Hernández
23. Javier Rosete Torres
24. Israel Ruíz Rodríguez

25. Mario Sánchez Ramírez
26. María Luisa Thome Lara
27. David Vargas Briseño
28. Lázaro Xochihua Atzin

María Elena Hidalgo Segura, emergency operator in Cocula of the 066 line, which is connected to the national system run by the Secretariat of the Interior, confirmed having received a call for assistance from the Iguala C4. In other words, the Army, the federal police, the Guerrero state police, the PGR, and the local Iguala police all had direct knowledge of this request for backup from Cocula local police.

The majority of the eleven Cocula officers who admitted going to Iguala claimed to have assembled at the Iguala home of Captain Nava González, who was on his day off. Officer José Antonio Flores Traín remained there on guard, while the rest of them left for the intersection of Periférico and Juan N. Álvarez, arriving between 22:30 and 23:00.

Officer Joaquín Flores Laguna claimed that when they got to the Pemex gas station on Juan N. Álvarez, at the corner of Industria Petrolera and Periférico—not far from the C4 base—there were about eight Iguala police vehicles blocking the road, which made room for the Cocula police to pass. Almost all the officers agree that three of the five buses that the *normalistas* were riding in were at this location. One of the students, *Pulmón*, was suffering an asthma attack, and officers helped him to an ambulance—surviving *normalistas* would corroborate this part of the story. From there onward, the story told by the Cocula men diverges in three key points: how they then proceeded to the Iguala police station, how they brought the students out of there, and to whom they turned them over.

According to officer Lagunas Franco, Nava González ordered him to go pick up his friend Flores Traín, who had remained at the police chief's house, and then, a half hour later, the three Cocula vehicles reunited in Mextitlán and returned to their town without further incident.

Officer Alberto Aceves Serrano recalled that on Juan N. Álvarez Street they came across "various people on the ground, of the masculine sex, presumably wounded by gunfire." None of the other police, or even the students I interviewed, would echo this claim.

Officer Nelson Román Rodríguez said that from that scene they went directly to Metlapa and then to Cocula.

Officer Ignacio Aceves Rosales claimed that when they were assisting the Iguala police, the deputy chief, Francisco Salgado Valladares, was present and called Nava González to give him directions. After they left Periférico and Juan N. Álvarez, they drove to the Iguala station and left the Cocula vehicles out front for security. Aceves Rosales and Nava González walked into the station, where they allegedly saw thirteen young people on the patio.

Officer Jesús Parra Arroyo, however, claimed that after they arrived at the station, patrols pulled up with thirty students on board and unloaded them one by one in the street, which accords with the testimony of Aceves Rosales, who claimed that the trucks entered the Iguala station empty.

And yet, according to Aceves Serrano, on arrival at the station Captain Salgado Valladares was already there along with more than thirty-five civilians, who were then split up between three Iguala and two Cocula vehicles, with around ten people to each vehicle.

Aceves Rosales said that, following an order from Salgado Valladares, they took thirteen students, loaded them in two

Cocula vehicles, and drove them to the outlying Loma de los Coyotes area, where they turned them over to officers riding in three Iguala police trucks. These delivered the students to one *El Pato*, who would transport them in a truck with a white cargo rack to the tiny village of Tianquizolco.

In the version according to Julio César Mateos Rosales, when they arrived at the Iguala station, a Cocula police truck drove into the courtyard and came out again with eight or ten students lying down in the back. Another Cocula truck was loaded with an undefined number of students out in the street. Mateos Rosales recalled that they drove them to Loma de los Coyotes and handed them over to Iguala police. He did not mention *El Pato* or a truck with a cargo rack.

Officer Aceves Serrano claimed that they drove the students to a police checkpoint in Loma de los Coyotes, where they loaded them into a double-wheeled "cattle-type" truck and three Iguala police trucks, which then took off in an "unknown direction."

Officer Parra Arroyo said that after unloading the students in the street, they straightaway put five each in two Cocula police vehicles and drove them to Loma de los Coyotes. He also mentioned the police checkpoint where they delivered the ten captives, and that police drove "with the kids" down a dirt road. He does not refer to a white truck, and he was the only officer to provide a time, stating that the transfer took place at 00:45 on September 27.

Of all the versions, that of Officer Roberto Pedrote Nava was the most divergent: he claimed that he drove a Cocula police vehicle without any students on board from Iguala to Metlapa, where he waited for Nava González and the other officers. At midnight Nava González arrived, along with Aceves Rosales, each in a truck with eight people loaded into the bed, some of whom were yelling for help. Nava González ordered him to wait there while the trucks went on to Iguala. Pedrote Nava claims that he waited twenty minutes for the trucks, now empty, to return.

Aceves Rosales and Reyes Barrera both said that at 02:30 Nava González and five other officers came out of the Cocula police station, dressed in street clothes. They then left in Aceves Rosales's personal vehicle, heading to a property belonging to the oft-cited gangster *El Gil*, in Pueblo Viejo, where he kept horses and gamecocks.

To try to understand what really happened in and around the Iguala police station that night, I interviewed the neighbors, asking if they saw or heard anything out of the ordinary, and they told me that they did not. But I was able to confirm that the portal leading to the courtyard at the station is low, so that police trucks—whether local or federal—cannot possibly enter. This means that when the police are transporting suspects, they need to stop in the street and walk them into the station.

On October 14, the PGR presented emergency operator María Elena Hidalgo Segura and legal advisor Magali Ortega as witnesses. Hidalgo Segura testified that on the evening of September 26 she was on duty in Cocula and realized there was a problem in Iguala when, at approximately 21:00, an operator from the Iguala C4, Sandy Ornelas, called her to ask which Cocula patrols had set off to provide the requested backup. She said that at 02:30, police officers returned to the station and burned a year's worth of service records. She said that her friend, Xóchitl García, confided that she saw the CCTV images and that they "were really ugly, everything that happened that night, and she heard there'd been about thirty people killed." Xóchitl, who was on duty on the night in question, quit her job four days later and was never summoned to testify.

Legal advisor Magali Ortega, meanwhile, admitted to having changed the names of the officers on the daily schedule and modified the registry to make it seem that Nava González was off on September 26 for medical reasons, which was untrue.

On October 13, Magali Ortega was detained as a witness, along with the twenty-four Cocula police officers. She claimed that she was forced to sign a statement incriminating the officers, being threatened with sexual abuse if she didn't. She also witnessed the torture of some of the officers. After her coerced testimony, Ortega was officially arrested on January 15, 2016 when she refused to ratify the same testimony. She is currently being held in Cefereso #16, in Morelos. Family members have confirmed that she did in fact obtain, by way of her sister who worked in public health, a false medical certificate for Nava González.

What is certain is that the official reports written by the Cocula police who were on duty the night of September 26 say nothing about going to Iguala to help the police there. Nor was the call from the C4 mentioned. Next day, the vehicle numbers of the three Cocula police trucks that went to Iguala were changed.

Just as with the detentions made by AIC under the direction of Tomás Zerón, the common denominator of the Cocula police who were arrested, besides their mutual contradictions, is that the majority of them, according to medical examinations conducted by SEIDO prior to their official statements, exhibited marks of physical violence.

Minerva Ochoa, wife of the Cocula officer Julio César Mateos Rosales, told me that her husband was forced to testify after being tortured both physically and psychologically. It was impossible, she said, for him to have participated in the events in Iguala on September 26, because he hadn't been working. They had spent the whole day together, cooking *pozole* for a church event. Minerva assured me that there were other witnesses who would confirm this.

None of the Cocula police officers who confessed their alleged participation in the events explained how they managed to subdue the students or mentioned that the students were injured. In none of the eleven accounts did the number of students they supposedly transported equal forty-three.

The PGR's internal ombudsman (Visitaduría General) opened an investigation on June 3, 2015 into allegations of torture committed by the federal ministerial police during and after the arrest of the Cocula officers.

The Version of the Iguala Police

The Iguala police officers who were not arrested on September 27 were sent on a training course in the 5th Regiment's Motorized Cavalry Unit of SEDENA, located in Tlaxcala. On October 14, ten of those officers were arrested inside the military camp and sent to the SEIDO.

Iguala police detained by federal ministerial police on October 14

Héctor Aguilar Ávalos*
Verónica Bahena+
Leodán Fuentes Pineda*
Alejandro Lara García*

Édgar Magdaleno Navarro*
Alejandro Mota Román
Enrique Pérez Carreto*
Óscar Augusto Pérez Carreto*
Santiago Socorro Mazón Cedillo*
Édgar Vieyra

*Officers not on duty the night of September 26, 2014
+Officer on vacation the night of September 26, 2014

Before they were taken away, Flor María Ayala, a surgeon working for the Regional Training Center of the 6th Military District, conducted a thorough medical examination on each of the officers. Not one of them displayed any contusions or wounds, though by the time they arrived before the Public Ministry, most of them had various injuries.

Federal ministerial police who arrested the Iguala officers

César Albarrán Beltrán
Daniel Cabello Vargas
Julio Pablo Cárdenas Ugalde
Carlos Espinosa Martínez
Rodrigo Refugio Hernández García
Julio César Herrera Sánchez

According to the policemen and their families, the beatings took place in the SEIDO offices, administered by burly men in black with hooded faces. They were all beaten and questioned about the disappeared students and the Guerreros Unidos in a similar manner.

Seven of the detained officers weren't working on September 26, 2014. One of those on duty that night, Édgar Vieyra, claimed to know nothing about the attacks against the *normalistas* or the disappearance of the forty-three. Alejandro Mota Román, the other officer on duty, explained that he was part of the crack police group known as Los Bélicos, The Warriors ("after we were certified by the Feds"). He identified the other members as Carlos, Prócoro, Captain Francisco Salgado Valladares, and (though he was no longer in it) Narciso. The group was set up to respond to calls for help made via C4. Without going into details, he confirmed that between 20:00 and 21:00 he went to the Iguala police station to recharge his radio and, as he was leaving, received a call about a stolen motorcycle:

"When I went looking for the motorcycle between nine-thirty and ten o'clock, I started hearing reports on my radio that various subjects were getting off a bus, without mention of what kind of bus or what company, and they were robbing passersby on Galeana Street close to the Estrella Blanca bus terminal, and it was also reported that they had taken over two buses, [informing] C4 over the radio."

He testified that a number of patrols, as he heard over the radio, offered to respond to the incident. "As I was going around I was listening to [these reports] and the C4 operator was announcing that there seemed to be shots fired, and I kept looking for the [stolen] motorcycle." Later, around 22:00, he spotted two people riding a motorcycle similar to the one reported stolen. He detained them, took them to the Iguala station, and put them before the prison magistrate, Ulises Bernabé García.

At approximately 22:30, according to Mota Román, there was a new call from the C4 warning that on Periférico Sur, near the 24 de Febrero neighborhood, "there were various armed people" and he went to the scene and saw a group of young men who ran towards the nearby hills when they saw the police. Mota Román claimed they were not armed but were carrying rocks. He did not pursue the fugitives.

At around 22:45, another call put out by the C4 warned that there were now "armed persons" in the Pajaritos area. At 23:00, he joined up with five police vehicles that agreed on a joint patrol in response to the reports, starting from near the state courthouse. Mota Román claimed that together they passed a point between Juan N. Álvarez Street and Periférico, where he saw a crowd of people gathering. According to his timeline, this would have been the *normalistas* getting ready to give their press conference just before the third attack.

At 23:30, Mota Román received the order to go to the federal police headquarters, where there were more than ten vehicles and about five police motorcycles, a fact corroborated by officers arrested on September 27. Soon thereafter he was instructed to assemble at the Regional Police Training Center.

Another of the ten Iguala officers arrested on October 14, Alejandro Lara García, asked the duty attorney to file an official complaint with the National Commission on Human Rights "against the federal police officers who detained us, beat us, and forcefully demanded to know where the bodies were."

By September 2016, the PGR had produced no evidence other than the self-incriminating confessions that "proved" that the detained local Cocula and Iguala police officers were involved with organized crime. Despite the torture they endured, none of the police officers yielded any information that would reveal the truth of how the forty-three students were disappeared or where they ended up.

In their testimonies, the Cocula officers and the alleged members of the Guerreros Unidos constantly referred to the deputy chiefs of the Iguala and Cocula police, Francisco Salgado Valladares and César Nava González, respectively. The latter was detained in Colima on November 15, 2014. In his statement to the PGR, he denied belonging to any criminal organization but admitted that on the night of September 26 Salgado Valladares asked him for help transporting "ten or eight people" to Loma de los Coyotes, on the outskirts of Iguala, where they turned them over to other Iguala officers.

Salgado Valladares was not apprehended until May 7, 2015, in Morelos. In his declaration to the PGR he admitted to having ties, since 2012, to the Guerreros Unidos. He also claimed to have learned of the incidents of September 26 through his Matra radio, on which he heard the voice of operator J. Natividad, who mentioned the apprehension of the *normalistas* on the order of "A5," the mayor of Iguala. When he arrived at the police station, around 23:00, he claimed to have seen about eight men handcuffed in the courtyard, their faces covered with their shirts, and then Nava González took them and drove them out of the station.

In December 2015, Nava González himself changed his original story before the judge hearing his case, giving it a very different turn, such that it accorded with statements Salgado Valladares's relatives submitted about that night.

The Leaders of the Guerreros Unidos—Another Dead End

Raúl Núñez Salgado, alias *El Camperra*, ran a butcher shop in the Iguala market; in his spare time he organized dances and rodeos. He was detained on October 14 by two marines, David Ramírez Alcaraz and Carlos Gutiérrez Silva, as he was leaving a mall in Acapulco, allegedly in possession of 299 packets of cocaine and 970 pesos. His testimony helped the PGR "strengthen" their case against the Iguala and Cocula police officers.

Núñez Salgado testified that in the middle of 2013 he began working for the Guerreros Unidos as a messenger for someone he only knew as Marcos, or *El Chaparro*, who recommended him to Mario Casarrubias, an alleged leader of the gang. He explained that since he didn't receive a salary, he organized dances and rodeos with one Rogelio Figueroa.

Contradicting the testimony of other detainees, he claimed that Gildardo López Astudillo, *El Gil*, was the head of Guerreros Unidos in Cocula, *El May* was the head in Teloloapan, and *El Cholo* in Taxco. When Mario Casarrubias went out of town, he explained, he'd send him money to hand out to Iguala police officers through Captain Francisco Salgado Valladares. *El Gil* was responsible for paying out the bribes to the Cocula police through César Nava González, according to Núñez. After Mario Casarrubias's arrest, in May of 2014, his brother José Ángel took over. At no point in his testimony does Núñez Salgado mention the name of Mario's other brother, Sidronio Casarrubias Salgado.

He was in the center of town, Núñez Salgado explained in his first declaration, went back to his house, and then, when one of his "employees" called him from the La Perinola bar to ask if they should close, "since the students are causing mischief in the streets," he went to the bar to help close up.

In his second declaration, however, he told a different story: he was eating in the market around 19:00 when some people rampaged past, some covering their faces, others bare-chested, carrying "sticks" and "irons." They ran into the bus station and started smashing windows. Half an hour later they came walking back, followed by three buses, down Galeana Street.

His story, however, doesn't match up with the actual events of that night. The security camera footage of the inside of the bus station, seen by the Interdisciplinary Group of Independent Experts, showed that when the students first arrived at 19:05, they had only stones (and no sticks) in their hands, they didn't break any windows, and they left close to seven minutes later.

At the same time as he gave his statement, Núñez Salgado filed a denunciation against the marines who arrested him and opened a complaint with the National Commission on Human Rights. The public defender, Jorge Carlos Heredia García, requested a medical examination to ascertain whether his multiple injuries were "the outcome of torture." The PGR complied and documented more than twenty-six lesions on different parts of his body, including blood in his eyes and contusions on his neck, face, hands, chest, and anal region. The PGR would later open its own investigation into the marines who arrested him.

At the time of his arrest, Núñez Salgado was carrying a paper with the inventory of the contents of La Perinola, signed by Carlos Canto Salgado, who was making over the bar to him. This document prompted a search of the bar, as well as further arbitrary arrests. On October 22, 2014, Canto Salgado was arrested by Navy officer Ariel Agustín Castillo Reyes and federal ministerial police officer Ezequiel Peña Cerda. In their arrest report they refer to Canto Salgado as *El Pato* (the nickname cited by Cocula police officer Ignacio

Aceves Rosales), the person to whom the *normalistas* were supposedly delivered in Loma de los Coyotes.

According to the report, he was arrested while walking down the street at one in the afternoon, but he wasn't presented to the Public Ministry until early in the morning of October 23, where he stood accused of organized crime and the kidnapping of the forty-three students.

Canto Salgado testified that he was a middle school teacher in Iguala and the owner of La Perinola bar, where he met Núñez Salgado. In his first official declaration, attended by a public defender, he "confessed" that his most frequent clients were Eury Flores López, *maestro* Aguirre, Osvaldo Ríos Sánchez, known as *El Gordey*, Ernesto Martínez alias *El Napo*, *El Camperra*, Captain Salgado Valladares, and three other men known as *El Chiquilín*, *El Goku*, and *El Pollo*, who "used to talk about being part of the Guerreros Unidos gang."

He claimed that he had also heard Núñez Salgado say that he was in the Guerreros Unidos, and that *El Camperra* delivered money from the criminal group to the Iguala police, who were, he said, "ready to obey any order."

On the night of September 26, Canto Salgado said that Eury Flores López and Osvaldo Ríos Sánchez were in the bar (although Ríos Sánchez had claimed to be in the street, following the *normalistas*) when *El Camperra* burst in, shut the door, and said that they were going after the students, because "this has gotten out of hand. It's not how it used to be. This is bad, but orders are orders."

Sometime after four in the morning, *El Camperra*, Flores López, Ríos Sánchez, and Canto Salgado himself left the bar. "Even if it's true," Canto Salgado stated, "that I knew about the workings of the criminal group named Guerreros Unidos and was acquainted with a few of its members . . . I never knew the destination or the final location of the Ayotzinapa students."

On October 29, 2014, in his preliminary statement to the judge, Canto Salgado retracted his previous declaration: he hadn't been arrested in the street, but in his parents' house, on October 22 at three in the morning. He went into detail about the torture he suffered and later, cowed by the presence of his abusers, he had signed his first declaration without even reading it. He claimed that the torturers put a list of names to him, and he didn't know them or even know if they were gang members, and he only said they were so they would stop hitting him. A doctor appointed by the PGR confirmed that he was visibly beaten. He prescribed painkillers and anti-inflammatory pills, also noting that officers were watching the prisoner at all times, even during the medical.

In his complaint to the Human Rights Commission, number 114113, it is noted that Canto Salgado was arrested without a warrant, taken to his house which was ransacked by the marines, and then taken to another location where they beat him and applied electric shocks to force him to confess to working with the Guerreros Unidos, with the collaboration of other federal officers. The PGR opened an investigation into these claims.

I was able to obtain the visitors' logbook for the Joyas del Pacífico residential building where Canto Salgado lived, and where the marines took him after arresting him at his parents' house. According to this log, which corroborates Canto Salgado's claims, two military vehicles (17325 and 17950) entered the grounds, whose drivers identified themselves as members of "Federal Police and Navy."

Based on the testimony given by Canto Salgado, on October 27, federal police officers Isaac Alejo Hernández and César Reyes Escobar arrested Néstor Napoleón Martínez, the son of an accountant who worked in the Guerrero health department. According to the arrest report, the federal officers had been sent to find someone in Iguala by the name of Ernesto Martínez, alias *El Napo*. The officers went to "public spaces" to ask around for someone by that name. In the central market, an unidentified person told them he didn't know anybody by that name but did know someone whose nickname was *Napo*, and that they could find him in the New Life Christian Center.

Napoleón Martínez, employed as an accounting intern, was arrested by the two officers in the Christian center. The officers claimed that he had tried to flee; they subdued him and found an AR-15 rifle in his backpack, plus thirty rounds of ammunition and marijuana. He was presented before the PGR on October 28 at 02:52, with at least ten visible wounds on the right hand and chest, as well as a 13.5 × 6cm bruise on his stomach and four gashes on the inner thigh, close to the groin. Accusing the two arresting officers of inflicting these wounds, he refused to make a statement. In October 2016, Martínez was set free.

It appears that the majority of the men apprehended and accused of being members of the Guerreros Unidos share a connection to the world of fairs and rodeos, cock-fighting, horses, and ranching.

The PGR Fabricates the Faces of the Alleged Killers

By the end of October 2014, by pressing hard on a number of detainees, the PGR had got itself the names and physical descriptions of the supposed intellectual and material authors of the attacks against the *normalistas*, as well as of their disappearance and likely murder: *El Chuky* or *Choky*, *El May*, *El Gil*, and *El Chaky*.

Comparing the physical descriptions provided by their supposed acquaintances with each other, and with identikit portraits drawn up by the PGR, it emerges that the SEIDO had not a scrap of reliable data about who the killers were or what they looked like. The same person was often described with completely different features. According to Macedo Barrera, the fearsome *Chuky* or *Choky* (the supposed lead assassin of the Guerreros Unidos who allegedly killed the students) was twenty-four or twenty-five years old, under five feet tall, brown-skinned, no beard, and with a shaved head. According to Núñez Salgado, he was between five-foot one and five-foot three, light-skinned, with an oval face, small eyes, thin eyebrows, and a military-style haircut. According to Ocampo Pineda, he was only four-foot nine, light-skinned, and aged about thirty.

El Chaky, meanwhile, one of *El Choky*'s gunmen who also allegedly participated in the attacks, was, according to Ríos Berber, just under five feet tall, stout, dark-skinned, with a slightly turned-up nose, shaved head, and the tattoos of a woman and an Indian on his body. Miguel Ángel Ríos Sánchez described the same man as being five-foot nine, round-faced and almond-eyed, with light eyebrows and short hair. *El Camperra* described *El Chaky* as being five foot three, with thick eyebrows, a stubby nose, large eyes, and a tattoo of two teardrops beneath his left eye.

The same discrepant descriptions were given by the PGR's "witnesses" for *El May* and *El Gil*, as well as for Gildardo López Astudillo, who was arrested in September 2015 but didn't match even the PGR's own previous description. *El Cepillo*, who supposedly burned the bodies of the students, and who has a deformity on his upper lip, was likewise wildly misdescribed by Núñez Salgado and *El Camperra* when they were trying to place him at the scene.

The PGR's investigation wasn't a hunt for the truth, but a blatant fabrication designed to bury the truth. Beyond using torture as a systematic means to "solve" the case, the Mexican government also resorted to murder.

7

The "Historical Falsehood"

"This one's fucked! He gave us the slip," said a member of the marines, wearing an infantry uniform bedecked with medals, with an air of surprise. He was leaning over the inert body of Miguel Alejandro Blas Patiño, known as *El Chiquis*, in a building at the corner of 10 de Abril and Emiliano Zapata streets in Jiutepec, Morelos on the night of October 26, 2014. Blas Patiño, a young man from Teloloapan, had recently been arrested in a raid conducted as part of the hunt for those who disappeared the forty-three *normalistas*. By his side, still alive, were Eury Flores López and Francisco Lozano Cuevas, who had just come to after a brutal torture session: electrical prods in their genitals, beatings, and suffocation by plastic bags that they chomped at in their desperation to breathe.

The testimony rendered, under torture and threats, by Carlos Canto Salgado had impelled the PGR to make further arrests. According to the arrest report (signed by Third Petty Officer Santiago González Velázquez and Corporal Iván de Jesús Montes Trujillo), Eury Flores López, who had studied business administration, owned a line of dump trucks, and helped organize rodeos, was arrested at five in the morning on October 27 when a squadron of marines driving through Iguala saw two "suspects" inside a white car speaking with a man standing in the street. According to the marines, when the man saw them, he pulled out a weapon and went into a nearby building. "Members of the marines descended from their vehicles and pursued him," according to the report.

When the marines entered the building, officer González Velázquez detained Flores López, who at once admitted to belonging to the Guerreros Unidos, knowing Ángel Casarrubias Salgado—presumed head of the organization—and working directly with *El Camperra*. Flores López also was supposedly in the confidence of the mayor, Abarca, to whom the Guerreros Unidos paid money to let them operate in the city; his personal cut was 40,000 pesos a month. Marines, including Montes Trujillo, also detained Francisco Javier Lozano Cuevas, who allegedly admitted to dealing drugs and working as a bodyguard for Flores López.

According to the marines, they discovered an M1 .30-caliber rifle (license 3.382.766) with a 24-capacity cartridge, a 9mm .84bb pistol (d38925), and two packets of heroin.

Witnesses to the arrest of the three men, however, would describe a very different scene: Flores López, Lozano Cuevas, Blas Patiño, and Paola Alejandra Rivera were in a third-floor apartment when a group of marines violently burst into the building at 22:00 on October 26. Without search or arrest warrants, they threatened the neighbors, warned them to keep their mouths shut, and began beating the men inside the apartment before continuing the assault in the courtyard. The neighbors reported hearing cries of pain.

Blas Patiño *El Chiquis* was a childhood friend of Lozano Cuevas, and the two played soccer together. He had come to Iguala to visit him and then proceeded to Morelos to close a business deal—having to do with construction—between Lozano Cuevas and Flores López. According to testimonies given later, the three men were tortured simultaneously, repeatedly losing and regaining consciousness. At one point, Flores López and Lozano Cuevas realized that Blas Patiño had died. They were soon taken to another location where their torture continued.

Trying to cover up the murder, the marines claimed that Blas Patiño died when he fell from the fourth story of a building in an attempt to escape. Family members were too frightened to even file a report, though the National Commission on Human Rights (CNDH) is investigating the death. Various neighbors, I was able to learn, also testified about the events, describing the violent irruption into the building of marines who ran up to the third floor and then dragged the three men back down the stairs. Their testimony directly conflicts with the marines' arrest report, which described the men as being found in the street.

Flores López and Lozano Cuevas were transferred to the PGR in Mexico City on October 27, where they stood accused of organized crime, crimes against public health, and the violation of the Federal Firearms and Explosives Act. In a statement submitted at 10:00 on October 27, Flores López confirmed that he had been on the third floor of his apartment building with three other people: Francisco Lozano Cuevas, someone who went by the name of *El Chiquis*, and a woman, when marines entered the apartment and arrested him and Lozano Cuevas. Though this part wasn't included in the statement, in a document submitted by the PGR, Flores López (in response to a series of questions asked by Antonio

Covarrubias Arce of the Public Ministry) "confessed" that he handed over half of the money he earned from the dances and rodeos he organized in Iguala to *El Camperra* so that the Guerreros Unidos would let him continue to work; he also allegedly gave up the names of other members of Guerreros Unidos.

Francisco Javier Lozano Cuevas, a thirty-five-year-old man who made his living selling mixed cement, reserved his right, at midnight on October 28, not to make a statement.

The PGR then produced their witness, Paola Alejandra Rivera Avilés, who, presumably under threat of torture, said that she heard nothing, was only aware that someone had entered her apartment, and, after the subject attempted to escape through the window, heard a loud thud.

According to the physical examination documented by the PGR, the two men presented recent injuries. Flores López had over 100 visible marks on his body, including bloody eyes and bruises and welts on his face, neck, shoulders, armpits, elbows, various parts of his chest, thighs, wrists, and buttocks. Lozano Cuevas had bruises on his right ribs, underneath his right eye, and his chin.

"How does the witness claim he received these wounds?" the public defender asked Lozano Cuevas.

"They tortured me."

"Who does the witness say he was tortured by?"

"By the soldiers who came to the apartment," Lozano Cuevas responded, adding that they were masked.

The public defender requested the Ministry to enable a forensic analysis of the wounds, "and if analysis points to the possibility of torture, the Istanbul Protocol is to be initiated." The Istanbul Protocol is a UN protocol for investigating and documenting instances of torture.

Both men denied being in possession of drugs or weapons when they were arrested.

I was able to track down the history of the M1 rifle that the marines claimed to have found in the vehicle Flores López and Lozano Cuevas were in at the time. This rifle had previously been decommissioned by police in Nayarit state in 2004. According to Bulletin DPE/4653/04, the same model of rifle with the same license number was confiscated from one Sabino Rivera López, who was in a vehicle on Principal de Ciudad Industrial Street in Tepic, and was later charged with a federal crime. The same weapon was planted on Flores López and Lozano Cuevas. The "historical truth," clearly, had to be cobbled together at whatever cost; the machinery of the state was just getting started.

The First Blunders of Jesús Murillo Karam

"On October 18, 2014, the Criminal Investigations Agency of the Attorney General's Office captured Sidronio Casarrubias Salgado, leader of the criminal organization Guerreros Unidos, who has yielded information concerning the occurrences in Iguala on September 26," Attorney General Murillo Karam triumphantly announced on October 22. Murillo Karam was accompanied by Tomás Zerón, director of the Criminal Investigations Agency (AIC). The announcement was part of the first press conference the PGR gave about the missing forty-three. "This leader of the criminal group Guerreros Unidos pointed to Mrs. María de los Ángeles Pineda Villa, the wife of the ex-mayor of Iguala, working in complicity with her husband, Mr. José Luis Abarca, and the chief of police, Felipe Flores Velázquez, as the principal organizer of criminal activity in city hall," Murillo Karam conclusively stated.

"Today we have identified at least three of the members of the criminal group Guerreros Unidos who received the captured individuals from the Cocula and Iguala police, and we now know the path that they followed to their ultimate fate. On the screen you can see the names and affiliation of those suspects whom federal agents are currently pursuing. We have names and photos. These are crucial for . . . their arrest is critical for the investigation." On the screen were projected photographs of José Luis Abarca, María de los Ángeles Pineda Villa, Felipe Flores, and the photograph of someone wrongly identified as *El Gil*.

Murillo Karam recapitulated that, on the night of September 26, the *normalistas* were traveling in four buses when they were attacked by Iguala police officers on the order of Mayor José Luis Abarca. "From the declarations that have been made, the investigations, the forensic analysis, [we conclude that] the events of September 26 in Iguala were a violent crackdown implemented by police officers from Iguala and Cocula, carried out in conjunction with the above-mentioned criminal organization, with the intention of preventing a group of people from disrupting the celebratory event to be held by the mayor and his wife on that night in Iguala."

The attorney general continued: "We have confirmed the actions performed by Sidronio Casarrubias and his co-conspirators, we have confirmed the location where the detained subjects were handed over to this criminal group, we have indisputably identified the Iguala and Cocula municipal police officers who commited the felonies of kidnapping and organized crime. Furthermore, we are diligently pursuing the investigation of crimes—including forced disappearance—committed by city officials."

What Murillo Karam did not mention, however, is that the arrest of Sidronio Casarrubias was carried out with the same irregularities as the other arrests. According to the federal police report, the alleged leader of Guerreros Unidos was arrested on October 16, 2014 on the Mexico–Toluca highway and was found to be in possession of drugs and illegal firearms. In his testimony given to the ministry's Juan Francisco Quezada López, however, Casarrubias claimed to have been arrested on October 15, between nine and ten at night while he was eating dinner in the restaurant Fogon do Brasil, in Toluca, and that the police planted the weapons inside his truck. He denied belonging to a criminal organization; he was a brother of serving soldier Alfredo Casarrubias Salgado, and also of Mario Casarrubias, another alleged leader of Guerreros Unidos. He said that he had been in prison in the United States for eight years, accused of drug trafficking, and that he had only returned to Mexico five months previously. He was given a loan by some former employees of Mario's, and he used this money to buy cattle.

Sidronio admitted to knowing Raúl Núñez Salgado, alias *El Camperra*, who had introduced him to *El Gil*, "the leader of the criminal group Guerreros Unidos." He allegedly also admitted to knowing the Benítez Palacios brothers, *El May*, and a number of other men among those detained by federal authorities.

He also claimed, according to his official testimony, that members of the rival criminal group, Los Rojos, were riding in the buses with the students, that José Luis Abarca gave bimonthly or monthly payments of four million pesos to the Guerreros Unidos, and that the mayor's wife, María de los Ángeles, was the lover of then governor of Guerrero Ángel Aguirre Rivero.

"On the day of September 26, 2014, at approximately 03:00, I received a message on my phone from *El Gil*, who told me, 'It's party time,' that Los Rojos had come by and they'd been fighting for hours . . . later, at 14:00, he told me that they had taken seventeen of Los Rojos," Sidronio supposedly admitted. But his timing was far off from the actual events of that night, as the *normalistas* didn't arrive in Iguala until 21:00 on September 26.

On October 18, he expanded on his previous testimony, providing names of members of Guerreros Unidos in other parts of the state. Then, on October 21, he stated to a judge that he was detained by a group of armed men on October 15 in a restaurant in Lerma, State of Mexico, along with three companions, including a woman named Teresa Rivera Díaz. On February 15, 2015, he wrote a twenty-six-page letter to the judge detailing the torture and rape he suffered at the hands of five federal ministerial police officers, including Gabriel Valle Campos, Juan Aarón Estuardo Flores Ramírez, José Ulises Torres Acosta, and Elpidio Raúl García Ramírez, all of whose names appear on custody reports. The UN opened an investigation into his allegations of torture.

In an interview, Sidronio's mother, Fracelia Salgado, told me that as a kid he wanted to join the Army like his older brother Alfredo, who was a second captain, but who had recently retired after suffering harassment because of his brothers' situation. Fracelia Salgado explained that Sidronio, rejected by the Army, went to live in the US when he was twenty, where he was arrested and imprisoned on charges of conspiracy to traffic drugs. He and his wife were in jail for eight years, and their two young children were practically left as orphans. When Sidronio returned to Mexico, in early 2014, all he wanted to do was make up for the lost time with his kids, work as a rancher, and open a car wash. When I asked if her son Mario was involved in drug trafficking, she wasn't sure; but she insisted that Sidronio certainly wasn't involved and that he was committed to starting a new life.

Until October 2016, Sidronio Casarrubias, who the government claimed was the boss of the Guerreros Unidos, was only accused of organized crime under the rubrics of committing crimes against public health, using resources of illicit origin, and being in possession of firearms reserved for military use. In mid-September 2016 a federal judge issued an enforcement of rights and threw out the charge of organized crime, after which he remained in prison only for the alleged possession of firearms. Not until two years after he was originally captured, at the same time as the PGR appealed the judge's decision to dismiss the charge of organized crime, was he officially charged with the disappearance of the forty-three students.

A few days after Murillo Karam's first press conference, officials at the AIC made further arrests and conducted more "interrogations" in an attempt to definitively wrap up the case.

The Meeting with Peña Nieto

As the government insisted the case was "solved," family members of the missing forty-three refused to continue meeting with Interior Secretary Miguel Ángel Osorio Chong and began demanding a direct meeting with President Enrique Peña Nieto. The first meeting took place on October 29, 2014 in the presidential residence of Los Pinos. By then, Attorney General Murillo Karam was ready with evidence to "clear up" the affair.

Also attending the meeting were Undersecretary of the Interior Luis Miranda Nava, legal adviser Humberto Castillejos, and head of the AIC Tomás Zerón. Conspicuously absent were Salvador Cienfuegos, the secretary of national defense, and Enrique Galindo Ochoa, the head of the federal police. As the parents and their attorneys waited outside the office before the meeting, the only representative of the forces of law and order was the national security commissioner, Monte Alejandro Rubido—and he was sidelined, standing with the families like just another spectator. Inside the office, the president and his cohort were the ones who really called the shots.

Undersecretary Miranda Nava chaired the meeting. Peña Nieto took care to write down each of the parents' names, looking sympathetic and engaged. The families kicked off with a series of accusations directed at the Army and the federal police, claiming that they knew what was happening all through the attacks and the disappearance—accusations that neither the president nor his team would even address.

"We have reached the absolute limit of tolerance and patience, and we are asking you, our president, as a last resort, to give us an immediate answer as to where the forty-three disappeared students have gone, and how the Army pulled them out of the hospital where they brought their class- mate . . . What is the Army's role when it encounters young people with such high hopes of becoming professionals . . . ?" demanded Felipe de la Cruz, leader of the parents of the disappeared, whose son was among the survivors.

De la Cruz had himself studied at the Normal Rural School of Ayotzinapa. Before the attacks of September 2014, he taught classes in Acapulco. In an interview he explained to me that though his son wasn't killed that night, he felt he'd lost him in a different way: two years later, he still has to calm the boy when he wakes up in the middle of the night, screaming from nightmares. Since he first berated Peña Nieto in the meeting, Felipe, like attorney Vidulfo Rosales, has become the target of a smear campaign.

"We see you as the representative of our nation, and believe that we are a moral nation, and as such, no matter who may fall, no matter what it takes, we demand justice. If someone had knowledge of the events and didn't act, they are guilty, and if you didn't act, you are just as guilty," de la Cruz continued. "We are here today to inform you that we will give you no more than two, three days, to provide concrete answers . . . You have seen the anger of each parent here, the despair. I doubt that even you will be able to sleep peacefully from this day on . . ."

The president's team watched aghast as de la Cruz spoke.

Peña Nieto responded by offering his "clear commitment" that his administration would fully investigate the matter. But the families wanted an explicit undertaking from the president, and Rosales had written out ten demands. The first and most important was that the Inter-American Commission on Human Rights would give technical assistance as an external and independent body of experts to the Mexican investigators and that Peña Nieto would issue an official invitation from the government. The family members had decided beforehand not to withdraw without getting at least this demand met. As they went down their list, Peña Nieto agreed to each point, but the parents also wanted him to sign the minutes of the meeting. It was decided that Castillejos and Rosales would draw up that document.

"There is not an inch of room for impunity," Peña Nieto proclaimed at the press conference after their meeting, positioning himself on the side of the parents in their effort to find the missing forty-three—a strategy with which he hoped to pacify them. Secretary of the Interior Osorio Chong, tasked with taking the first concrete steps, formed a commission to oversee the investigation consisting of six parents, three students, and, representing the government, Osorio Chong, Miranda Nava, and Enrique Galindo of the federal police. The commission, however, never materialized, because the government didn't hold up its end of the bargain.

The meeting with the parents, along with the marches that were taking place in the street in support of the missing forty-three, spurred the government to announce a new version of the events of that night—and it was this version, despite all the scientific evidence and witness testimony refuting it, that the government would stick to.

The Builders of Cocula Who the PGR Turned into Assassins

Patricio Reyes Landa, also known as *El Pato*; Jonathan Osorio Cortés, or *El Jona*; Agustín García Reyes, or *El Chereje*; and Felipe Rodríguez Salgado are young men who, besides living nearby each other in Cocula, Guerrero, have four things in common: they are construction workers, they are poor, they were tortured, and they were accused of being members of Guerreros Unidos and the authors of the killing and cremation of the forty-three *normalistas* in a Cocula trash heap.

On November 7, Murillo Karam announced at a press conference: "Today marks thirty-three days since the state of Guerrero turned the investigation into the criminal acts committed on September 26 and 27 in Iguala, Guerrero, over to the PGR. They have been thirty-three very difficult and painful days, especially for those who do not know the whereabouts of their children. But they have also been thirty-three days in which we have not stopped searching, in which the authorities of the republic have not paused in our efforts to find the disappeared."

Murillo Karam, visibly irritable and impatient, was speaking to a room filled with Mexican and international journalists. "They have been thirty-three days in which all Mexicans have lived in anguish, in indignation over the disappearance of the forty-three students, with whom we all feel such solidarity. The federal government has led a great effort into what could be considered one of the most complex investigations in recent history: ten thousand people, including police, soldiers, marines, prosecutors, investigators, and forensic experts have been to the region, turning over every clue that might indicate the whereabouts of these young men."

Murillo Karam, speaking with what seemed a forced solemnity, then affirmed that Reyes Landa, Osorio Cortés, and García Reyes "are members of the criminal organization Guerreros Unidos, and, in making their confession, have admitted to receiving and executing the group of people that the Iguala and Cocula police officers handed over to them."

"The government of the republic concurs with the families and with society at large about the need for transparency in this investigation, and for this reason we have considered it important to relay to the public, step by step, each advance that we make . . . I know that the information we have collected so far has caused immense grief, a grief that we share, in solidarity with you all. The confessions we have heard, in addition to the investigations we have made, point, very sadly, to the murder of a large number of people in the vicinity of Cocula."

207

In the displayed photographs of the latest "confessed" assassins, Reyes Landa appears visibly beaten up, his left eye is half shut, and his face is bruised. Murillo explains to the crowd that the *normalistas* had been traveling in four buses when they were attacked. "The ex-mayor, at that moment, was attending the event in which his wife was explaining her [charity] work outside the DIF [federal service program] building . . . After the first attack against the *normalistas* . . . Iguala police officers violently captured them and transferred them to the police station. From there, with the help of the Cocula police, they moved the young men in police vehicles to a breach point between Iguala and Cocula where there is a road to an area called Loma de Coyote."

"It has been confirmed through investigations by the Public Ministry that at this spot, between Iguala and Cocula, the local police delivered the detainees to members of the criminal group, Guerreros Unidos . . . Our most recent arrests, which include the three material authors already mentioned, have enabled us to grasp the last link in the criminal chain of events of which we have knowledge so far. These latest detainees confess that by the breach road leading to Loma de Coyote the municipal police showed up with a number of people, though they couldn't precisely say how many . . ."

Murillo Karam continued by projecting fragments of video showing an interrogation of one of the new "material authors"—a video that had clearly been edited. He did not show the official police confessions, the only ones with any legal value, if lawfully carried out. Annoyed at the delay before the projection started, Murillo Karam snapped, "Wake up whoever's on video!"

"How many students did you have?" a masculine voice asks in authoritarian fashion; the face of the interviewer is not shown.

"There were, they said there were forty-four, I heard . . . We didn't count them one by one," García Reyes responds nervously.

"Who told you?"

"They did."

"Who?"

"*El Pato, El Güereque*, they were saying, 'There's forty-four or forty-three of them.' That's all I heard, but I didn't count them. But there were a lot, and *El Pato* had them."

"And how did they get there, these forty-three or forty-four?"

"They came in the big truck."

Murillo Karam explained: "Two of the detained stated that some of the people who were transferred to the dump site in Cocula arrived already dead or unconscious and that the others were interrogated by members of the criminal group to determine who they were and why they had come to Iguala."

He then showed photographs of two vehicles, one smallish Nissan and the other a three-and-a-half-ton truck, supposedly the vehicle used to transport the students.

The video continued: "Were any of them already dead in the truck before they were taken out?"

"Yes. When I was pulling out the kids, some of them were already dead," Osorio Cortés responded, hunched over and stammering. "There were about fifteen dead."

"Had they been killed by gunshot, or what?"

"They'd suffocated, been asphyxiated."

Murillo Karam continued: "The detained said that they killed the remaining survivors at this location and then dragged them down to the dump, where they burned the corpses. They stationed guards and took turns making sure the fire burned for hours, pouring on diesel, gasoline, tires, wood, plastic, and other items they found in the area . . . The fire, according to these testimonies, lasted from midnight until approximately 14:00 the next day. According to a statement made by one of the detained, and one other, the fire lasted until 15:00 on September 27 . . . When investigators analyzed the location, they found ashes and pieces of bone, whose characteristics correspond to human bone fragments." Based on interviews conducted with the "confessed" killers, the PGR chief explained how they removed the bodies from the trucks, one claiming that they grabbed them by the arms and legs and tossed them into the trash pit. "Those who were alive stood up, they grabbed them, then they walked them over," Osorio Cortés alleged in a video recorded at the trash site.

"Continuing with the sequence of events, the detained claimed that when they went down to the place where they had thrown and burned the bodies, they received an order from someone nicknamed *El Terco* to break up the charred bones and put them in black trash bags. According to the testimonies, these bags, except for two of them, were emptied into the San Juan River, and, one of the men stated, the other two were thrown in complete."

"How many bags did you take?" a federal ministerial police officer asks García Reyes in the video.

"There were eight of them, but they weren't full, they were like half-full."

"How big were the bags?"

"Trash bags, big ones."

"Black ones?"

"Yeah, plastic."

"The kind with drawstrings?"

"No, not those, the thicker ones."

"Okay. Where did you buy them?"

"*El Terco* brought them, boss."

"Eight bags?"

"Yeah, we brought them in the [Nissan] Estaquitas and we came to the bridge at San Juan, it's called, but before coming to the village, just before getting there, they said, 'Get out and throw the bags.' It was *El Terco* told us. When he said 'Throw out the bags,' I grabbed two and just chucked them in, the others grabbed the bags, made holes in them, and emptied them out, and they . . ."

"So you threw two complete bags in?"

"I just chucked them in."

"And did they . . . did they sink or float?"

"No, there was that much water."

"They washed away."

"Yes, they washed away."

"And the other ones?"

"The others, some sank and some floated away."

"The other ones you ripped apart and threw in?"

"Well, it was fast. I mean, I took two, I threw them in, and then I got back in, and then I saw a couple sank down and the others I didn't see."

Murillo Karam concluded: "As the forensic investigators explained, the high level of deterioration caused by the fire makes it very difficult to extract DNA to allow us to make identifications." He seemed to anticipate no further questions.

The government's attempts to "solve" the case, however, remained full of irregularities and incongruencies.

The attorney general couldn't publicize all of the confessions of García Reyes, Osorio Cortés, and Reyes Landa, because each of them told such different versions of the story. It all added up to what seemed like a comedy of errors, except that the PGR tragically invented connections where there weren't any.

Agustín García Reyes, Jonathan Osorio Cortés, and Patricio Reyes Landa were all arrested on October 27, 2014. García Reyes and Osorio made their statements early on the morning of October 28, but Reyes Landa held out until November 3, when he finally succumbed to the pressure. The three men each gave distinct timelines about when they were told to get together to go kill and burn the *normalistas*.

Jonathan, twenty years old and said to be the lookout, claimed that they met up at 20:30 and he, along with Patricio, Agustín, *Huasaco*, *El Primo*, and some other men, went in the Nissan Estaquitas to Loma de los Coyotes. Patricio, twenty-five, said that at 23:30 Felipe Rodríguez Salgado, known as *El Cepillo*, came by to pick him up in the Nissan. Meanwhile Agustín, twenty-two, said that at about three in the morning on September 27 he met with *El Pato*, Jonathan, and *El Güereque*, who picked him up in the Nissan.

Jonathan went on to recall that around 21:00 they arrived in Loma de los Coyotes, where they met up with the white three-and-a-half-tonner that *El Cepillo*, *El Rana*, and *El Duva* were riding in, and "in which about forty people were loaded." And yet, at that time the attacks against the students hadn't even begun.

Agustín, meanwhile, explained that when they came to collect him at three in the morning, there were four people tied up with rope in the back of the Nissan van, all of them alive. They then drove towards Metlapa and on the highway met up with a white pickup truck driven by *El Cepillo*. In the back were some people shouting that they were Ayotzinapa students.

212

Jonathan said that in Loma de los Coyotes *El Cepillo* transferred four *normalistas* into the Nissan where he was riding with Patricio and Agustín, and that one of the students was dead from a gunshot wound to the head. However, according to Patricio, at Loma de los Coyotes they met up with an Iguala police vehicle, and it was from that vehicle that the four students were handed over. Neither Jonathan or Agustín mentioned the presence of any police in Loma de los Coyotes.

According to Jonathan, when they arrived at the trash dump, some fifteen of the approximately forty people packed into the bigger truck had died "from asphyxiation." Agustín, however, said that when they unloaded the students at the garbage dump they were all alive, while Patricio thought that there were only about thirty people in the truck. Patricio was also the only one to mention that it was raining that night.

Jonathan claimed that as each student was brought out of the truck, they were shot in the head one by one. Agustín claimed that they made the students lay on the ground and then *El Cepillo*, *El Güereque*, *El Primo*, and *El Bimbo* all started firing at once into the heap, killing *El Cochiloco* as well. Jonathan said that they killed *El Cochiloco* and one infiltrator separately.

Agustín said that those who were alive walked into the trash pit. Jonathan said they were all dead when they threw them in, grabbing them by the hands and feet.

Agustín said that *El Cepillo* doused them in diesel and lit the fire. Jonathan said that *El Cepillo* left before the fire was ready and didn't come back until the next day.

Agustín initially said that on September 27, at 17:00, they shoveled the charred remains into eight trash bags and threw them all in the San Juan River. In the PGR video of his confession, by contrast, he says that he threw two whole bags in, whereas the others ripped holes into them before emptying the contents. Jonathan said that at 17:40, when he was at Patricio's house, *El Primo*, *El Cepillo*, *El Rana*, and *El Bimbo* showed up with four black sacks of ashes that they were going to throw in the San Juan.

Patricio said that it wasn't until September 28 that they went to collect the ashes from the dump and that he wasn't present when they threw them into the San Juan. Though Jonathan had recalled that the night they killed the students was a dark one, and they worked by the light of cell phones and flashlights, when he was shown photographs of the forty-three students he confidently claimed to recognize eleven of them.

Reading through the testimonies submitted by Jonathan, Agustín, and Patricio to the Public Ministry, it's striking that none of them mentions smashing or grinding up the inciner-ated bones. These actions were invented by Attorney General Jesús Murillo Karam to bolster the government's argument that it was difficult to scientifically identify the remains of the *normalistas*.

As if it were a sort of stamp with which the PGR marks its detainees and exhibits its investigative methods, the medical reports of the three young builders reveal that each of them had multiple contusions and wounds.

On November 3, 2014, Patricio Reyes Landa complained that his arrest report contained false information and that he was the victim of blows, electrocution on his genitals and inside his mouth, and asphyxiation by water and plastic bag. Jonathan Osorio Cortés also said that the multiple wounds on his body were caused by the police who detained him. All three men were held at the PGR jail until January 2015, when they were transferred to Cefereso #4, in Tepic, Nayarit.

According to the PGR dossier, the three were key players in the Cocula branch of Guerreros Unidos. They traveled, armed, by car or motorcycle, worked as security, conducted kidnappings and assassinations, and received a monthly salary of 7,000 pesos. During my research into the case, I visited their homes and interviewed their families. The young men accused of the murder of the forty-three students were construction workers and peasants who lived in extreme poverty. They had very little education and no means to pay a lawyer to defend them in court.

According to the PGR, an anonymous call came in on October 25 denouncing two subjects, "Patricio, alias *El Pato*" and *El Cepillo*, as being members of Guerreros Unidos, and thus started the hunt: federal ministerial police went out combing the streets of Cocula for anybody who knew *El Pato*.

The Story of the Three "Assassins"

Mrs. Eliodora Landa, mother of Patricio Reyes Landa, lives in the San Miguel neighborhood of Cocula. She said that her son had been nicknamed *El Pato* since he was a kid. For more than fifteen years, due to their poverty, his family has received benefits from the Opportunities Program run by the Secretariat of Social Development (SEDESOL). They have spent twenty-two years in a crumbling adobe hut loaned to them by an uncle. Until recently they had a dirt floor, but, with the help of SEDESOL, they were able to lay cement.

Patricio studied only up until middle school, married young, and managed to fit with his wife and daughters into a small room with a leaky laminate roof—they hang buckets from the ceiling when it rains. As poverty is inherited in Mexico, his family also relies on the Opportunities Program.

I was able to consult the SEDESOL list of beneficiaries, updated to September 2015, and confirmed that Patricio's wife and mother remain eligible due to their lack of resources.

Patricio's wife, who didn't want to use her name for fear of reprisals, maintains that her husband is not the man the PGR invented. She's known him since she was sixteen and he eighteen, and they have been married for seven years. She claims that she's never noticed anything suspicious about him or his friends and that he had very little money. "He was a builder's assistant and sometimes he worked with Felipe Rodríguez Salgado's father-in-law. When there was no other work he would help out with the cattle in Apetlanca or Apipilulco," she told me.

He had a broken-down motorcycle that hadn't been running since the beginning of 2014, but which, when the PGR searched their house, they hauled away. His other possessions were a bed, a fan they were paying off in installments (which the PGR also seized), a refrigerator they were still paying off, and a dresser that she had been given.

"Since there wasn't any work, a teacher came by, a neighbor from here, and asked if he could go put in some fencing in Apetlanca. He went [to work there] and came back every week to give us money," his wife said. Patricio would return on Saturdays and leave for work again on Sunday.

She said that on September 25 Patricio came home to Cocula. On the 26th they went together for dinner to his sister's house, which was close to the center of town, at around 19:30. At 23:00 they left because "it was ugly out, about to rain." They arrived home and didn't go out again. At 23:30 or midnight it started to pour down, continuing until four in the morning.

The next day Patricio went to work putting down cement at a gas station, returning in the afternoon to spend the evening at home with the family. On Sunday, September 28, he went back to Apetlanca.

The PGR first came to Patricio's mother's house on October 20, looking for weapons. They told her that Patricio was a member of Guerreros Unidos and that he had participated in the attack against the students. After they left, Patricio's wife called him to ask if he had been involved, and he assured her that he had nothing to do with it.

On October 26, at nine in the morning, federal authorities arrested Patricio at the Apetlanca home of the schoolteacher, Yesenia Delgado. He told his family that when the officers came into the house, they pushed him into the bathroom and roughed him up. Later they took him to the hills along with Jonathan Osorio Cortés, blindfolding both of them, and beating them for hours. They put plastic bags over their heads, nearly suffocating them, doused them in water, and electrocuted them in the mouth, on the testicles, and in the rectum.

"He says they were telling him he had to talk about things he didn't do," his wife told me. "And he'd refuse, and they'd hit him worse. 'You're going to say what we're telling you, not what you want,' and if he didn't confess to what the police were saying, they were going to come after the whole family."

Months later, Patricio sent me a personal letter describing the horrors he went through. The UN is currently investigating his case for human rights violations.

Jonathan Osorio Cortés, twenty years old, only got as far as middle school because he couldn't afford to continue, and then went to work as a builder's assistant (as well as working part-time at a taco stand) in Mexico City, where he has relatives. Elena, his mother, told me that when there wasn't other work he would clear cornfields or spread fertilizer. He lived seasonally between Cocula and Mexico City and had no car, motorcycle, or even bicycle. He had been living in Cocula for a few months when the same teacher who offered Patricio work, Yesenia Delgado, told him that he could come and lay fencing in Apetlanca. He accepted. There, according to Elena, he met Patricio, who he'd crossed paths with before but hardly knew.

"My poor son never had any money," she explained. "When he got a little he'd give me some for food, but he almost never had a cent. He'd ask me to lend him twenty pesos or to buy him a Coca-Cola."

Jonathan told his mother that men in civilian clothes stopped him and Patricio around nine in the morning, beat them, and tortured them. "The guys who grabbed him said it was because he ran, that that was why they got beat up," Elena explains. "They blindfolded them, started torturing them, and then he heard them digging, and they told him they had a bag and they were going to bury him in it. It hurts me so much," she said.

Her son told her that they tied his hands and asphyxiated him with a plastic bag and that he lost consciousness at least three times. They threw cold water and ice at him to bring him round. They also electrocuted him.

"He came out with scabs on his testicles. With the other boy they stuffed a pistol in his mouth," Elena said. "When they put them in the helicopter to transfer them, they told them that they were going to throw them out, and nobody would ever know." Jonathan told his mother that while he was in the helicopter he heard someone say, "With these idiots we're going to put the lid on the case."

Jonathan was offered money by the PGR, his mother said, and they even wanted him to incriminate some of the elementary school classmates they found on his Facebook page.

"I was able [to see him] the day after they detained him. They held him longer there. I only saw him for five minutes, there was a bruise on his face, on the left side, and I asked him, 'Did they hit you?' He just said, 'Don't worry, Mom.'"

Overcoming her fear, she went to Mexico City in December 2014 to file a complaint with the CNDH.

A few days after his arrest, officials flew the young man by helicopter to the trash dump in Cocula, where the PGR recorded the video that Murillo Karam would later show at the November 7 press conference. Elena told me that before making the video they told him everything he needed to do and say and that by the time he arrived there were already human remains laid out in preparation.

Agustín García Reyes, also known as *El Chereje*, twenty-four years old, was a *campesino* and builder who typically earned 130 pesos a day (about $7) to support his wife and son. His wife told me in an interview that they would sometimes have to ask for credit, because they didn't have the money to buy food. Agustín knew Patricio and Felipe from soccer games, but they weren't friends. He didn't own a car or a motorcycle. "They [the PGR] say that he goes around on his motorcycle with a gun. He's never ridden a motorcycle. He's never had a gun. He doesn't even have a bike," his wife said.

His wife, who asked me not to reveal her name, told me that they were together at home all day on September 26, along with her parents who, as they lived far away and it was raining hard, spent the night with them. She affirms that they slept all night and her husband never left. "It's impossible for him to have done everything they say," she told me, "because he was with me all the time."

During Murillo Karam's November 7 press conference, he showed a video billed as a "reconstruction of events," showing federal ministerial police officers taking García Reyes to the San Juan River.

"Tossed them here, just past here I tossed them in," García Reyes says to the camera. He is surrounded by federal ministerial police officers, one of whom holds onto his cuffed hands.

"Here?" an officer asks.

"Yes."

"Where did you dump them?"

"I tossed them here."

"Okay."

"The water was deep, so it took them away."

"Perfect," the officer is heard saying, as if Agustín had recited the script to his satisfaction.

The images show a black bag, like those supposedly containing the remains of the *normalistas*, snagged on the riverbank as if it had just then been found. Words appear on the screen: "Reconstruction of Events."

Agustín's family members described to me, for the first time, the events leading up to his appearance on that video. After a group of marines, at 04:00 on October 26, without a warrant, first searched his in-laws' house, hit his brother-in-law and forced him to tell them where *El Chereje* lived, they arrested him. His wife described how men, some in uniform and some in civilian clothes, entered their rented home, threw García Reyes to the ground, and started beating him, even pointing a gun at the head of their five-year-old son. His wife asked the men why they were taking him away, and they proceeded to push and hit her. "They were marines. I saw their trucks," she told me. Days later, Agustín told his wife what happened next. "They tied him to a chair with his hands behind him, they suffocated him with a bag, they put electric wires all over his body, on his testicles. Everything, they did everything to him. He fainted, and his ears still hurt, and he has a headache.

"They told him that they knew what he'd done, and he said no, they should talk to me, because we were together the whole time," his wife said. "And then later they started telling him that he had to say everything he'd done because if not they were going to come for me, for my son and my family, they already knew where we lived, and they were going to kill me and nobody was going to find where they dumped my body and my son's."

Agustín also told her that when they took him to the San Juan River they kept on threatening him. They ordered him to repeat what they had been saying. "He told them, 'I really don't know what happened here. What are you after?'" The federal ministerial officers warned him they were recording and that he had to say what they wanted, or else they would go for her and the boy and disappear them.

She explained that she had a very low income and it took her a while to get to Mexico City to lodge a complaint with the CNDH, but when she eventually made it, they triggered the Istanbul Protocol for the investigation of torture cases.

I was able to see García Reyes's arrest report, signed by federal ministerial police officer Jazmín García Martínez and marine Vidal Vázquez Mendoza—the same pair who had captured the first alleged murderers, Osvaldo and Miguel Ángel Ríos Sánchez and Carlos Pascual Cervantes Jaimes.

"I haven't spoken to a lawyer," García Reyes's wife told me. "We don't have the money to pay one, that's for rich folks. How could I, earning hardly enough to eat? I know he didn't do it," she added hopelessly. "I know it wasn't him because he was with me the whole day. I don't know why they're accusing innocent people. I don't know what more the president wants."

The PGR Finds Zero Evidence of the
Normalistas in the Trucks

I was able to obtain access to the forensic analysis conducted on both the Nissan Estaquitas and the bigger truck that the PGR claimed were used to transport the *normalistas*. On October 16, 2014, the PGR inspected the vehicles, which were located in the Lomas de Pueblo Viejo neighborhood of Iguala on the property of Gildardo López Astudillo, who the PGR identified as *El Gil*.

The Nissan, which was parked in the Grúas Meta car lot and was displayed by Murillo Karam as one of the vehicles used to commit the crime, was subjected to the luminol test, but there were no blood traces or fingerprints that could link it to the students. Nor would such a truck have been of much use to transport them: according to the PGR report, the roof was sunken in, the hood partially broken, the bumper falling off, the headlights shattered, and the tires flat, as if it had come straight from a junkyard.

The PGR conducted the same luminol test on the large truck on November 3, and, again, they found no trace of the students. More tests were conducted on other potential transport vehicles on *El Gil*'s property, all with the same results.

On January 14, 2015, Felipe Rodríguez Salgado, alias *El Cepillo*, twenty-five years old, was arrested in Cocula. His appearance, however, did not at all match the description given by his supposed accomplices. Felipe's wife—whom he's been married to since 2008—is a middle school teacher. Before he was detained, Felipe worked as a construction worker with his father-in-law, earning 150 pesos a day, or about $8 dollars. If there wasn't enough construction work, he would take farmers' goats and cows to pasture. The few possessions he and his wife had squeezed into their rented room, on General Cuéllar Street in Cocula, were a bed, a crib for the baby, a refrigerator, a small dresser, a table, a television, and an electric stove. His wife told me that they were still paying 500 pesos a month for the refrigerator and 200 a week for the bed and crib.

On September 26, according to his wife, Felipe came home from work at 14:00 and, around 21:30, they went to eat at a food stand close to where they lived. According to the PGR, this was when Felipe was leading the operation to kill and cremate forty-three students.

After eating, Felipe stayed outside, having a beer with a friend. Afterwards he went into the room and spent the rest of the night with his wife, who said that he left the next morning for his grandmother's house at around 08:30. He came back at noon, and they returned to his grandmother's house together, where they spent the afternoon.

In October, Felipe had told his wife that he was fed up with not finding work and was going to go to the United States, where he had two brothers. He left on October 20. One week later, the police showed up at his house.

His wife called Felipe after the police came: "That's why you left, right?" He said that it wasn't, and she mustn't worry. Weeks passed and she didn't hear from him. Felipe tried to cross the border, but got lost in the desert. Eventually he got in touch again and finally returned on January 11, 2015. They saw each other for only a few hours before she went to work. Three days later, Felipe was arrested while heading to work in Cocula. The PGR, however, claimed that they arrested him in Morelos in possession of marijuana. When his wife was able to visit him, on January 17, he was visibly bruised, but he didn't want to tell her what had happened. He did, however, tell his mother.

On January 18 he was put in the maximum-security prison, El Altiplano, where he soon filed a complaint that the officers who detained him beat him, tortured him, and forced him to confess in a video that the PGR would later use in its claim to having solved the case.

His wife told me, "He already knew they were looking for him. If he was guilty, he never would have returned." She showed me the more than thirty letters that his Cocula neighbors sent to the judge to testify to Felipe's upstanding conduct. I picked a name signed on one of these letters at random and phoned a man who told me he'd known Felipe for three years. They played soccer together, organizing games in Cocula every Saturday or Sunday. He affirmed that Felipe wasn't a violent person; he had never seen him with a weapon or acting suspiciously.

Felipe submitted his official declaration on January 16, and, like the other confessions given to the PGR, it is full of absurdities and contradictions. Not aligning with what his co-confessors claimed, Felipe said that eight police trucks with more than thirty officers delivered between thirty-eight and forty-two students. Not a single detained policeman or supposed accomplice described anything similar. He claimed that the *normalistas* arrived bloody and beaten, but he didn't say that any of them were dead, as others recalled. He never mentioned giving the order to incinerate the students or, later, to break up their bones, though the PGR maintained that he did both.

In parallel to his official statement, Felipe was also filmed for a video, in which he contradicts his own written declaration, but which Murillo Karam would use as evidence for the closure of the case.

In that official statement he also denounced rough handling by the federal police officers who arrested him: "They put me in a room, threw me on the ground, they began beating me . . ." His assigned counsel asked the Public Ministry to initiate the Istanbul Protocol to determine whether he had been tortured.

On December 6, 2014, the PGR announced the first results of the tests they conducted on the trash bags supposedly thrown into the San Juan with the remains of the students. There was a DNA match for one of them: Alexander Mora Venancio.

The First Confrontation between the Official Version and Reality

On November 13, 2014, Secretary of Defense Salvador Cienfuegos met with members of congress for the first time to discuss the Iguala case. According to later media reports, Cienfuegos affirmed that when officers from the 27th Infantry Battalion called the Iguala chief of police, Felipe Flores Velázquez, to ask whether local police officers had attacked the *normalistas*, he lied to them.

Cienfuegos told legislators that the Army didn't learn about the attacks until two hours after they began, and he asked them not to blame Colonel Rodríguez Pérez (responsible for the battalion) for this lapse, because he had given forty years of "irreproachable" service to the military.

On December 14, I published my article "The True Night of Iguala" in *Proceso* magazine, exposing several falsehoods that the PGR had claimed in their official account of the events of September 26. This was before the Interdisciplinary Group of Independent Experts (GIEI) from the Inter-American Commission on Human Rights came and began their independent investigation.

The *normalistas* did not come to Iguala to disrupt the mayor's wife's presentation. By the time they arrived in the city, the event had been over for more than an hour, and the attacks against them took place later still. This eliminates the motive imputed by the government to Mayor Abarca.

The *normalistas* were traveling in five buses, not four, as the PGR claimed.

I also revealed the existence of the Iguala C4, the Center for Control, Command, Communication, and Computers, through which all law enforcement agencies—the 27th Infantry Battalion, the federal police, the PGR, the state police, and the local Iguala police—were informed in real time of any emergency in the area. The C4 was run by the Guerrero governor's office and connected to the Interior Secretariat's National System of Public Security. I explained how on the night in question, via the C4s in Chilpancingo and Iguala, all three levels of government, including the Army, the federal police, and the PGR, had been monitoring the students ever since they left Ayotzinapa in two Estrella de Oro buses. At the end of the night, these two buses were the principal targets of the attacks, and it was in them that the majority of the seized students had been riding.

I was the first to interview radio operator José Natividad Elías Moreno, who explained that all the reports incoming to the C4 were relayed simultaneously to the federal police, the Army, and the other federal law enforcement agencies. A day after the publication of the article, on December 15, the PGR issued a warrant for Elías Moreno, and soon thereafter arrested him. As with the other arrests in this case, the officers who picked up Elías Moreno (at the same time as seven other municipal police officers) were later subjected to criminal investigation.

Accompanying the article, we released previously unseen videos in which students and other witnesses testify to the presence of federal police officers during at least one of the attacks against the students. We quoted a local resident who claims to have seen the federals with his own eyes, and Ayotzinapa student Luis Pérez Martínez's statement of 27 September, describing how the federal police attacked his classmates.

The article proves for the first time that the Army, despite the denials by Cienfuegos, did go out into the streets of Iguala while the attacks were taking place and that the military were informed of what was going on by the C4. It also showed that Captain José Martínez Crespo—a key actor on that night— was in command of two platoons on the Iguala streets during the hours when the disappearances occurred, and, what is more, went to the Iguala municipal police station.

The article uncovers the existence of a state government report which includes three state police dispatches. In dispatch number 02370, dated September 26, 2014, the operating coordinator (José Adame Bautista, of the North Zone of Guerrero's Department of Public Security and Civil Protection) reports that at 17:59 the Chilpancingo C4 noted that two Estrella de Oro buses, numbers 1568 and 1531, were leaving Ayotzinapa "carrying students from the Normal Rural School of Ayotzinapa and heading towards Iguala." The dispatch also included the fact that at 20:00, federal and state police officers arrived at toll booth #3 on the federal highway, where one of the student buses had stopped. Another dispatch reflects the

C4 reports that the *normalistas* got to the Iguala bus station at 21:30 and that there were "gunshots" at 21:40.

In one of the dozen known videos recorded by the *normalistas* with their cell phones, you can clearly hear alarmed comments on the federal police presence during the attack on Juan N. Álvarez Street, before any students were disappeared: "The cops are leaving! . . . The feds are staying and they're going to want to mess with us!" These videos were in the possession of the State Prosecutor's Office, and hence of the PGR when it took over the case, but they have been omitted as evidence and completely ignored throughout the federal government's investigation.

We also published, for the first time, the names of two federal police officers who were involved that night, Luis Antonio Dorantes and Víctor Manuel Colmenares Campos, revealing that they both had left Iguala's federal police base a few days after the attack against the students.

The report put together by the Guerrero government included the flight plan of a UH-1H helicopter, number XC-LLK, which, under state jurisdiction, conducted a flyover of Iguala and its environs on September 27, 2014. The pilot was Andrés Pascual Chombo, with years of experience in the Mexican Air Force and the PGR. The flight occurred within the span of time when, as Murillo Karam would have it, a massive trash and tire fire was consuming the students, and yet the pilot didn't register anything of interest. A fire that large would surely have produced enough smoke to be clearly visible from the sky.

I divulged the medical reports that found evidence of torture on the first round of suspects arrested in the case.

"The True Night of Iguala," with its radical rethink of the Iguala affair, made the rounds of the Mexican and international media and caused much discomfort within the federal government. Two days after its publication, on December 16, the families of the missing forty-three held a press conference in which they demanded the federal government open a line of investigation into the participation of the 27th Infantry Battalion and the federal police in the attacks against the students. Likewise, legislators from the opposition Party of the Democratic Revolution (PRD) and Labor Party exhorted Peña Nieto to come clean about the same two institutions' role in the attacks. Congress members also suggested that the chiefs of SEDENA and the PGR could be subjected to a "political trial," a congressional hearing to hold politicians and public officials to account for lying to Congress.

Congressman Silvano Aureoles, referring to a related article I published, said in a public statement: "Given the reports coming out in the media and documentary evidence pointing to the intervention of soldiers and federal officers, it would seem that the head of the attorney general's office, Jesús Murillo Karam, lied to the public and to the legislative commission investigating the case." Miguel Alonso Raya, PRD member and legislative deputy, said, "I recognize that the report in question introduces grave and serious doubts about the official version of what happened this past September in Iguala."

The then director of federal police, Enrique Galindo, felt compelled for the first time, three months after the events, to acknowledge that the federal police were indeed aware of the arrival of the students in Iguala and of the attacks against them, though he insisted that none of his men took part, cautiously stating: "We at least have no evidence of their active participation in the concrete events of September 26." With more bravado, Attorney General Jesús Murillo Karam publicly attempted to refute my research.

"The Army is beyond the control of the president"—Miranda Nava

Faced with the lies of the federal government and the refusal of the 27th Infantry Battalion to permit the family members of the disappeared to search their base, the movement opted to take further and much more drastic steps. After touring the Costa Chica looking for support, the relatives of the forty-three met in Ayutla with representatives of the Popular Guerrero Movement, the State Coordinator of Guerrero Education Workers, the Union of Pueblos and Organizations of the State of Guerrero, and other community defense groups. The coalition vowed to expel the Army from their region. At this time, the federal government was saying that members of guerrilla organizations had infiltrated the group of family members at the meeting with Peña Nieto, to manipulate them.

On December 17, 2014, some of these organizations, along with the families of the forty-three, resolved to go and remove a military checkpoint set up against the local guerrilla movement. Another massacre—this time of the parents—seemed imminent. When the protesters arrived in Ayutla, one of the witnesses told me, "the place was crawling with soldiers, riot cops, tanks, like there was going to be a war. Nobody knew how they found out [we were coming]. It didn't matter. The decision had been made." The protesters strategized and decided to break into smaller groups to descend on the checkpoint.

As they were approaching, lawyer Vidulfo Rosales received a call from the undersecretary of the interior, Luis Enrique Miranda Nava. "Now then," Miranda Nava said aggressively. "What's this about expelling the Army from their post?

What's come over you?" But Miranda Nava didn't scare Rosales, who was neither his lackey nor his employee.

"I don't know what you're talking about," Rosales responded, trying to gain time.

"What do you mean, you don't know what I'm talking about? I have it down right here that you're leading this, you're with those people, that's what I'm hearing. Talk to them, it's insane what you're about to do, and I'm holding you responsible for whatever may happen. If you think we won't respond, or the Army won't respond, you are badly mistaken," Miranda Nava blustered. "These things are out of my hands. You understand me. It's up to the generals. If you think they won't shoot, you're wrong." He hung up, and Rosales continued walking with the crowd. Helicopters buzzed in the sky. More troops appeared. At least 300 armed troops stood in formation. The protesters, meanwhile, numbered around 5,000. The atmosphere was tense as a bow. The soldiers raised their weapons, and some of the protesters had firearms of their own. A bloodbath seemed likely.

The protesters divided into three groups, while another contingent of troops encircled them from the rear. People called on nearby communities to start ringing their church bells. More people came, some of them erecting barricades in the street to stop any reinforcements from the military base in Chilpancingo.

The stand-off lasted for three hours until a small committee, led by Rosales, approached the checkpoint. Experienced in this sort of campaign, the lawyer calmly announced, "We have a document." He began reading out the reasons why the Army should not be working in public security or occupying indigenous territory, and in light of these arguments, he asked them to retreat to their bases. The captain in charge replied that they were not going to accept the document and that they weren't leaving.

"We have a constitutional mandate to be here," the captain said.

"That's debatable," Rosales said.

"And who are you?"

"I'm these people's lawyer." He went on to explain that the only way for the Army to lawfully conduct public security operations was with a judge's order. If such an order was produced, the protesters would depart peacefully.

"I've got one," the officer lied.

"Show me."

"And why should I show it to you?"

"Not to me, to everyone here," Rosales said, turning to the crowds. "Isn't that right, *compañeros?*"

"Yessss!" they cried.

The protesters resolved they would give the Army thirty minutes to accept their document. Otherwise, they would be faced with a decision.

"You are not going to push us out of here," the captain barked. The committee withdrew.

Half an hour later, a helicopter arrived with the commander of the 9th Region of Acapulco to make an announcement to the leaders of the protest.

"Okay, gentlemen. There's no problem, I'll accept your document. I'll take it, but we're not moving from here. No. It's our duty . . . There are drug traffickers around, delinquents, and we have to provide protection."

The protesters objected that the Army only ever harassed their community security groups.

"It's a presidential order to deploy the military in this zone, and no matter what, we're not moving," the commander said.

The protesters insisted that the checkpoint had to be lifted and moved somewhere else.

Miranda Nava called Rosales again. His message was clear: not even the president could control the military. Over the years following the attacks in Iguala, this has become abundantly obvious.

"You have to back away from this, you jackass, or it's going to get out of hand. There's still a chance to sort things out. I repeat, this is beyond my control, beyond the president's control. This is a military matter now, and they are pissed. They're not about to budge. You're going to kick me out before you kick them out."

"Sure, but we're not asking them to move a whole brigade. This is the villagers' territory, and they came and put up a checkpoint in response to the death and disappearance of the students. What's the objective?"

"I told you," Miranda Nava responded.

Government officials called the directors of the Tlachinollan NGO and warned they were going to "see to them" and that they'd do better to back down with dignity. The directors responded that, even if it was only temporary, the Army needed to leave, and then the protesters would do the same. Miranda Nava suggested that the recently arrived soldiers could withdraw, but the demonstrators weren't satisfied.

"That's no way to persuade the people to leave," Rosales said. "They're not going anywhere."

"Well, I warned you."

"Fine."

Fifteen minutes later the undersecretary suggested that the Army make a tactical retreat and that the people back away as well, so as not to aggravate the situation. Within twenty

minutes the Army began their departure, and the crowds celebrated. It was a momentary victory.

The Interdisciplinary Group of Independent Experts (GIEI)

On January 27, 2015, in another press conference, Attorney
General Murillo Karam responded to questions about my
article, "The True Night of Iguala," by insisting that the case
was closed and repeating his "historical truth."

According to the unswerving official version, the students
were attacked solely and exclusively by the municipal police
of Iguala and Cocula, following orders from the mayor, José
Luis Abarca. They were then taken to the Iguala police
department, ferried all together to a location outside the city,
and handed over to *El Cepillo*, *El Chereje*, *El Pato*, and *El
Jona*, who, that same night, killed them and burned their
bodies in the trash dump of Cocula, finally disposing of their
remains in the San Juan River.

In March 2015, the GIEI began its own investigation, as
promised by Peña Nieto during his meeting with the families of
the disappeared. In both their first and second reports
(September 2015 and April 2016), the five experts making up
the GIEI team—Carlos Beristain, Ángela Buitrago, Claudia
Paz y Paz, Francisco Cox, and Alejandro Valencia—echoed
the conclusions published in *Proceso* magazine, arriving at practically the same version of events as I had posited in my series.

The GIEI team categorically concluded that the fire in the
Cocula trash dump could never have happened and that there
was no scientific proof to back up the PGR's claims. The only
explanation for the nonsensical stories offered by the four
builders is the systematic torture they suffered before submit-
ting their "confessions."

In April 2016, in its last report, the GIEI presented a previously unseen video showing the director of the AIC, Tomás Zerón, visiting the San Juan River with Agustín García Reyes (*El Chereje*) at around noon on October 28, 2014. In footage taken by journalists that day, black plastic bags are conspicuously present in the river, inside of which were found the supposed remains of the *normalistas*. The GIEI pointed out that standard procedures for the handling of evidence were never mentioned in the PGR dossier, and it accused Zerón of contaminating and manipulating the evidence, undermining the reliability of the alleged discovery. The families of the disappeared promptly accused Zerón of planting the remains of Alexander Mora in those bags.

The team also noted that Agustín García Reyes showed clear marks of torture. The new video corroborates the story told by García Reyes's wife, that he had been taken to the river where he was threatened and forced to speak to camera of events he knew nothing about.

My examination of this aspect of the PGR dossier showed that the only acknowledged procedure regarding the allegedly accidental discovery of black plastic bags containing human remains is dated October 29, when the intervention of the Public Ministry and a forensic expert were solicited in order to certify the find and to include the evidence in the official preliminary investigation. The forensic investigator noted that Navy officers placed "in clear view of the forensic team and the DA, three meters northwest of the tree on the riverbank, a bag of synthetic material, black in color, subsequently labeled Bag 1, open on one side, and containing a humid lump of what appeared to be dirt, brown and black, unidentifiable at first glance, and which the forensic anthropologist proceeded to inspect, discovering fragments of human bones that had been directly exposed to flame."

The collection and bagging of the bones occurred, according to the report, on October 29 and 30 at the same location. This means that after the initial discovery on October 28, there was an entire day during which the bags could have been tampered with or evidence could have been planted.

The forensic report also notes that the marines claimed to have found the bag earlier, inside the river. In other words, it had already been moved at least once from its original location.

To lend credibility to their "discovery," the PGR claimed that the Argentine Forensic Anthropology Team (EAAF) was present when the bags were found, but the Argentines have always denied this. This was the second time that the EAAF had undermined the government's attempts at a clean resolution to the case.

Three separate scientific studies—one by the EAAF, one by an independent team consulted by the GIEI, and one by the Autonomous University of Mexico—confirmed that the Cocula trash dump offered no real evidence of the cremation of the forty-three students, indeed no evidence of a fire fierce enough to have cremated anything.

The remains identified as belonging to Alexander Mora Venancio, which the PGR used to try to clinch the case, turned into yet another piece of evidence incriminating the federal government. If there was never any fire in Cocula, and if the evidence found along the San Juan was tampered with, then how did the federal authorities obtain those remains, and where did they come from?

8

In Mexico's Dungeons

He doesn't know if it's night or day. He's lying face down, hands tied, unmoving. He feels carpet under his face. He knows he's not in some clandestine location, but in PGR offices, in the custody of federal ministerial police from the AIC. It's October 15, 2014. A few hours ago he was seized from a restaurant on the Mexico–Toluca highway, where he was eating with two friends. His captors said he had something to do with the forty-three missing students.

Just a few minutes ago, a man dressed in a suit came into the room where they had him tied to a chair. The man approached slowly, leaned down, and spoke into his ear, telling him that he had been sent personally by the attorney general, Jesús Murillo Karam, to solve the case of the disappeared *normalistas*. He added that he could help him set things right before it was "too late." He warned: "You have three minutes to decide." But there was nothing to tell. He didn't know what happened on that night in Iguala. Next, a group of seven federal ministerial police officers came into the room with rolls of bandages, wooden planks, dildo-shaped metal bars, and plenty of black plastic trash bags. "These people are going to make you do what we tell you. That's an order from the attorney general," the man in the suit said, and he gave the signal for the infamous ritual to start, telling his men not to stop until they got what they wanted. And then—expertly, rapidly—the officers blindfolded him, pushed him face down on the floor, and tied his wrists with gauze strips.

They leave him like that for a while. He still doesn't understand what's awaiting him. The minutes seem interminable. The men come back, flip him over, face up. His body is like a puppet, the officers manhandling it as they please. One of them pulls his arms up above his head so his back is flush against the floor, another sits on his legs to stop him from kicking, and yet another officer sits on his stomach and puts a plastic bag over his head until he loses consciousness. For a few moments he feels nothing: not pain, not life. And then they revive him with blows to the chest.

"Whatever happens, you're going to die," one of the men tells him. He begs for mercy. "This is just the beginning." They flip him back over so he is face down, then pull off his pants and underwear. They undo the bandages they had tied his legs with. They splash water on his testicles and then slip another bag over his head to asphyxiate him again. A hard metal object is thrust into his anus, and then, slowly, pulled out. The pain is indescribable. They continue to rape him. Another officer periodically slips the bag back over his head and others apply electrical shocks to his testicles. He passes out again.

They revive him again. As the blindfold has slipped down he is able to see the man sitting on his chest, who is sweating, and seems to be nervous or agitated. "The son of a bitch already woke up," one of the others says. They order him to stand up and pull up his pants. He realizes he is soaking wet.

He feels excruciating pain in his anus, his stomach, and his chest around his heart.

The man who ordered the officers to begin the torture, who said he was sent by Murillo Karam, asks him if he's ready to tell them what they want. He is. "I'll do whatever you like. Just don't torture me anymore, for the love of God." They hand him over to other agents who run him through another torture session. Every inch of his body throbs with pain. When they let him go to the bathroom he realizes he is bleeding from the anus and that he has open wounds on his thighs. He can't stop shaking.

After more than twenty-four hours of physical and psychological torture, on the morning of October 17, Sidronio Casarrubias Salgado signed a detailed confession for the PGR. He was forced to say he was the leader of the Guerreros Unidos and that he had given the go-ahead for the murder and cremation of the forty-three Ayotzinapa students in the trash dump outside of Cocula, Guerrero. He also had to confess that his brother, Mario Casarrubias Salgado, was also a Guerreros Unidos leader. Other members of the gang included the mayor of Iguala, José Luis Abarca; the mayor's wife, María de los Ángeles Pineda Villa; and Iguala police officers. Under duress, Sidronio said that the students were accompanied in the buses by members of the rival gang, Los Rojos, and that Gildardo López Astudillo, *El Gil*, along with local police officers acting on the orders of Abarca, attacked the buses to stop Los Rojos from invading Iguala.

This testimony was used by the government to hasten the closing of the case. During his trial, however, Sidronio Casarrubias described the abuse he suffered at the hands of the federal ministerial police officers who detained him. At an identity parade before the judge, he specifically identified Gabriel Valle Campos as the officer who raped him.

Valle Campos had joined the discredited and corrupt federal judicial police in 1993 and remained in the force even as, in futile attempts to hide its dark past, it changed names and acronyms. He had been stationed in Aguascalientes and in Durango, and then, in 2013, was transferred to the Attorney General's Office of the State of Mexico where, despite the serious accusations against him, he remained on active service until at least May 2016, when he presented his last declaration of assets.

The case of Sidronio Casarrubias was extreme enough that the PGR's Inspector General opened an individual investigation into the torture he endured.

Casarrubias wasn't the only suspect in the case who was tortured. At least thirty-one other detainees suffered beatings, asphyxiation, sexual violence (including electric shocks on their genitals and anal penetration), and rape threats against their families (which were sometimes carried out). All of these actions and threats were intended to force the suspects to implicate themselves or others, as well as sign formal confessions that had been already typed out by the PGR.

According to a report that makes up part of the preliminary investigation AP/PGR/SDHPDSC/OI/2015, which I was able to see, in just the case of the disappearance of the forty-three students there were ninety-five instances in which the Istanbul Protocol was initiated to verify accusations of torture.

Coercing false confessions through torture to construct its so-called "historical truth," the Mexican government's dogged insistence on violence distracted from an actual truth. Two years after the disappearance of the students, the PGR remains without a single scientific piece of evidence that the students were burned. From the very beginning of the investigation, the PGR had already drawn its convenient conclusion: "it seems that [the students] were completely burned, which means that should their remains be found it may be impossible to identify them." This statement appears in the first pages of the PGR's dossier. To this day the government has been unable to explain how they arrived at that conclusion. The only evidence that any of the students have been burned—as the treatment of the remains of Alexander Mora show—were planted by the PGR, along with tampered evidence "found" near the San Juan River.

The "historical truth" has been exposed as a lie by my own investigation, by the lack of evidence in the Cocula trash dump, and by the Interdisciplinary Group of Independent Experts (GIEI) that the Inter-American Commission of Human Rights sent to Mexico at the request of the families of the disappeared students. While the government of Peña Nieto has shown no real interest in solving the case, it has presented unlikely suspects in a desperate attempt to staunch the gaping wound that exposed to the world how Mexico abuses its authority and fails to uphold justice.

Taken together, from the GIEI team's investigations and my own research, there are thirty-three confirmed detainees who the government used to construct its historical truth— and who it also brutally tortured. The documents and interviews I obtained showed that federal office buildings had basically become torture chambers. The information on the systematic torture of the detainees that I published in *Proceso* was later used in reports by the GIEI and the Associated Press and, finally, investigated by the UN through its Working Group on Arbitrary Detention, the Working Group on Enforced or Involuntary Disappearances, the

Special Rapporteur on the Independence of Judges and Lawyers, and the Special Rapporteur on Torture and Other Cruel, Inhuman or Degrading Treatment or Punishment, which, in July 2015, sent a letter to the Mexican government informing it of its investigation into the "arbitrary detention, torture, and cruel, inhuman and degrading treatment" of twelve of the men and women detained in the Ayotzinapa case, including Marco Antonio Ríos Berber, Raúl Núñez Salgado, Agustín García Reyes, Jonathan Osorio Cortés, Patricio Reyes Landa, and Carlos Canto Salgado (who were accused of being members of the Guerreros Unidos and of having participated in the attack and disappearance of the students), as well as the Iguala police officers Verónica Bahena Cruz, Santiago Manzón Cedillo, Héctor Aguilar Ávalos, Alejandro Lara García, Edgar Magdaleno Cruz Navarro, and Jesús Parra Arroyo (likewise accused of involvement in the affair).

On top of the twelve subjects whose torture sparked investigations from the UN, the following detainees also claim to have been subjected to torture: Iguala police officers Honorio Antúnez and David Cruz Hernández, and alleged members of Guerreros Unidos Gildardo López Astudillo, Felipe Rodríguez Salgado, Eury Flores, Luis Alberto José Gaspar, Francisco Javier Lozano, Napoleón Martínez Gaspar, and the brothers Miguel Ángel and Osvaldo Ríos Sánchez.

In the first report submitted by Carlos Beristain, Ángela Buitrago, Claudia Paz y Paz, Alejandro Valencia, and Francisco Cox of the GIEI, in September 2015, they observed that 80 percent of the detainees showed signs of mistreatment.

The thirty-three victims pointed to federal police, federal ministerial police, and Army and Navy officers as the perpetrators of their abuse, with the presumed complicity of the

242

three top government officials responsible for the investigation into the disappearance of the *normalistas*: Attorney General Jesús Murillo Karam; AIC Director Tomás Zerón; and the director of Specialized Investigations on Organized Crime (SEIDO), Gustavo Salas Chávez.

The disappearance of the forty-three students revealed the brutal reality of the Mexican state, which is rife with disappearances, murder, corruption, impunity, and the systematic use of torture by law enforcement agencies to lock up innocent people and protect the guilty. The crimes committed on that night in Iguala remain concealed beneath a pact of silence that the Mexican government doesn't want to break. While the witnesses remain silent because of a justified fear of violent reprisal, the perpetrators remain silent to protect one another, and this silence, in the end, impedes us from knowing the ultimate fate of the students.

Though Mexico has seen more than 25,000 disappearances in the past eight years, the forty-three Ayotzinapa students are not just another case. And the difference isn't only in the profile of the victims—young and very poor, supported by families and civil organizations fighting to get to the truth—but because it is the only case of collective disappearance in which there is clear evidence of the active participation by state forces, in both the event and its subsequent cover-up.

The number of victims of the attacks of September 26 and 27 is over 100. There were six murders, forty-three disappearances, twenty people wounded by gunshots, and dozens more detained, tortured, and accused of committing crimes they claim they had nothing to do with.

The terrifying stories of the detainees who were brutalized in the dungeons of Mexico demonstrate that when forces of law and order are trained to inflict pain on every centimeter of a victim's body, they are worse than a hyena with its prey.

The Bribes

Minutes after being raped and tortured, Sidronio Casarrubias was taken before the director of the AIC, Tomás Zerón, whose Criminal Investigations office was in the same building. Zerón then took Casarrubias to see the woman he had supposedly been with when they were seized in a restaurant a few hours previously. Zerón told Casarrubias to start talking with her. This woman, named Dulce, was not the person he had been eating with. Trembling with fear, she told him that she had been tortured. He never saw her again, and her present whereabouts are unknown.

In front of Zerón, the same officers who had tortured him warned that he'd better not denounce what had happened: "If you do, you know what we can do to you and your family. Think of your kids, your wife, your parents."

On October 17, 2014, an agent from the Public Ministry typed out Casarrubias's confession, telling him, "You just have to sign and put your fingerprint on it." On the same day Murillo Karam, flanked by Zerón, held a press conference announcing Casarrubias's arrest: "He will help us solve the case of the six people killed in Iguala and the subsequent disappearance of the forty-three students from the Normal Rural School of Ayotzinapa."

Days later, Casarrubias was transferred to the maximum-security prison, Cefereso #1, known as El Altiplano. His wounds had yet to heal, and his nightmare was not over. During his first month inside, he was visited three times by PGR officials who pressured him to repeat before the judge the same confession he signed after being tortured. One of his visitors was Murillo Karam himself.

"I am the Attorney General of the Republic, Murillo Karam," he told Casarrubias in one of the prison's offices. The PGR chief was smoking a cigarette, seemingly nervous. "I know that you were tortured and I want you to tell me if you could recognize the voices of any of the men who tortured you. Because those who did that to you are themselves criminals. Were you also raped?"

"Yes," Casarrubias responded.

Murillo Karam then offered him 66 million pesos if he would tell him where the students were. Casarrubias said that he didn't know.

"I'm going to lock you away in solitary for eighty years. You're never going to get out. I know you're not guilty of the crimes . . . but it looks like you don't want to help yourself. I know you don't have any money, and that you need the best lawyers there are, but apparently you're not going to get one," the attorney general said, and then he left.

On February 25, 2015, Casarrubias denounced the bribery attempt before a judge. Two days later, Peña Nieto fired Murillo Karam.

That same February 25, the UN sent the Mexican government a letter signed by five of its special rapporteurs in reaction to the treatment of Casarrubias: "We wish to express our grave concern about the detention, torture (including sexual), and the restrictions of the right to legal defense suffered by Mr. Casarrubias Salgado." The letter was signed by Mads Andenas, of the Working Group on Arbitrary Detention; Ariel Dulitzky, of the Working Group on Forced and Involuntary Disappearance; Gabriela Knaul, of the Working Group on the Independence of Judges and

Lawyers; Christof Heyns, of the Working Group on Extrajudicial, Summary, or Arbitrary Killings; and Juan E. Méndez, of the Working Group on Torture. "We also wish to express," the letter continued, "our grave concern related to the allegations that the torture and ill-treatment was intended to extract a forced and false confession. We fear that these methods may not be an isolated case, and that the investigation into the disappearance of the forty-three students from Iguala may equally be based on information obtained through acts of torture."

Confessions of Nonsense and Absurdity

Marco Antonio Ríos Berber, Martín Alejandro Macedo Barrera, Luis Alberto José Gaspar, and Honorio Antúnez were detained on October 3 and 4 by Guerrero ministerial police, in a joint operation with the federal police and the Army. According to the police report, they were captured while walking down the street. They were the first supposed members of the Guerreros Unidos to be arrested.

Ríos Berber and Macedo Barrera admitted, under torture, to having taken part in the attacks against the students. Macedo Barrera claimed that some of the students died in the shootout in Iguala, while others were taken to a safe house in Loma de los Coyotes, where they were killed. Ríos Berber said that the Iguala police transferred twenty of the students to the police station and that the rest of them were killed in the mountains near Pueblo Viejo.

Ríos Berber also told representatives from the UN that he was seized without a warrant and driven to the PGR office in Chilpancingo. There he was threatened, stripped naked, and, "multiple times during his torture, he was almost suffocated."

The following day he was transferred to the Mexico City SEIDO, where he signed his confession under duress.

Just Sitting on a Bench

Luis Alberto José Gaspar, eighteen years old when he was arrested, explained that he had been working as a builder's assistant to support his wife, one child, and two younger brothers who depended on him for food, board, and school fees. He said that when he was detained in Iguala on October 2, 2014, he was just sitting on a bench in front of a school. He told a judge on November 25: "In relation to the actions imputed to me, I had nothing at all to do with it. I'm a good man, a working man, and I'm innocent." He said that six ministerial police vehicles were involved in his arrest, on grounds that he looked "suspicious." After pushing him into one of the cars, they asked him where he was on the night of September 26, and he responded that he was in his house. Soon the blows began, and the bag over the head. His torturers kept saying that he was a member of the Guerreros Unidos. When he claimed not to belong to any criminal organizations and to have proof that he worked as a builder, the response was, "We don't care about your proof." They then took him to the offices in Chilpancingo so he could sign his confession.

"In the morning," José Gaspar went on, "they blindfolded me and took me to an empty space. And then they stripped me naked, tied me up with bandages, put a cloth over my face and told me that I better tell them all I knew about the students. I asked them, how could I tell them anything if I didn't know anything about the students, and they asked how come I didn't know anything if I was from Iguala. And then they put water on the rag on my face and they hit me in the ribs and on the head for hours." When they took him to make his confession, he instead described how he had been arrested. They ignored him and, telling him that they were going to take him back and beat him some more if he didn't comply, forced him, without consulting a lawyer, to sign a statement. "I signed because I was scared," he told the judge.

The next night they flew him to Mexico City. At the SEIDO they tried to get him to make another statement, but he refused, still not understanding what he was being accused of.

How to Dig Your Own Grave

On October 8, 2014, federal ministerial police arrested brothers Miguel Ángel and Osvaldo Ríos Sánchez in Cuernavaca, Morelos, for alleged suspicious activity. According to the police, they were carrying guns and drugs. After being informed of their rights, both immediately stated that they were members of the Guerreros Unidos, that they sold drugs, and that the *normalistas* had been killed and buried at La Parota, on the outskirts of Iguala.

Due to supposed mechanical failures affecting the police vehicles, they were driven very early the next morning to the PGR offices in Mexico City. During the medical check, Miguel Ángel presented with ten wounds on his body and Osvaldo with fourteen. At 06:30 the same day they were flown by Navy helicopter to the Iguala–Teloloapan highway and then driven in military vehicles to the wasteland known as La Parota.

Viridiana Ramírez, Miguel Ángel's wife, confirmed to me that her husband and brother-in-law were tortured by the police for hours. En route they told him that they were going to throw him out of the helicopter and nobody would ever know, and they bullied him to confess to the death and disappearance of the students.

Miguel Ángel told his wife that when they arrived at La Parota, the marines ordered him to start digging his own grave. "They wanted us to sign a confession that they had already written," Osvaldo said, adding that as they were digging the grave they shot towards them. When he tried to pull himself out of the grave they fired again, barely missing his hand. The officers periodically slipped plastic bags over their heads and administered electric shocks. In the end, both men signed the confession.

Disturbingly, on October 23, activists in a Guerrero community organization found recently dug graves in La Parota, containing the remains of flesh, blood, shoes, backpacks, and pencils.

Tied to a Chair

After twenty years in the Army, Honorio Antúnez retired and got a job as a local Iguala police officer. On September 26, 2014, he was off duty to take a training course. On October 3, as he was clocking in for work, a team of both state and federal ministerial police came in and arrested him. "You're a municipal, so you're fucked," they told him. They put him into a white truck and took him to a place where several cars, including a cargo truck with the words "Mobile Dental Unit" printed on the side, were parked. Though the federal ministerial police participated in his arrest, only state officers' names appear on the arrest report: Fidel Rosas Serrano, Alfonso Casarreal Morales, and Rodolfo Peralta Millán.

Antúnez said that two men, who he'd seen before at the state police station on September 27, now showed up. One of them was the state prosecutor general, Iñaki Blanco Cabrera.

The officers proceeded to interrogate him about Iguala mayor José Luis Abarca and his wife, as well as asking him where the disappeared students were. He told them that he didn't know. "You know where they're buried!" they yelled at him between insults. The federal police then cuffed him, hustled him into the dental truck, tied him to a dentist's chair, and began torturing him. "Nobody knows you're here. If you die in the middle of this, it's no big deal," they told him. "After they put the bags over my head they put a cloth on my face, over my nose and mouth, and they started to splash water in my face so I was breathing in the water through my nose and mouth. They were also beating me in the stomach," Antúnez explained at his first hearing before a judge.

Later, the federal ministerial men pulled him out of the truck and handed him over to the federal gendarmerie, at the turn-off to Rancho del Cura on the Chilpancingo highway. "Heading towards Tepecoacuilco, [the gendarmes] turned off the highway into the brush where they started torturing me again, hitting me in the stomach and asking me about the *normalista* kids." They finally took him to Chilpancingo, and, that night, he signed a confession.

Investigators started running the names of local policemen past him. "Since I wasn't telling them anything and not answering their questions, they took me to another office and showed me photographs." Presenting photographs of colleagues he knew only by sight, they asked him if these were members of the Guerreros Unidos. He told them that he didn't know. "I don't stand by the confession they made me sign in Chilpancingo," he told the judge. "I don't stand by it because I signed it after being tortured."

Honorio Antúnez's confession, pre-prepared and signed under duress, enabled the PGR to arrest twenty other Iguala or Cocula police officers who they accused of engineering the students' disappearance.

Cries from the Dungeon

The federal ministerial police officer put the blindfold on her, dragged her to an office, and threw her in a chair. They would take her house away, they told her, rape her family. They beat her in the ribs, kicked her legs, and applied electric shocks to her body. Terrified, the Iguala police officer Verónica Bahena (who had been on vacation at the time of the events) soiled herself, at which her tormentors laughed, humiliating and insulting her. Her cries echoed those of the other ten municipal policemen who were arrested along with her on October 14.

As corroborated by multiple testimonies from family members of the detained police officers, the torture sessions took place in the PGR, at the hands of brawny men dressed in black and with masked faces. During the beatings, they repeatedly asked about the disappeared students and the Guerreros Unidos. The treatment seemed to follow a pattern: "Why did you kill them?" A blow. "Why did you take them away?" and another hail of blows, repeated until the officers were semi-conscious and on the floor.

Sue Martínez has been married to police officer Héctor Ávalos for thirteen years. They've lived all that time in a pasteboard and laminate house in a crowded suburb of Iguala. Héctor had been in the Army before becoming a police officer, working mostly as a driver. He didn't like law enforcement, but it was the only way he found to keep afloat and support his family. Sue told me that her husband wasn't working on the night of September 26, which I was able to confirm by the police logbook.

Héctor and Sue were at home all day on the 26th. On the 27th, which was their son's birthday, they took him to eat at McDonald's. They returned home at 20:40 and didn't leave again until the following morning.

It wasn't until four long days after his arrest that Sue was able to see Héctor, who had been taken to a prison in Nayarit. "When I saw my husband, I thought he was going to die there and then, that's how badly he'd been beaten." He told her that he had passed out twice while the PGR officers had been beating him and that they kicked him to wake him back up. After the session they dragged him and the others out into the hallway and left them there. "They wanted them to confess. They kept asking where the students were." Her husband swore he didn't know anything, since he wasn't working that day. "You have to confess," they repeated.

Laura Martínez, the wife of police officer Alejandro Lara, told me that her husband also had a day off on September 26 and that they were together the entire time: "Wherever I go, he keeps me company. On his free days he was always with me and I was always with him." That Friday, she told me, they went together to pay the installment on the loan they took out at a pawn shop. At around 21:00 (close to the time of the first attack) they were watching their daughter's basketball practice, well outside the center of town. She was now gathering letters attesting to her husband's good character; people who had seen him at basketball practice also went to confirm his alibi.

After Alejandro Lara's arrest, it was a long time before they could see each other again. When Laura was finally allowed to visit, Alejandro broke down sobbing. Hardly able to speak, he told her what they had done to him: severe beatings all over his body, especially his stomach, electric shocks, and asphyxiation with a plastic bag. The UN rapporteurs, summarizing Lara's case, wrote: "This violent episode lasted about four hours, during which Mr. Lara could hear others who had been detained with him also being tortured." Lara would be one of the first victims to file an official complaint of torture with the National Commission on Human Rights "against the federal police officers who arrested us, beat us, and tried to force us to tell them where the bodies were."

Of the ten arrested male officers, eight bore multiple marks, according to their medical examinations, especially around the pelvis and upper thigh—evidence of electric shocks. Verónica Bahena was found to have at least five wounds and suffered from a severe uterine hemorrhage for several days.

"We are going to rape your daughters"

On October 27, 2014, Patricio Reyes Landa and Jonathan Osorio Cortés (two of the young builders framed by the PGR) were stopped in Apetlanca. The arrest was made by federal police officers Jesús Emanuel Álvarez Alvarado, José de Jesús Palafox Mora, and Jorge Edmundo Samperio Rodríguez. One of the officers split Reyes Landa's head open with his gun. Instead of being booked straight away before the law, they were helicoptered—along with Agustín García Reyes, the third builder, who had been seized earlier that day in Cocula by the Navy officers Vidal Vázquez Mendoza and Jazmín Edith García Martínez—to an official military building.

In a handwritten letter sent to me for this investigation, as well as in testimony to the UN, Patricio Reyes Landa wrote that he was left on the floor in this military building for a long time. He could hear the screams of pain of the other two, until it was his turn. "Two people in Navy uniforms came and put me in a room. They tied my hands behind me with a bandage and tied up my legs . . . then they started applying electric shocks to my testicles, inside my anus, and in my mouth . . . they also put a plastic bag over my head so I couldn't breathe, and when I lost consciousness they beat me in the chest and the stomach. This lasted for about three hours, and all the time they were telling me what I had to say." During the torture session they showed him various photographs of his family. "They told me I had to cooperate, and if I didn't they were going to kill my wife and two daughters, but before killing them they were going to rape them, they were going to stick a pistol into their rectums, and they were all going to rape my wife . . . and whatever, I was a worthless piece of shit."

The GIEI team found at least seventy wounds on Reyes Landa's body. Jonathan and Agustín suffered the same treatment: the GIEI counted ninety-four separate wounds on Jonathan's body. These are the men accused by Attorney General Murillo Karam—men who "confessed" only after suffering severe beatings, torture, and threats against their families—when he claimed that the case was solved.

Agustín García Reyes told UN investigators, as they wrote to the Mexican government in July 2015, that he was "forced to memorize certain dates and names to later include in his confession before the Public Ministry." He also described how officers from "the Attorney General's Office took him to the Cocula trash dump to reenact how the events would have occurred, what people would have taken part, and where, and told him what to say." The GIEI team announced (in April 2016) that Tomás Zerón himself, the director of the AIC, took García Reyes to make the video, and that by the river his men planted a black plastic bag containing the remains of Alexander Mora—the only missing student who is definitively known to be dead.

According to the PGR, the immediate boss of the three men accused of killing and burning the students was twenty-five-year-old Felipe Rodríguez Salgado. He was detained on January 15, 2015 in Cocula, though the federal police claimed to have arrested him in Morelos. In a letter he wrote a few days afterwards, he explained that Tomás Zerón came to the Nayarit prison where he was being held: "He wanted me to incriminate myself in the disappearance of the students and also sign some documents and recognize some people I don't even know, someone named Sidronio and the ex-mayor of Iguala. He wanted me to say that they were my bosses and the ones who paid me. In exchange he'd give my family money and buy them a house . . . He said I'd be sentenced to [just] eight years in prison." Salgado wrote that on February 18, Zerón returned to the prison to repeat his offer. When he refused again, Zerón said, "You're missing a great opportunity. Careful, now, don't tell anybody about our chat because it could be really bad for you and for your family."

All four of these men signed confessions claiming that they had killed the forty-three students in the Cocula trash dump, burned the bodies, and then got rid of the ashes in the San Juan River. The confessions, however, do not agree on the facts, the times, the location, or even on the names of those who were allegedly involved.

For two years Amnesty International and Juan Méndez, the UN special rapporteur on torture, have produced reports elaborating on the widespread and systematic use of torture by Mexican law enforcement agencies and the military to extract false confessions. Offices of the PGR, the Army, the

Navy, and the federal and state police have been converted into torture chambers like those in Abu Ghraib and Guantánamo, though it seems the cries of the victims in Mexican dungeons have not been heard by the international community or been reported on in the press.

The reasons for torturing someone are always perverse, but the case of the men and women tortured during the state's investigation into the disappearance of the forty-three students evinces a deeper level of moral degradation. The Mexican government arrested and tortured innocent people, wrenching false confessions out of them just so it could proclaim the case was closed.

At the time of writing, the PGR has been forced to open investigations into dozens of public officials for torturing the so-called culprits in the disappearance of the forty-three *normalistas*. The majority of those officials belong to the Navy. In September 2015, an internal PGR investigation pointed to nineteen different officers who had engaged in torture. I include a complete list at the end of the book. Not one of them has been charged with a crime.

9

The Killing Hours

Next to his classmates from the Raúl Isidro Burgos Normal Rural School of Ayotzinapa, Fernando Marín is lying on the ground near Estrella de Oro bus 1568, soaked in his own blood. The barrage of gunfire that rained down on them minutes earlier nearly ripped off his right hand, and the tendons are flapping from his wrist. It doesn't hurt too bad yet, but his breath is coming in gasps. At twenty years old, Marín has no doubt that tonight is the last night of his life.

It's past 22:40 on September 26, 2014, and Iguala's Juan N. Álvarez Street is deserted. Shopkeepers and clients are cowering behind stores' metal roll gates, which came down as soon as the shooting began. Those who could get away have scattered.

Nearby residents are lying face down in their own homes. It's as if the walls were made of paper instead of brick. The bullets that were aimed at the students could just as easily pierce through their walls. A few of them, in the darkness, creep up to the windows to catch a glimpse of the nightmare outside.

"You're fucked, you know that?" a state police officer barks at Marín. "Finish him off, go on, he's cooked. Just kill him," the officer says to the other state police. And now Fernando, nickname *Carrillas*, feels the cold metal of a barrel against his left temple. He thinks, I'm going to die, I'm going to die, I'm going to die tonight.

State and local police, as well as armed men in civilian clothes, have surrounded three buses full of *normalistas* on the corner of Juan N. Álvarez and Periférico Norte. A few streets away, federal police officers divert traffic and turn away curious onlookers. The officers would rather perform their operation out of public view, but there will be witnesses.

As if by a miracle, the officer with his gun pressed to *Carrillas*'s temple doesn't fire. Instead, he steps back and calls an ambulance. The paramedics who arrive on the scene, however, assume that the *normalistas* are armed and aggressive, and keep their distance.

"How are my *compañeros* going to shoot when they don't have guns," *Carrillas* thinks to himself. "When we don't have anything." But he doesn't speak. He is consumed by terror. The seconds beat away in his chest, pulsing in his shattered forearm, pulsing in his head.

That same beat began counting down earlier in the day, at 13:00.

Carrillas

Following his cousins and older brothers, Fernando Marín began his studies at the Ayotzinapa Normal Rural School on July 25, 2013. Like all the freshmen, he started with "initiation week," during which the older students helped him forge a political and social consciousness, as well as inducting him in collective labor. Mostly the children of poor farmers, new students cut brush, tend to the pigs, and lend a hand on the neighboring farms owned by *tíos*, the so-called aunts and uncles who live close to the school. They also learn the history of the school and tour the communities to raise funds.

"The Normal [school] has had a ton of problems with the government," *Carrillas* told me, in the only interview he has given to the press. "They teach us that we have to be ready to join the struggle at any moment, from the first year to the fourth year. [The government] wants to keep us submissive, poorly educated. It always wants the children of *campesinos* to be submissive, they don't want us to get ahead."

Carrillas is clear about one thing related to the attack he and his classmates endured: "Why us? Because those who graduate from here have strong ideals, they're people who speak hard truths to the government . . . Men like Lucio Cabañas or Genaro Vázquez, they're like Che Guevara, like our founder, Raúl Isidro Burgos . . . People who join the guerrilla movement, who have that vision. That's why the government doesn't want more of us in here. This school is huge, it's greater than the government even imagines."

After a year in the teacher training school, *Carrillas* was elected by his fellow students to lead the Committee on Order and Discipline. "My work," he explained, "consisted in keeping everything in order at the Raúl Isidro Burgos Normal Rural School of Ayotzinapa, to make sure my classmates didn't drink alcohol and kept good discipline from the first year to the fourth."

He was great friends with Bernardo Flores Alcaraz, or *Cochiloco*, elected secretary of struggle. They were inseparable—until that night in Iguala.

On the morning of the 26th, *Carrillas* woke up at nine, went to Chilpancingo on an errand, and returned to the school. He sat down at his cubicle in the common area known as "La Gloria" and then went to one of the covered sports fields, where he ran into *Cochiloco*.

13:00—The Army in Chilpancingo: The Prelude

With time running out for getting enough buses to transport the students to Mexico City for the annual protest in commemoration of the student massacre of October 2, 1968, *Cochiloco* left Ayotzinapa just after noon with a group of classmates to see what he could rustle up at the Chilpancingo bus station. He little imagined that, later that night, there would be another massacre and that they would be the victims.

The previous day, the Estrella de Oro bus company had lodged an official complaint, BRA/SC/06/2630/2014, with the state PGR in Chilpancingo for the recent theft of seven of its buses, including numbers 1568 and 1531. The state and federal police had tried to thwart these previous attempts, but *Cochiloco* and his classmates had succeeded. Later, on October 28, an attorney for Estrella de Oro would make this declaration to the PGR: "It's important to stress that the theft of the property of Estrella de Oro, S. A. de C. V., by students of the Ayotzinapa Normal Rural School, has been an ongoing issue for more than seven years, during which time the company has promptly filed the corresponding complaints, although, to our knowledge, no penal action has been taken against anyone."

When Bernardo *Cochiloco* and his classmates showed up at the Chilpancingo bus station, they were dismayed to see that the entire station was surrounded by Guerrero state police and Mexican Army soldiers who, as can be seen in photographs obtained in the course of this research, were equipped with heavy-caliber weapons. Both the PGR and the Secretariat of National Defense would conceal this fact, and even the Interdisciplinary Group of Independent Experts neglected to include this information in its report.

The presence of the Army in the center of town was, according to local witnesses, exceptional: never before had it been involved in stopping the students from taking the buses. It is clear that federal forces were on the alert and coordinating with each other, hours before the attacks. Equally obvious is the spirit of animosity towards the students.

According to an editorial published in *El Diario de Guerrero* on September 27, "The mere presence of state police and Army troops dissuaded the students from the Raúl Isidro Burgos Normal Rural School of Ayotzinapa from their umpteenth attempt to take buses from the station."

According to the same paper, the students were about to board a bus when state police and soldiers approached them. The *normalistas* tried to provoke both groups of officers. The passengers fled, but no more than a verbal skirmish occurred.

"After the incident," the article continued, "in the immediate vicinity of the bus station, police officers in anti-riot gear, along with military personnel, were deployed to the surrounding streets and undertook to remain in the area to stop the students from stealing other private passenger buses."

Bernardo and his friends were stumped; they returned to the school frustrated and without buses. They called a meeting for that afternoon with the few students that were at the school, mostly first-years, as many of the older students had already left. The discussion centered around the need to go and look for more buses in Iguala. "We knew we were being monitored, which is why we decided to go to Iguala, because there had been too many problems in Chilpancingo," Ángel de la Cruz, nineteen years old and a survivor of the attacks, told me. "Whenever there was trouble in Chilpancingo, we went to Iguala. I mean, it was already our plan B."

Ángel, in his second year, had just returned from his practicals the day before and still had to write a report when *Cochiloco* came up to ask for help with the buses. Ángel, along with some other students, thought it was getting late, but the majority voted to go. "Out of discipline, we had to go," he said. Ángel had already helped commandeer some of the other buses on September 22, and, on the 26th, he personally persuaded a third-year student to come with them.

He had experienced showdowns with the police while taking buses before, but it was never much more than officers surrounding them and throwing tear gas. "Nothing as serious as this, I mean, they never did that kind of thing to us before."

17:59—Departure from Ayotzinapa

At 17:15, when the students were boarding the Estrella de Oro buses 1568 and 1531, Bernardo met up with *Carrillas* on the sports field and invited him to go collect money and try to get a few other buses. It was a request from his best friend, and Fernando couldn't refuse. Along with about 100 other students, *Cochiloco* and *Carrillas* boarded the buses. Though nobody knew it yet, they were vehicles of death.

As soon as the two buses left the school grounds, all levels of the government were alerted through the Chilpancingo C4. According to report 02370, from the Guerrero Secretariat of Public Security (SSP), the government was monitoring the situation. "At 17:59 a telephonic notice came in from C4 Chilpancingo about the departure of the two Estrella de Oro buses, license numbers 1568 and 1531, with students from the Ayotzinapa Normal School, heading towards the city of Iguala de la Independencia," wrote Adame Bautista, a coordinating operator of the SSP, in his report.

At the same time as Adame learned of the *normalistas'* departure, soldiers from the 27th Infantry Battalion, state and local police officers, as well as federal police and federal ministerial police, were being updated in real time. According to what I was able to glean thanks to the Federal Transparency Law (Freedom of Information), the Secretariat of the Interior, led by Miguel Ángel Osorio Chong, also had access to this information through the Executive Secretariat of the National Public Security System's National Information Center.

Let us recall that Osorio Chong told the parents of the disappeared students, during their first meeting in October 2014, that the federal government had no knowledge of the attacks until hours later. The documents I managed to uncover during this investigation provide clear proof that this was a lie.

The buses were full, Fernando Marín said: "My first-year classmates were on their phones talking to their moms, their siblings, maybe their sweethearts . . . we were in high spirits." They had no idea how closely they were being tracked.

After about two hours on the road, the 1531 bus stopped at the Huitzuco turn-off, outside the village of Rancho del Cura. The 1568 bus, in which both *Carrillas* and *Cochiloco* were riding, continued until the Iguala-Puente de Ixtla toll booth, fifteen minutes outside Iguala. At that moment, according to communications protocol, the Huitzuco police would also have been aware of the presence of the *normalistas*.

The students' plan was simple: the two groups should take as many buses as possible at that point on the highway.

20:30—The Outskirts of Iguala

Carrillas and *Cochiloco* are standing by the toll booth when three federal police trucks with five officers arrive, led by Víctor Manuel Colmenares, along with three state police officers, under the coordination of Adame. At the same time, a man in civilian clothing riding a red motorcycle showed up, hovering close by.

In the PGR's investigation, Colonel José Rodríguez Pérez, chief of the 27th Infantry Battalion, testified to the existence of a crack team within the Army called the Information Search Organ (OBI), in which soldiers in civilian clothes conduct undercover operations. On the evening of September 26, he ordered an OBI soldier to the toll booth to keep track of the students. Inexplicably, the PGR did not delve further into the operations conducted by the Army on that night.

"The motorcycle started patrolling, circling around us," *Carrillas* explained. And then another unmarked vehicle appeared and started doing its rounds, obviously monitoring the students as well. Seeing how closely they were being watched, *Carrillas* became uneasy and reckoned they wouldn't be able to get any more buses. After talking it over with *Cochiloco*, they were about to abort the mission and return to Ayotzinapa empty-handed once again, when they received an unexpected call from the students who had stopped in Rancho del Cura, alerting them that some classmates had gotten a bus in Iguala but were trapped inside the station. Both Estrella de Oro buses took off quickly from their separate points, meeting up along the way and entering Iguala together, intent on rescuing their trapped classmates. Night had fallen. Every step the students took was closely monitored by the Iguala C4.

21:16—The Bus Station

By the time they arrived at the bus station, most of the students had covered their faces with t-shirts or bandannas. It is clear from CCTV footage that none of them was armed. The rescue of their classmates was easier than expected, and Bernardo decided to use the opportunity to go for a few more buses.

This wasn't so easy, and the students resorted to sticks and stones. According to the statements given on September 27 to the public prosecutor by the drivers, the students hit, insulted, and threatened them. One of the drivers was bodily forced into one of the buses so he could drive them. Another was pulled out of his cabin in his underwear. Another was trussed up and left inside his bus. Nevertheless, in response to insistent questioning from state prosecutors, all the drivers affirmed that the students were unarmed, brandishing nothing but stones.

The students took a Costa Line bus from terminal 5, another Costa Line that was in the parking lot, and an Estrella Roja from Cuautla that was parked at terminal 12. It was a random selection, and the 100 students soon divided up among the new buses to head back to Ayotzinapa. Hugo Benigno Castro Santos, who drove the Costa Line bus in his underwear, told the public prosecutor: "A group of approximately thirty males arrived and boarded my bus. When I, the undersigned, saw them, I took the key out of the ignition. One of the youths told me to start it up or get out the way, and I told him I didn't have the key and they started yelling at me to get out the way or get off, because if I didn't they were going to smash my face in, and one of them snatched the key out of my hand and pulled me out of the driver's seat and one of them started the engine and I told them that I'd better drive, because otherwise they would mess up the bus, and so I started driving."

Nobody wrote down who went into which bus—they wanted to get out of there as fast as possible. Specifying which students were in which bus is further complicated by the history of repression in Guerrero. Many of the *normalistas* didn't know each other's real names only their nicknames: besides *Cochiloco* and *Carrillas*, there were also *Teletubi*, *Manotas*, *La Ambulancia*, *El Canelo*, *Komander*, *Chiquito*, *Beni*, *Acapulco*, *Fresco*, *Chaner*, and *Jenny* in the buses—another reason why even the students found it hard to draw up an initial list of who exactly had been disappeared that night.

Two buses, the Estrella de Oro 1531 and the Estrella Roja, exited the station through its main gate and started down an express route to Chilpancingo, heading for Ayotzinapa. Two other Costa Line buses and the Estrella de Oro 1568, in which *Carrillas* and *Chochiloco* were riding, took the wrong exit, onto Galeana Street in downtown Iguala, where they were beached in traffic before hundreds of witnesses and under the watchful eye of the local Iguala police.

"The guys were telling me to head for Chilpancingo," one of the drivers would testify, "and I told them I didn't know which road to take, as they'd made me exit the station onto Galeana, so we were in the center, and they told me not to act stupid, of course I knew how to get out and I should go straight there. And, let me add, they all had their faces covered with their t-shirts and handfuls of rocks and as we were moving they threw rocks at passing cars, and about ten of them got off and started walking on the right side of the bus asking people the way out of town towards Chilpancingo."

It was a Friday evening, and the center was busier than usual because the presentation of María Pineda Villa's good works with the federal service program (DIF) had just finished. Pineda Villa and her husband, Mayor José Luis Abarca, had already left at this point and were eating tacos a few miles outside of downtown, where the three buses were lost and stuck in traffic.

Vidulfo Rosales, the Tlachinollan lawyer who would represent the families of the disappeared, commented in an interview: "The strange thing is that they get to the bus station and leave right away, and within ten minutes the police are already outside. This allows us to conclude that they were being tracked, that [the police] had been following them. You can't mount an operation in ten minutes."

The students tried to open up a lane in the traffic for the buses to pass through, as they themselves and other witnesses would later recall. The local police, communicating with the C4, tried to block them in. "I was in the second bus, which then pulled ahead, and we were down [on the street] making way for the bus, stopping the traffic so we could get out of there sooner, because what we most wanted to avoid was a set-to with the police. We wanted to get out as quick as possible because we didn't know Iguala," Ángel de la Cruz said.

More police started to arrive. They cocked their guns and pointed them at the students. "We're students. Why are you aiming at us?" Ángel yelled at the police. Thanks to a salvo of rocks, they pushed the police back and were able to continue.

21:30—The First Attack

"I didn't notice if they were state or local police, and so I stopped the bus, and as the door was open the youngsters started to get down and they started throwing stones and the police started shooting at them and at the bus, so what I did was turn on the cabin lights and shout that I was the driver so they wouldn't confuse me with the youngsters around me, and then I ducked down under the wheel," one of the drivers said.

That was the moment the first gunshots rang out in Iguala, on Galeana and Bandera Nacional Streets. The bangs sent people running in all directions, uncertain if they were hearing fireworks or gunfire. No bystanders were injured.

Francisco Chalma, one of the surviving students, testified before the state prosecutor on September 27: "When we got to the main square we got down from the bus and, to buy us some space, we threw stones. They kept on following us . . . We surrounded the police because they were after our classmates in the third bus, the Estrella de Oro, and I got behind one of the police officers who had cocked his gun and was aiming at our *compañeros* ready to fire, and more officers came, and they saw that we were behind him and they aimed at us, and we had a little scuffle and I grabbed the butt of his rifle, and then he threatened me, if I didn't let go he was going to shoot us and we kept struggling . . . the guy I was scrapping with fired his gun in a burst, first at the ground, and then he raised it and fired towards my *compañeros*, about a meter away, but when he raised his gun at them they had already started to split. The other two cops, when they saw their fellow officer start shooting, they started shooting at my *compañeros* as well."

At the same moment, there was another shooting nearby. Shoppers and storekeepers at the corner of Juan N. Álvarez and Emiliano Zapata, one block away from the central plaza, didn't realize what was going on until they saw, standing in the middle of the road, a young man with a bandanna over his face. He was wearing jeans, a ripped shirt that looked like it had just come out of a fight, and he was visibly upset. At that moment a dark Suburban and a police truck showed up. Five armed men dressed in civilian clothes got out of the Suburban. Witnesses would recall that all five sported buzzed, military-style haircuts. "I just assumed they were soldiers. They looked really mean. One of them had a beard," a witness said.

Six officers dressed in black, wearing bulletproof vests and equipped with anti-riot gear, were riding in the police vehicle—they were not local Iguala police. "Stop, motherfuckers!" one of them yelled, and someone started firing. One witness recorded the moment in audio, on a phone. You can hear more than fourteen shots, with a brief pause between each.

"They're going, they're going," cries a woman's voice amid the noise on the recording. Nobody was injured, but three cars had bullet impacts. A few of the men from the Suburban chased after the young man with the bandanna, and then the Suburban took off towards Periférico Norte, with the police trucks following behind.

After that a dark-blue Ford Focus, without plates, arrived on the scene. Another military-looking man got out and started collecting the bullet shells that were scattered in the street. No authorities ever followed up this lead—yet another deficiency of the PGR investigation.

"The shops and stalls closed up because there was a lot of gunfire right there in the plaza," Ángel, still traumatized by the episode, would later recount.

21:40—Cornered

The three buses had almost made it to Periférico Norte when Iguala police blocked the street with one of their trucks and got out. At least three more patrols were blocking the buses from the rear. The students might have been able to ram the police truck out of the way with their bus, but they were scared that someone would get hurt.

Five students, including Ángel de la Cruz and a nineteen-year-old first-year called Aldo Gutiérrez, got out of the first bus to try to move the police truck. "We were about to start pushing when they started shooting," Ángel said. The *normalistas* were trapped. When the gunfire began—coming from both sides of the bus—local Iguala police, state police, armed men in civilian clothes, and undercover military were all present at the scene.

And then Aldo hit the sidewalk. "I thought [he'd slipped] moving the police truck," Francisco Chalma said. "Then I saw that it was because he got shot, and blood was coming from his head, so I went over and tried to cover the hole. The police kept firing their weapons to try to get us away from there, and we took cover between the first and second buses . . . every time we peeped out they shot at us."

"The first [police officers] were local . . . here in Guerrero, we know which police are state, local, and federal by the way they dress, or more than anything by the way they look. For example, the first policemen had nothing but guns and caps, that was it, and their trucks were clunkers. But then the other lot came and even the officers looked different, these ones were like federal types," Ángel de la Cruz explained.

In one of the videos taken by the students, the small local police pickup is visible blocking the street in front of the first bus. In other videos, you can see that there are more police trucks.

From on board the third bus, Fernando Marín aka *Carrillas* had a clear view of the local and state police. He perfectly distinguished the insignia on the backs of their uniforms. The local police wore standard police attire, while the state police were in anti-riot gear with the words *"Policía Estatal"* on their backs. Despite this first-hand testimony, the state secretary of public security, Lt. Leonardo Vázquez Pérez, told the PGR that none of his officers went out that night, because there were not enough of them, and so they stayed in to protect their station. The PGR never investigated the state police who were on shift that night.

Carrillas described the barrage of gunfire that popped the tires and shattered the windows of the third bus. Almost all of the bullets were aimed at the Estrella de Oro 1568: according to the state prosecutor's review of clues and evidence, it was left with at least thirty bullet holes and many shrapnel impacts.

"The police were trying to kill us all," *Carrillas* said.

Panic broke out, the residents recall, as vendors and retailers hurriedly closed up and lowered their metal blinds.

"You bastards already killed somebody!" one of the students cried out. "Get down! Get down!" screamed another.

"Call [the school]!" a student urged.

"I don't have any credit, Vega."

"You already killed somebody! You already killed somebody!" The accusation rang out as Aldo's arms were shaking in the last spasms of life. "You killed a guy! Call an ambulance! An ambulance!" the same voice shouted.

Francisco Chalma picks up the story: "As time went on I crept closer to a car, on the left side, to check on my *compañero*, if he showed signs of life or if he was dead, and his body was still reacting because he was shaking, so I went to him again and put my t-shirt on his head where he was bleeding."

The shooting continued for more than thirty minutes. Inside the stores, people were crying. The students in the streets were crying too, and those with phones were calling their classmates back at school, begging for reinforcements. Julio César Mondragón, a twenty-two-year-old freshman, began recording on his phone.

Witnesses and neighbors would attest that armed plainclothesmen, as well as the police, were firing at their targets. None of the students fired a single shot. They were unarmed.

One of the police vehicles was outfitted with a machine-gun turret, blasting directly at the youngsters, one resident recalled. Ángel de la Cruz also described such a vehicle. Neither the Iguala nor the Cocula police have a vehicle with a machine-gun turret.

The sound of assault rifles continued to echo throughout the streets. Seconds later came volleys from some higher-caliber, more potent weapons, and onlookers ducked down behind their windows.

"We're unarmed! Don't shoot!" the students screamed.

One of the drivers, Castro Santos, described the last moments of the first attack: "When I stopped hearing gunfire I got off, crawling down the steps and ducking underneath the bus. All I could hear was the kids shouting, shouting to be let go, and then, about forty minutes later, when I didn't hear any more noises I got out from under the bus to see if the other drivers were okay, and on one side of the street there was this kid laid out bleeding, and I didn't know if he was alive or dead."

The worst was still to come.

10

The Last Breath

Twenty *normalistas* are trapped inside the Estrella de Oro 1568 bus on Juan N. Álvarez Street. With gunfire coming from all directions, they flatten themselves in the narrow aisle.

Carrillas thinks that if he doesn't do something fast to save his friends, they're done for. He grabs the fire extinguisher and jumps off the bus to try to push the gunmen back. He can't see Aldo, bleeding on the pavement just ahead of the first bus. Amidst a hail of bullets, he lobs the extinguisher at the police, then takes a bullet in the arm and falls. He manages to scramble back into the bus, leaving a trail of blood.

"At that point, in my head I was thinking there was no hope. I thought if they'd got me in the arm, they're gonna kill my *compañeros* in a second," he recalled.

Carrillas tells *Cochiloco* to call David Flores—*La Parka*, the acting secretary general of the school who has stayed behind in Ayotzinapa—for help. A terrified Miguel Ángel Hernández Martínez, *El Botas*, one of *Carrillas*'s friends in his first-year class, fixes a makeshift tourniquet. Blood pools in the central aisle of the bus.

At the sight of his wounded friend, *Cochiloco* makes the hardest decision of the night: it's time to surrender. "You know what?" he says to the driver. "We're beaten, they've already shot *Carrillas*. You can't go on with us. So please, help us out." *Cochiloco* asks the driver to go out and try to negotiate with the police.

But when he climbs down and identifies himself, the police call back contemptuously: "We don't care who you are. You're one of them. You're just the same . . . Just another *ayotzinapo.*"

Police officers begin pulling the students out, clasping their hands behind their heads and moving them to the left sidewalk. *Carrillas* recognizes the same twenty or so state and local officers who had been shooting at them. One of them says he's going to kill him and puts the cold barrel of his gun against his temple.

The people who live nearby have listened in terror to the sound of gunshots and blows, but what they will never forget is the sound of the *normalistas* weeping. Ángel de la Cruz, in the first bus on the other side of the street, can glimpse his classmates as the police usher them down into the street. He can't see much further, blinded by the headlamps and flashlights. He can't see what's behind the convoy of buses.

22:30—*Los Federales*

A resident of central Iguala leaves his house and begins walking towards Juan N. Álvarez Street. His brother, who was inside a nearby restaurant when the attack began, has called him asking for help. Reaching the corner of Juan N. Álvarez and Revolución, he meets a number of federal police vehicles. Their lights are not flashing. Only a few meters away, he can

274

clearly distinguish the shields on their trucks and even the insignia on their uniforms. He has no doubt. The *federales* are armed.

Intent on helping his brother, he takes a roundabout way to avoid the police, but the other nearby streets are also blocked off—the entire vicinity of the first attack is under well-organized police control. He can't get any closer, and so he calls his brother, who has fled into a nearby home—the residents let him in when the shooting began. His brother tells him that he saw buses go by and then civilian cars chasing after them, guns blazing.

On Juan N. Álvarez, the shooting seems to have stopped. Next to the last bus is a cluster of police trucks with their lights flashing. Outside the first bus, Manuel Ángel Espino Honorato, aka *Pulmón*, who's only been at Ayotzinapa for two months, is having an asthma attack. "Call an ambulance!" another student cries out.

Espino Honorato survived to tell the State Prosecutor's Office the next morning: "A number of us were yelling at our attackers that they'd already taken the life of one of our *compañeros* and injured others, and they had to stop shooting. Ignoring our pleas, they kept on. We cried out that we were defenseless and unarmed, some of my *compañeros* even raised their hands as a signal of surrender, and still they kept shooting at us . . . I started having trouble breathing and, earlier, I had suffered a collapse, and my *compañeros* were worried it would happen again and so they yelled to the police to stop so I could get medical attention, but it was no good, they went on firing at us. Minutes later a Red Cross ambulance arrived, and the [medics] were able to get to me to take me to the General Hospital in Iguala, where I received oxygen and nebulization."

"The police are leaving!" a voice rings out from between the two buses. "Hold on, wait," calls another. "The *federales* are still here. They're going to keep messing with us, man."

The initial attackers, their work complete, begin to leave the scene of the crime as new personnel arrive to relieve them. Another student, upon seeing a few shadows step into the street to collect scattered bullet shells, shouts: "Why are you picking up the shells, assholes? You know what you did, shit." Another calls out: "Why are you hunting us?" There is no response. "Fucking ass-licker," spits the same student who asked about the bullet shells.

At the other end of the caravan, matters are even worse.

10:45—The Subjugation of *Cochiloco*

After the state police officer lifts the pistol away from *Carrillas*'s head, the police start laying down all the students from the third bus, the Estrella de Oro 1568, which had been closely monitored since leaving Ayotzinapa hours earlier. In a last bid to express his leadership as secretary of struggle, *Cochiloco* refuses to submit. "You know what? I'm not lying down," he says to one of the policemen, who brutally clubs him on the head with the butt of his rifle, spraying the nearby wall with blood. He is pushed to the ground with the rest of the students.

Seeing their leader fallen, the other *normalistas* stop resisting. Even though they are not handcuffed, they don't try to escape. *El Botas*, one of the youngest students, can't contain his panic and starts whimpering tearfully to *Carrillas*, who is next to him on the ground: "What are we going to do? Why are they doing this?"

"Calm down, *compa*," *Carrillas* says. Trying to instil hope, while having none himself, he adds, "Our comrades are coming to get us out. Don't worry, don't panic."

And then an officer comes over and starts kicking *Carrillas* in the face and the ribs. More police arrive, and at the same time there is a cry from the first bus: "The *federales* are coming!"

Tonight, providence has a gift for Fernando *Carrillas* Marín: the gift of life. An ambulance appears and takes him away to the General Hospital.

Near the first bus, close to Periférico, more ambulances are coming for the injured students. At this point, extermination is not yet the objective.

The last image *Carrillas* sees before the ambulance doors close is of his friend, Bernardo Flores Alcaraz, *Cochiloco*, and another nineteen students from the third Estrella de Oro, number 1568, stretched out on the ground at the feet of local and state police officers, with federal police and armed civilians milling nearby. He will never see any of them again. All of them will be disappeared, nearly half of the forty-three. *Carrillas* is the only survivor from the third bus, and the weight of that knowledge sits today like an anvil on his chest.

"Maybe it was God's wish they didn't take me, who knows," *Carrillas* says, months later. "I don't know what came over that policeman, I really don't." He wasn't previously religious, but he has no doubt that some supreme power is what saved him that night.

At 23:14, according to videos taken by locals, the police leave Juan N. Álvarez Street. This is when the disappearance of the occupants of the third bus occurs.

22:30—Federal Police at the State Courthouse Attack

While three of the buses were trapped on Juan N. Álvarez Street, the two others, the Estrella Roja and the Estrella de Oro 1531, managed to make it onto the federal highway in the direction of Chilpancingo.

At approximately 22:30, as the attack was beginning on Juan N. Álvarez, federal police officers stopped the two buses in front of the state courthouse. The state prosecutor and the PGR would maintain that only four buses were attacked that night, never mentioning the Estrella Roja, but, in reality, all five buses were targeted.

Student Alexander Torres Pérez, who was on the Estrella Roja, from which no students were disappeared, described the situation to the State Prosecutor's Office on September 27: "There were only fourteen of us from the school on that bus. At that moment a classmate nicknamed *El Pato* received a call on his cell phone telling him about the shootout between our *compañeros* and the local police and that one of ours had died, which filled us with fear and anger. Later, the driver got onto the Iguala–Chilpancingo federal highway, going about sixty kilometers per hour, and just about one hundred meters before the pedestrian bridge, where there are hardware stands, we suddenly saw [that] a local police truck was blocking the road, and the driver had to brake to a halt. He got out of the bus and started talking to the police. And then my *compañeros* and I decided to voluntarily get off the bus and, once on the street, they started insulting us, telling us, 'Damn sons of bitches, you're going to die like dogs.'"

But there were not only local police present. Federal police and one vehicle from the 27th Infantry Battalion, carrying soldiers of the crack Information Search Organ team dressed as civilians, were helping to block the street and stop the *normalistas'* bus.

There was obvious coordination between the various agencies to set up checkpoints and stop the buses. The first checkpoint was about one kilometer away from the state courthouse, according to family members of the Avispones soccer team. There, federal police redirected traffic onto a dirt road leading to another highway. State and federal police operated the second checkpoint, in front of the state courthouse. Traffic soon piled up, setting the stage for dozens of witnesses, both drivers and people who worked and lived nearby, to clearly see federal police officers pointing their weapons at the *normalistas* getting off the Estrella Roja bus, amid insults and curses.

Lawyer Vidulfo Rosales, who reconstructed the events that took place on the highway, summarized the scene to me: "The federal police aim at them, threaten to shoot, signal them to stop, they get off, they throw stones, there is a confrontation with the *federales* and [the *normalistas*] run for the hills . . . The fourth bus, the Estrella de Oro, is surrounded by local police. Behind, as backup, are the federal police."

The driver of the Estrella Roja explained in a written testimony submitted to the Attorney Gernal's Office (PGR): "We were headed toward Chilpancingo, but leaving Iguala, right by the state courthouse, there were two highway patrols [federal police] and four officers already out of their vehicles with guns in their hands pointing at the bus." A witness who was driving and had also been blocked by the checkpoint told me: "The federal police aimed at the students and, with much verbal abuse, ordered them to get off."

Just ahead of the Estrella Roja was the Estrella de Oro 1531. Uniformed officers bashed at the bus with truncheons to force the students off, spraying tear gas inside and stabbing its tires. Federal, state, and local police were all present, though their dark-colored uniforms were easily confused in the night. In later interviews, Iguala municipal police officers explained that they hadn't had access to anti-riot gear (including truncheons) for months and that they had no tear gas. They claimed that their station was even low on cartridges.

"You could hear the thunks against the metal. They were hitting the bus, and you could hear that they were knocking out the tires," one witness would later recall. "We were scared. We didn't know what was happening." Another witness, an employee of a nearby store, said, "At that time the federal police were there . . . Yes, definitely the federal police."

Of all the people in cars who were witnesses to the attack, nobody dared help the students, given the police deployment. Not even the security guards at the state courthouse came to their defense. A few of the students broke away from the bus and ran to the courthouse where they begged the guards to let them in: "They're trying to kill us, they're kidnapping us!" they yelled. Nervous, the guards refused to open the gate, telling them to go around to the other side of the building to the Public Ministry office. The students never got that far. Though these guards were direct witnesses to the attacks against the students, as well as to the participation of federal police, the PGR has never interviewed them.

After the approximately twenty students who were riding in Estrella de Oro 1531 were herded out of the bus, nobody knows where they ended up. In their place were left piles of stones, bloody clothing, and the whiff of tear gas.

The driver, whose eyes were damaged by the gas, was temporarily detained inside a state police truck. He would later declare to the Interdisciplinary Group of Independent Experts: "From the vehicle I was able to see how they were pulling the students off the bus one by one, brutally hitting them on the head with their truncheons. Those who could walk they pushed into the trucks, and those who couldn't, two officers would drag them and throw them in."

Seeing the aggression against their classmates, the students in the Estrella Roja bus started amassing rocks, but the police shined their flashlights on them and took aim, sending the students running for safety to an abandoned house, where they would remain for forty minutes.

Months later, a captain and information director of the 27th Infantry Battalion would declare to the PGR that he was present, supposedly as a mere observer, as the local police dragged the students off Estrella de Oro 1531. The same captain would neglect to mention, however, that federal police were also present. Much of what the Army reported about that night was half-truths or completely contradictory.

23:45—The Attack Against the Avispones

After the family members of the Avispones passed the first federal police checkpoint in their cars, the team bus went through behind them. Hired from Castro Tours, it was white with green stripes, similar to the two Estrella de Oro buses in which the *normalistas* were riding.

According to reports from the families and one of the adults riding with the team, the bus was not diverted from the checkpoint, thus passing close to the Estrella de Oro 1531, whose passengers had already been disappeared. The players saw nothing but an empty, window-shattered bus. Ten kilometers up the road, close to the Santa Teresa exit—a stretch of highway that was under the jurisdiction of the federal police—the Avispones bus would be brutally attacked.

When the *normalistas* who managed to escape from the Estrella Roja came out of their hiding places and returned to the highway, they ran into more police who, once again, started chasing them. According to one, Alejandro Torres Pérez, they "decided to hide in the undergrowth again, for another half hour."

An employee of one of the nearby stores recalls that at midnight he was on his way back from Chilpancingo, and, when he passed the state courthouse, the Estrella de Oro bus was still there. Another local employee, who passed the spot in the early hours of the 27th, said: "Almost under the bridge there was an abandoned bus, with the windows broken. The place was deserted, no sign of any authorities." Other people told him that students had been attacked there and that some of them had been able to flee but others were taken away.

The *normalistas* who fled the Estrella Roja once more risked emerging from their hiding places. Torres Pérez recalls: "We decided to walk along the road towards the bus we'd been taking to Chilpancingo, but we didn't want to get back on in case there were any police inside who would get us. We walked back to Iguala on the highway."

Midnight—The Manhunt

The witnesses to the attacks on Juan N. Álvarez Street said the students were kept on the ground for more than half an hour. In a video taken by a neighbor, the police vehicles' flashing lights flooding the streets disappear at 23:11, after which the street is empty: the state and local police, as well as the armed civilians, have all gone. The students in the third bus disappeared with them, but no witnesses report seeing what vehicles they were taken away in. *Carrillas* remembers only that they were loaded into police trucks.

Minutes later a Chevy and a Nissan truck drive up, full of *normalistas*: reinforcements from Ayotzinapa, responding to the calls for help. But they're too late. The survivors of the first two buses tell them what happened, and then the journalists begin trickling in. To the best of their ability, the students try to safeguard the scene of the crime; they begin collecting the bullet shells that have been sprayed everywhere. They take photos that, a couple weeks later, they'll pass on to me. Though the 27th Infantry Battalion, the federal police station, and the Mixed Operations Base of the PGR are only minutes away, not one public law enforcement official shows up to protect them.

Still in shock, the *ayotzinapos* are somehow able to improvise a press conference, right there on the corner of Juan N. Álvarez and Periférico Norte. One journalist recognizes an official from the Center for Investigation and National Security (CISEN), as well as undercover soldiers—he knew them from covering other stories in the area.

Documents I was able to obtain from CISEN confirm that, due to the historical ties between the Ayotzinapa Normal School and past guerrilla movements, the students were under constant surveillance. In the Floresta neighborhood, only about 400 meters from the state courthouse, where the second group of students were disappeared, is CISEN's branch office.

At their improvised press conference, the students angrily denounce the attacks to the journalists. Among the audience, besides the lurking undercover men and the newly arrived students from Aytozinapa, are teachers from the State Committee of Education Workers in Guerrero. It is against this press conference that the last attack of the night is launched.

First-year student Brayan Baltazar Medina recalls: "First I noticed two suspicious vehicles, one a white Lobo truck with a man in the back and another truck with an antenna that sped away, and about fifteen minutes later another car, like a [Ford] Ikon, black, came up with its windows down and you could see cameras flashing, which alerted a few of my *compañeros* . . . And then came rifle shots, and they started firing at us and we ran towards the highway, heading towards the boulevard, and we had to duck down because they kept on shooting, so we hid between some vehicles, a group of about fourteen of us."

It is a storm of bullets. An armed group in dark clothing gets out of unmarked cars, first firing into the air, and then directly at the crowd. A stampede follows, with bullets whizzing through the air—journalists and students indiscriminately targeted.

Sophomore Omar García told me: "It was obvious that they were trained, highly trained, by the way they were shooting. I've seen, I've witnessed, lots of shootouts in lots of places, not because I'm involved in that stuff, but because it's around you, I've seen it and I know how someone acts who isn't a professional. . . . These people here, they had perfect aim, [they were] in formation. Let's not kid ourselves, they were trained marksmen."

Omar was the leader of the Committee of Political Orientation and Ideology—a working group founded by the guerrilla leader Lucio Cabañas and the political heart of the school. He was one of the contingent of students who rushed from Ayotzinapa after receiving calls for help.

At one point, the attackers pause to reload. "Because there was this space of seconds, all of us got up and started running.

Of course, you could tell that this was something really organized, that it was professional," Omar said, in November 2014. "Run! I ran with everybody else. We made it to Álvarez Street towards the center of town. There were about twenty-seven of us."

The commando unit chases after those who had fled. Not content with just dispersing the group, they pursue them, hunting them through the streets. Two students hit the asphalt: Julio César Ramírez and Daniel Solís, who cries "Help!" just as the bullet pierces his back. The rest of them scatter. One of the students, heroically, tries to save the life of a female reporter, throwing himself on her to block the bullets.

"As we were running, since they were still shooting, I hit the curb and threw myself on the ground with another classmate. And then I turned my head to the right and saw, about ten meters away, two of my *compañeros* laid out," José Santiago de la Cruz, one of the surviving students, would tell Guerrero's prosecutor general later that day, the 27th. "We were all running, and with me was a friend of the ones who'd already died, I saw him hit the ground, all bloody. I wanted to help him but I couldn't. Those guys were out to kill us, they were shooting so much . . . I hid under a parked car, and after a bit the shooting stopped . . . I came out from where I was hiding, and then six of us went to hide in a little hut that was abandoned, a white hut. Then, to be safe, we jumped a fence and climbed up to a roof."

Omar runs and runs. "I was just running wherever I could, we had nowhere to escape to. That's what we were all thinking, run for it, because sooner or later they're going to catch up." He feels sure he's going to fall at any moment, like the others. As he races past the third and now empty bus, he notices fellow student Edgar Andrés Vargas, whose jaw has been smashed by a bullet. "The impact was so great, he didn't even realize how serious the wound was. He couldn't feel it, I remember, he only realized a bit later, when he felt that he was wet" from his own blood.

Some students go to help Vargas, carrying him to Juan N. Álvarez Street. Neighbors begin peeking out, and the students ask the way to a hospital. One family compassionately directs them to the Hospital Cristina, not far away. Other students beg to be let into houses. Like cats, they try jumping gates and fences, climbing into trees. Some of them make it to safety. Others do not.

00:50—"Please, help us! They're killing us!"

"Please help! They're killing us! Help!" the students shout as they run through the streets, down Juan N. Álvarez, away from Periférico. Behind them are the sounds of automatic gunfire—dry, constant, merciless. Captain José Martínez Crespo and his squadron are currently on these same streets.

The neighbors hear the cries, but nobody opens their doors. A woman peering through the window doesn't have the courage. Her eyes are full of terror, her heart full of guilt. She's got her grandchildren at home, and if she opens the door, those who are killing the students might kill her and her family too.

It begins to rain. A dark Suburban, a siren on its roof, is seen prowling the streets. More armed plainclothes men join the hunt for *normalistas*. Among the forty-three will be some who are swept up at this stage. No authorities intervene.

Finally, one neighbor takes pity and opens her door to some of the students. She holds a finger to her mouth to hush them as they slip inside. Another cluster of eight students crouches down between cars on a side street. They spot their friend

Julio César Mondragón, who has been recording the attack on his cell phone. Just then somebody opens their door to let them in, and they wave at Julio César to come with them, but he doesn't see, and keeps on running.

"When we got to the Cristina Hospital, they explained they couldn't give medical assistance because they're closed this time of night and there weren't any staff . . . We understood, and asked if we could have shelter just for the night because people were after us, and they let us, I mean, it was really kind of them, the people there at least gave us a refuge, and a bit later their boss came," Omar recalled.

Soon after the *normalistas* get to the hospital, the Army arrives. Omar doesn't know it, but the squad is led by José Martínez Crespo, a key player in those fateful hours. "The Army burst in, cocking their weapons as if, I don't know, looking for criminals. They accused us of breaking into the building and said they were going to take us all away, that we were delinquents, and we told them, 'No sir, we came just to get help for our wounded friend.'" The soldiers retort that they were asking for it; serves them right for being trouble-makers. "Have the balls to face up to all the havoc you've caused," one of the soldiers says.

The soldiers round up the students and a teacher, ask them to lift up their shirts, check to see if they are armed, and take their photographs. Omar remembers thinking, "Now the Army can do whatever it wants with us, we won't have a chance to defend ourselves."

"Give me your real names!" the captain orders. "I don't want any false names, because if you give me a false name, you're never going to be seen again." At this point, Omar and his classmates don't know about the forty-three students who have already been disappeared.

"Yeah, we were scared," Omar would later remember. "They were hinting that they were going to disappear us, or that they were going to hold us someplace . . . We know our history, the Dirty War, here in Mexico. Obviously, those who disappeared most people and were the experts at not leaving any traces were precisely them, the Mexican Army and armed forces, the Navy and all them, right? I mean, I could hear his insinuation, that they were going to disappear us." Omar was referring to the still-bleeding open wound in Guerrero.

The students again request medical help for their friend, because the hospital can't provide it. The soldiers tell them they'll call the local police, before heading back outside, towards the corner where the bodies of Daniel Solís and Julio César Ramírez are lying.

By the end of that tragic night, as the sun begins to rise, the surviving *normalistas* start to realize that some of their class-mates have disappeared. They lodge a formal complaint with the Guerrero governor's office, whose own police were involved in the disappearance. Some of the students provide their real names as they file the complaint, others use false names, and some, understandably, refuse to give any name at all.

Shortly after nine in the morning on September 27, Infantry Lieutenant Jorge Ortiz Canales reports to the Public Ministry the discovery of another *normalista*: the body of a male subject in a red polo shirt, black jeans, and white-and-gray sneakers, abandoned a few meters off Industria Petrolera Street, home of Iguala's C4, from which all levels of government—local, state, and federal—have been monitoring the students. Showing clear signs of torture, including a fractured cranium and a partially skinned face, the body will later be identified as that of Julio César Mondragón.

In the massacre of Iguala, three students and three local citizens were murdered. At least twenty-nine people (ten of them students) received gunshot wounds. And forty-three *normalistas* were disappeared.

During those dark hours of fear and desolation, as the Mexican state hounded, murdered, and disappeared young students, eight householders opened their doors to save the lives of at least sixty other students, enabling them to tell the tale of that night.

11

The Dark Hours

The Squadron of Captain Martínez Crespo

The first minutes of September 27, 2014: At the corner of Juan N. Álvarez Street and Periférico, the third attack against the *normalistas* and others gathered for a press conference has just occurred. Military-looking men in civilian clothes jump out of dark SUVs to follow the students down the side streets. Julio César Mondragón is missing—he will turn up the next day with a fractured skull and a skinned face.

A squadron from the 27th Infantry Battalion shows up in two of Secretariat of National Defense (SEDENA) Chevrolet Cheyennes: fourteen troops equipped with bulletproof vests, helmets, and G3 assault rifles. The squad is commanded by Second Captain José Martínez Crespo; under him is Second Lieutenant Fabián Alejandro Pirita Ochoa. The names of the other troops (one of whom remains unidentified) are Gustavo Rodríguez de la Cruz, Francisco Narváez Pérez, Eduardo Mota Esquivel, Juan Sotelo Díaz, Ramiro Manzanares Sanabria, Juan Andrés Flores Lagunas, Eloy Estrada Díaz, Uri Yashiel Reyes Lasos, Emanuel Peña Pérez, Roberto de los

Santos Eduvigez, and Omar Torres Marquillo. At least one of the Cheyennes has a machine gun installed on the roof.

The two trucks pull up next to the defenseless forms of two *normalistas*, Daniel Solís and Julio César Ramírez, lying soaked on the ground. The occupants observe no other authorities, assume there are no witnesses, and proceed at leisure. Three soldiers jump down from one of the trucks. One of them aims his G3 at the students; the other two start kicking them. None moves to assist the students, to call an ambulance or the Public Ministry. They seem immune to the horror surrounding them: random sandals, truncated fingers, puddles of blood. The trucks soon take off into the darkness, turning onto Juárez Street, parallel to Juan N. Álvarez. The soldiers still have work to do.

A witness who requested anonymity, for fear of reprisals, told me that the whole operation lasted only minutes: "I think they wanted to check if they were still alive," the witness murmured, still shaken by the brutality of the troops.

On September 27, Guerrero's Secretariat of Health conducted an autopsy on the bodies of Daniel Solís and Julio César Ramírez, estimating that Solís died at about 00:50 and Ramírez at about 01:00. Given the estimated times of death and the witness's statement, it is probable that the two students were still alive when Captain Martínez Crespo and his men came by.

According to the report from the state prosecutor, it wasn't until 02:40 that Corporal Juan Carlos Peralta, of the 27th Infantry Battalion, called Iguala's Public Ministry to inform them that "between Periférico Norte and Juan N. Álvarez, in the Juan N. Álvarez neighborhood, two lifeless bodies of the male sex have been found, both gunshot victims, as well as various vehicles damaged by gunfire." The corporal requested personnel to come to the location.

Martínez Crespo and eleven of his subordinates later

confirmed to the Attorney General's Office (PGR) that they did indeed pass by the location where Daniel Solís and Julio César Ramírez were lying, but claimed that they didn't stop. And yet one soldier, Uri Yashiel Reyes Lasos, has contradicted that claim, admitting to me that a few soldiers did get out of one of the trucks: "Passing through on Periférico we came upon two buses obstructing traffic on the street towards Álvarez, I also noticed that in front of the buses there were two bodies, face down, of two people, seemingly deceased, and so one truck halted to check out the location and the bodies."

According to the same witness, this was likely the moment when the soldiers dropped off one of the trucks and kicked the students.

Second Lieutenant Pirita Ochoa, for his part, admitted that he saw "the buses that were found with the windows shattered by bullets . . . And there we saw two bodies on the asphalt, seemingly dead, both male, as well as various vehicles with bullet impacts, [and then] received the order from Second Infantry Captain José Martínez Crespo to leave the location without making any notes or asking what had happened."

The Ministry questioned one of the other soldiers, Óscar Cruz Román, about the discovery of the two *normalistas* on the ground: "What does the respondent have to say about why, when the two bodies were discovered, you did not stop to provide assistance or perimeter security?" Cruz Román responded: "I don't know, the person who gives the orders is my immediate superior, Commander Pirita."

Soldiers in Iguala

It would have been around midnight when Martínez Crespo was ordered by Colonel Rodríguez Pérez to leave the barracks.

The first scene they claimed to have come across was the state courthouse, but, according to soldiers' accounts, neither students nor police were present. As we've seen, the stories told by Martínez Crespo and his troops diverge on significant points. The majority of the soldiers who testified claim that one truck stopped in front of the Estrella de Oro bus and another behind. Two of the soldiers say that an inspection of the bus was carried out, which took between twenty and thirty minutes, but nine others, including Martínez Crespo, do not mention any inspection of the bus.

I was able to read the official declarations of thirty-four soldiers from the 27th Infantry Battalion, including that of Colonel José Rodríguez Pérez, who was commanding the base. According to these declarations, the Mexican Army had been monitoring the students since they arrived in Iguala at 19:30, two hours before the first attack. The declarations also acknowledge that both their base and the base of the 35th Military Zone, in the state capital Chilpancingo, had been keeping track of the attacks against the students in real time.

The PGR didn't summon Rodríguez Pérez to submit a declaration until December 4, 2014. He expanded on this declaration on March 2, 2015, confessing that from 19:00 on September 26 until 10:00 the following morning, there were troops on the streets of Iguala.

His admissions, however, contradict the official version provided by the PGR, which maintains that neither the Army, nor any other federal agency, participated in any way or had knowledge of the attacks until a few hours after they had been carried out. Rodríguez Pérez's statement likewise contradicts the claim made by the secretary of defense, Salvador Cienfuegos, on November 13, 2014, when he said that "the Army acted in good faith on the basis of the information they had at the time . . . It is a lie to say they knew what was occurring and did not come" to the scene.

Before members of congress in the Special Commission to investigate the disappearance of the *normalistas*, Cienfuegos declared: "They followed a protocol, and this protocol stipulates that the Army may not intervene in civil actions concerning public security without a petition from a local authority." According to the Labor Party congresswoman, Lilia Aguila, Secretary Cienfuegos requested that Colonel Rodríguez Pérez not be charged with nonfeasance, as he had an irreproachable record.

And yet Rodríguez Pérez himself supplied a very different account. He explained that the military officers assigned to the Iguala C4, Felipe González Cano and David Aldegundo González Cabrera, informed him in real time what was occurring. Furthermore, he revealed that the 27th Infantry Battalion had an Information Search Organ (OBI) team to respond to "situations ongoing within the city of Iguala," and he admitted that two OBI officers, Ezequiel Carrera Rifas and Eduardo Mota Esquivel, had been monitoring the students since they entered the city. One of them was present when at least twenty students were seized from the Estrella de Oro bus 1531 in front of the state courthouse.

Rodríguez Pérez also admitted that, around 22:30, two squadrons went into the streets of Iguala as the attacks were taking place. One of the squads was led by Captain Martínez Crespo and the other, a Rapid Response Team manned by fourteen soldiers, was led by Lieutenant Roberto Vázquez Hernández.

A high-ranking military source (who spoke to me on condition of anonymity) explained that each battalion, military zone, and military region, as well as SEDENA itself, has its own OBI team. Information obtained from a battalion is passed along to the chief of operations and then transmitted to the colonels who command the military zones and on up the chain to the central offices of Defense. OBI teams are part of the second section of SEDENA, which conducts intelligence and counterintelligence operations. The same source confirmed to me that officers who work in information units wear street clothes to camouflage themselves among civilians. Many of them don't have their hair buzzed and don't even sleep at the military bases, although they are part of the Army and enjoy military benefits.

Witnesses who were close to the intersection of Juan N. Álvarez and Emiliano Zapata, near the Star Gym, at 21:00, described men in civvies who began firing their weapons. "They were civilians, the ones chasing after the students," one said. Likewise, witnesses a few blocks away made similar claims, that men dressed in civilian clothing participated in the armed attack.

Colonel Rodríguez Pérez stated that he had been invited to the presentation given by María de los Ángeles Pineda Villa but was unable to attend and sent in his place Second Captain Paul Escobar López, along with Carrera Rifas, the OBI officer. Before the presentation was over, he ordered Escobar López to go to the toll booth on the Iguala–Puente de Ixtla highway to verify an OBI unit's report (as well as word from a military officer at the C4) that there were Ayotzinapa students there.

The colonel explained that just minutes later he was informed that students had seized a bus and were headed to the Iguala bus station; once there, he heard, "they robbed two buses and smashed the place up." "We knew that the local police had already arrived because the students had taken three buses . . . [and] they stopped them on Hermenegildo Galeana and Melchor Ocampo streets, we were informed that the local police detained them there, and the students got off and attacked the local police." It was Carrera Rifas who told the colonel of these events, as well as of the shooting that was going on in the streets; but the OBI officer omitted this part of the story in his statement to the Public Ministry.

Carrera Rifas was not questioned by the PGR until September 11, 2015. On this occasion he claimed that on the day of the attacks he was in the center of Iguala, on Galeana Street, where the first attack took place. However, he was only there by chance, and he didn't see a thing, though he did overhear some talk about a confrontation between local police and students involving gunfire.

The other member of the OBI team, Eduardo Mota Esquivel, made his statement on December 3, 2014. On September 26, at 22:00, his superior officer, Lieutenant Joel Gálvez Santos, ordered him to confirm whether there was "an abandoned bus that maybe had a few students" on the highway to Chilpancingo. Mota Esquivel went to the location on his motorcycle. "Pulling up . . . just below the bridge that crosses the highway towards Chilpancingo, close to the state courthouse, I saw a passenger bus from the Estrella de Oro line [the 1531 bus], surrounded by local Iguala police officers, who had come in pickup trucks with municipal police insignia. [They] were trying to get the passengers off the bus, but since . . . they were being really aggressive, they couldn't do it."

Mota Esquivel relayed his observations to Gálvez Santos, who instructed him to stay "for a little while longer to see what there is to see, but don't take risks, or get too close." He explained that he stayed for about an hour, during which time he saw students throwing stones from inside the bus as the police tried to force open the door. Later, he saw "three other Iguala police trucks come to back up the officers who were already there, but the new arrivals were more aggressive and threw two tear gas grenades through the bus windows."

"Get out, fuckers!" the police yelled, according to Mota Esquivel, who went on to describe the students being pulled out, handcuffed, and pushed face down onto the ground. At 23:30, Mota Esquivel allegedly left the scene. According to the time line of events, the students were disappeared sometime between 22:30 and 23:00.

Eyewitnesses would describe federal police blocking the path of the students' bus and swearing at them, shouting into a megaphone for them to get off.

Mota Esquivel, who did not mention the presence of the federals, said that he returned to the base at 23:40, where he reported to his superior officer. Later he joined the squad commanded by Martínez Crespo, who asked him to show him where the bus was. Mota Esquivel's testimony about his second trip to the scene is full of omissions when compared to what other squad officers described.

On September 11, 2015, Mota Esquivel, in a new official statement, changed his story: he claimed to have spent less time at the scene of the attacks and added that the local Iguala police confiscated his motorcycle. In this version he joined Martínez Crespo's squad in order to recover his motorcycle, not at the captain's request, as he originally stated. In the first version he claimed to have gone with Martínez to the state courthouse and from there they went straight to the Hospital Cristina, after hearing reports of the presence of armed men; but in his second testimony, he said that from the state courthouse they went to the Iguala police station, which is a key point in this case.

Three soldiers in the squad declared to the PGR that after

leaving the state courthouse, Martínez Crespo did head back to the local police base, though Martínez Crespo himself maintained otherwise in his own testimony of December 2014. After the squad arrived at the Iguala police station, Mota Esquivel explained in his second statement, he received a phone call informing him that armed men had barged into the Cristina Clinic to take away some of the wounded victims and ordering him, along with the rest of the squad, to that location. It was on the way to the clinic that they would have stopped to kick two *normalistas* stretched out in the street.

When they first arrived at the clinic, Captain Martínez Crespo and his second lieutenant, followed by other officers from the team, formed a V—"a formation used to enter buildings when there is reason to expect the imminent danger of being fired upon," as Mota Esquivel explained. He said that five soldiers entered the clinic and that he took a photograph of the student who had been shot in the mouth. However, no such photograph was included in the PGR dossier or the reports sent by the 27th Battalion to the 35th Military Zone.

This is the same moment referred to by Omar García, the student leader of the school's Political and Ideological Orientation Committee, when he recalled that after his wounded classmate was denied medical treatment, soldiers came and aimed their weapons at them, ready to shoot, ordering them to take off their shirts, searching them for weapons, taking their photographs, demanding their real names, and threatening to arrest them on charges invented on the fly. The insinuation was that if they didn't provide their full names, they might never be heard of again.

The troops were in the clinic between 00:55 and 01:10, and then, according to their statements, they went to the corner of Juan N. Álvarez and Periférico.

In another part of his testimony, Colonel Rodríguez Pérez explained that through C4 he learned that three gunshot casualties had been admitted to the General Hospital of Iguala. He explained that the information came from Rapid Response's Lieutenant Roberto Vázquez Hernández, who himself declared that he went to the hospital on orders from Lt. Colonel Benito Cegueda Hernández, who in turn claimed to be following orders from Rodríguez Pérez.

Vázquez Hernández left the base at 23:00, leading a squad of fourteen troops. "Personnel from the C4 informed us," Rodríguez Pérez said, "that some of the students were on Periférico, blockaded by local police. Another vehicle, which appeared to be filled with students, was in front of the state courthouse, on the Chilpancingo-Taxco highway, also blocked by municipal police." The colonel added, in self-justification, that upon receiving this information he got in touch with the chief of Iguala police, Felipe Flores Velázquez, asking him "if he had any problems with the students, and he told me no, he didn't have any problems, and that his officers were already at the roadblocks."

Lieutenant Joel Gálvez Santos, assigned to the base's Center of Information, Instruction, and Operations, said he was in charge of receiving calls, beginning on the afternoon of September 26 until the following morning, from Felipe González Cano, who was on duty at the C4. Nine detailed reports came in between the arrival of the students and the discovery of the body of Julio César Mondragón. Gálvez Santos confirmed that he relayed the information to his superior at the battalion and to the 35th Military Zone in Chilpancingo. At 21:30, according to Gálvez Santos, he was notified by González Cano that a confrontation was underway between the local Iguala police and the *normalistas*. "For this reason soldier Eduardo Mota Esquivel was ordered to scout the location on Periférico, informing me at approximately 22:30 that in front of the state courthouse there was a bus with *normalistas* on board, which was surrounded by various local police vehicles, with the police shouting in offensive terms at the *normalistas* to get off the passenger bus, [but] they didn't obey . . . in response the police officers launched tear gas."

Gálvez Santos's account alludes to the attack against Estrella de Oro bus 1531, which resulted in the disappearance of some twenty students, in full view of at least one Army officer.

In accordance with other testimonies, Gálvez Santos said that one of the calls he received from González Cano, at around 23:00, concerned injured subjects admitted to the Dr. Jorge Soberón Acevedo General Hospital. In response, Colonel Rodríguez Pérez "ordered the Rapid Response Team to deploy and verify the information." González Cano's own testimony, compared to that of Gálvez Santos, was terse.

The Army Tampers with Iguala's Security Cameras

Infantry soldier David Aldegundo González Cabrera didn't submit his testimony to the PGR until August 2015, yet his role was key: on the night of September 26, 2014, he was in charge of Iguala's security cameras. According to him, only four of the city's twenty-five cameras were working that night, and "I was the only one monitoring the security cameras," which would make him the sole viewer of any live footage.

According to González Cabrera, one of the cameras was on the corner of Periférico Poniente and Prolongación Karina, only a few meters away from where the attack against the *normalistas* took place on Periférico and Juan N. Álvarez. Because of its strategic placement, this camera should have recorded the moment when the students were taken away, offering a clear view of the perpetrators. But only a single minute of recording exists from it, and the video has been clearly manipulated.

There were also cameras on the Iguala–Taxco highway, at the corner of Periférico Norte, another in the Ciudad Industrial neighborhood on Avenue C (which was even closer to Juan N. Álvarez Street), and another on the Iguala–Taxco highway, near the main supply warehouse.

I was able to obtain all five of the C4 recordings that ended up in the State Prosecutor's and the PGR's official dossiers. Four of those recordings are from the camera on the Iguala–Taxco highway and Periférico Norte, and one from the Prolongación Karina. The four highway recordings are between thirty and fifty-six minutes long, whereas the fifth recording is only one minute.

In the short and rather vague testimony provided by González Cabrera, he doesn't specify the exact times of the events he saw on the cameras, and some of the occurrences he mentions are not recorded. He claims, for example, that he watched via video feed from the Periférico and Prolongación Karina camera three patrol vehicles heading in the direction of Periférico Norte, towards Juan N. Álvarez Street, and then later returning to Periférico Oriente, with the middle truck transporting civilians in the back. And yet this is the recording that lasts only one minute and only shows half of what Cabrera described—when the trucks return with civilians in one of them. There is no recording of the empty trucks. (The surveillance footage can be viewed on YouTube under the title "La noche de Iguala: el video escondido.")

According to his testimony, González Cabrera manipulated the camera to focus exclusively on the three patrol vehicles.

302

As he was the only one working that night, he was the only one who could have changed the recording from color to black-and-white or changed the angle of the camera, pointing it up and away from the street when the rest of the convoy passes by. He does not mention the convoy at all, nor does he explain why the recording lasts only one minute. "The events that I saw seemed typical," he remarked, "the municipal police respond all the time to public complaints." He added that the recordings remain saved in the surveillance system for seven days.

Cabrera claimed that at 07:00 on the morning of September 27, he ceded control of the surveillance operation to a colleague, though he didn't provide his name. This official—who would have been the one to hand the recordings over to the state ministerial police—remains unidentified to this day.

It's striking enough that the Ministry's Víctor Manuel Reséndiz never questioned González Cabrera, even though he was one of the key witnesses of the attacks. But it is even more telling that the witness who signed off on González Cabrera's testimony was Lourdes López Lucho, one of the heads of the investigation into the disappearance of the forty-three students—long notorious for conducting the previous administration's dirty work and a trusted associate of Tomás Zerón de Lucio.

The First Squad

According to various soldiers' testimonies, the first Rapid Response Team left the 27th Infantry Battalion base between 22:15 and 22:30. They departed in two Chevrolet Cheyennes under the command of Roberto Vázquez Hernández, section commander in charge of twenty-seven troops.

This first foray was not registered in the battalion logbook. Officially, the squad was going to the General Hospital, close to the base, to find out whether gunshot wound victims had been admitted. Vázquez Hernández told the PGR that at around 21:00, three or four casualties had been admitted to the hospital; he then returned to base to report to Lt. Colonel Cegueda Hernández, before receiving an urgent order to head out again with his squad to respond to the attack in Santa Teresa. They left the base for the second time at around 23:00, in an armored Sand Cat, with the following soldiers: Francisco Morales Merino, Eduardo Castillo Rea, César Augusto Martínez Ocampo, Rodolfo Antonio López Aranda, Jesús Marbán González, Eusebio Jiménez González, Cruz Javier Gómez Nicasio, José Luis Rodríguez Ortega, Camilo Espinoza González, Francisco Montaño Juárez, and Erik Abel Márquez Bahena. Infantryman Morales Merino explained to the PGR: "We received the order from Commander Vázquez, who told us, 'Load up, we're leaving.' He also said, 'On the alert, dicks hard—there are armed men out there killing people.'" This was the soldiers' state of mind when they went out into the streets that night.

They headed for the Iguala–Guerrero highway, via the state courthouse. A few of the soldiers in the squad testified to driving past the Estrella de Oro 1531 bus, which was by then empty, its windows shattered and its tires flat. According to their testimonies, as they were driving towards Santa Teresa, there were federal police officers next to two shot-up taxis, a few meters away from each other, and further ahead another passenger bus in which the Avispones soccer team had been riding. The soldiers all concurred that as the squad reached the scene, the survivors were beginning to come out of their hiding places.

Section Commander Vázquez Hernández left the base a second time, he said, at 23:00 to respond to the emergency in Santa Teresa; but according to the Avispones players, they were attacked around 23:40 by unidentified armed men, which would suggest that the squad left the base before the attack took place.

The troops allegedly remained at the Santa Teresa location until three in the morning and then returned to base, arriving at 03:30. They almost immediately set out again to the nearby hospital to once more check the names of the wounded, who by then numbered more than a dozen.

Soldiers Inspected the Police Station

Ulises Bernabé García, Iguala police's prison magistrate, was a key witness to the events of the night of September 26. During our interview, he affirmed that, contrary to the claims made by the PGR, the forty-three students were never taken back to the Iguala police station.

Bernabé García started working at the station in July 2014, after his predecessor requested a three-month leave. His work consisted primarily of setting fines or jail time (typically counted in hours) for misdemeanors such as drunkenness, urinating in public, or disorderly conduct. The plan was that when the former magistrate returned, on September 30, Bernabé Garcia would go back to his former position as a legal advisor. "I mean, it was bad luck more than anything, bad luck to be in that job at that moment," he said to me in April 2015, before fleeing to the United States.

Part of his first testimony was published in *Proceso* magazine in December 2014, and immediately afterwards the PGR issued an order for his arrest. His name had featured in the preliminary enquiries of state and federal prosecutors, which made out that Bernabé García had interrogated the *normalistas* in the courtyard of the police station and was working in concert with the Guerreros Unidos. In reality, he was the first witness to assert that the Army was indeed in the streets during the attacks that night and the first to mention the name of Captain Martínez Crespo. Since April 2015 he has been in an immigration detention center in Florence, Arizona, waiting a decision on his asylum claim. Renowned attorney Margo Cowan, who is representing him, told me: "Bernabé García's case is very solid, no doubt about it. The asylum laws in the US offer refuge to those in danger, and this man is in great danger for being an honest lawyer. He talked about what he saw that night, even though telling the truth put him in peril. He reported what happened, and because of that his safety and his life are in danger in Mexico."

When he showed up for work on September 26, there were only two detainees at the station: they paid their fine by cleaning the station and were released before noon. Throughout the afternoon and evening, police brought in six more people, between thirty and thirty-five years old, for drinking or brawling in public. Bernabé García issued each of them with a fine and they were locked into the men's cell. The last man arrested that night came in at around 21:30.

The magistrate's version accords with the declarations made by other Iguala police officers on September 27. These officers likewise mention the arrest of six people: one on Nayarit Street and five more at a sobriety checkpoint on the Iguala–Chilpancingo highway.

Bernabé García claimed not to have found out about the attack at the time, because he didn't have a radio. Nor, as he worked in an administrative capacity, did he have a weapon, uniform, or vehicle. However, sometime between 23:00 and midnight, the sentry at the station announced that a soldier wanted a word with him: it was Captain Martínez Crespo.

Martínez Crespo entered the station with five other soldiers, all armed. On the pretext of looking for a white motorcycle, they combed the entire place: cells, bathrooms, and offices, as well as Bernabé García's small office. The six drunks who had been arrested earlier were still in their cell. According to the PGR, this was the hour when the forty-three students were assembled at the police station, before being transported to Loma de los Coyotes.

"It was the first time I'd ever seen him," Bernabé García said of Martínez Crespo. "He made me suspicious when he slapped me on the back, chatty, like we knew each other . . . I gave him complete freedom, 'You can search the station.'" The inspection lasted about fifteen minutes, and around midnight, the two military vehicles pulled away. Shortly afterwards, the chief of police, Felipe Flores, along with the state deputy prosecutor, Ricardo Martínez Chávez, arrived and called a meeting for everyone who was at the station. They announced a "red alert," due to the shooting of the students. Armed officers were asked to turn in their weapons for forensic investigation.

According to Bernabé García, Flores and Martínez Chávez saw for themselves that there were only six people locked up in the station. Shortly afterwards, the deputy prosecutor left, while the local station remained under the control of the state ministerial police. Family members of the arrested men then showed up, wanting to pay the fines. Bernabé García explained: "They gave me their names, paid the fines, the minimum . . . They [Flores and Martínez Chávez] had just told us what was happening. I mean, I didn't want them coming here and targeting us, attacking the station and causing loss of life in my cell." When the last family member had paid and the cell was empty, it was around 02:20. Afterwards, the deputy prosecutor returned to the station and was displeased that Bernabé García had let the men go, though he had never told him not to. Bernabé García showed him the intake and release paperwork he had signed for the offenders. Days later, he was asked for a report and submitted copies of the paperwork to the State Prosecutor's Office.

At the Regional Police Training Center, Bernabé García said that he was interrogated just like the Iguala police officers were. "They pushed me in front of the deputy prosecutor and demanded, 'Where are the students?' 'What students? I don't know what you're talking about.'" Officials from the Prosecutor's Office told him that there had been students at the police station, and he responded that that was incorrect. He wanted to testify before the Public Ministry, but they wouldn't take his statement: it would obviously have undermined the version that state and federal officials were in the process of fabricating.

When the PGR called him in to make a statement on November 21, 2014, in their Iguala offices, he told them of the Army's visit to the station and reconfirmed that no students had been there. The PGR let him go, but, afterwards, the Army started looking for him. "A *compañero* mentioned it," Bernabé García told me, "that they were asking at the station about me. And [on hearing he was no longer there] they said, 'Get him in.' With what intention? To beat me up, disappear me, or what? I don't know why the Army is asking about me. I'm not afraid of talking to them, I'd even be glad to. But I am afraid they won't let me, and say, 'The magistrate is saying things, that the Army came out to inspect the station . . . so maybe they had something to do with [the attacks].' I'm not saying they had anything to do with it, but I'll vouch that they did come out when they claim they didn't." Maximiliano Martínez García, the sentry at the police station, backed up Bernabé García's statements in an interview with me.

Bernabé García's second testimony was published in June 2015. Three months later, Captain Martínez Crespo expanded on his own declaration to the PGR and, for the first time, admitted to having gone to the police station on the night of the attacks. According to him, however, they didn't get there until approximately 00:55, and only to ask about the white motorcycle: "I was there for no more than five minutes, without noticing anything else." And yet he had omitted even this brief mention of his visit in his two prior statements, and gave a different time line of the events in each statement.

Moreover, Guerrero's State Commission of Human Rights confirmed that there was no evidence that the *normalistas* had ever been held at the local police station. Ramón Navarrete, the president of the commission, confirmed that on the morning of September 27, he went to the station to investigate: "We conducted a very detailed search, looking for the slightest clue that would indicate the presence of the students." Ramón Navarrete also pointed out that on the following day, when they sought to inspect the base of the 27th Infantry Battalion, they were not allowed access. "If there'd been nothing to see," he said, "they would have let us in."

The *Federales* Participated in the Attacks

From documents I was able to obtain from the federal police base in Iguala, I confirmed the names of the seven federal officers who were deployed to the streets on the night of September

26. They are Deputy Chief Luis Antonio Dorantes Macías; Sub-inspector José Carlos Hernández Romero; officers Víctor Manuel Colmenares Campos and Arturo Gómez Gómez; and sub-officers Emmanuel de la Cruz Pérez Arizpe, Marco Antonio Pérez Guzmán, and Alfonso Ugalde Cámara.

According to PGR documents, Colmenares Campos and Pérez Arizpe were the two federal officers recognized by the driver of the Estrella de Oro 1531, Gregorio Jaimes Reyna, as accomplices in the disappearance of between fifteen and twenty *normalistas* when their bus was blocked near the courthouse. In April 2016, the National Commission on Human Rights (CNDH) specified that, according to Jaimes Reyna, between 22:00 and 22:30, federal officers Colmenares Campos and Pérez Arizpe stood idly by—on a highway under federal jurisdiction—while municipal police officers assaulted students in his bus, forcing them off and loading them into Huitzuco police vehicles.

"What happened with the kids?" Colmenares asked local police officers in front of the state courthouse. "Back there they fucked with our *compañero*. They're going to take them to Huitzuco, and the boss will decide what to do with them," an Iguala police officer allegedly explained. "Ah, okay, okay. That's fine," Colmenares said, watching the *normalistas* being driven away.

In April 2015, the CNDH detailed how the two federal agents "had acquiesced to the indiscriminate operations of two municipal police forces within a zone under federal jurisdiction. They allowed the detained *normalistas* to be transferred by the Iguala police to a different town, relying on the help of a police force operating outside of its jurisdiction, as was the case with the Huitzuco police."

Other witnesses interviewed in September 2015 noticed that the federal agents, too, aimed their weapons at the students outside the state courthouse, in plain view of dozens of motorists.

Instead of being investigated for these infringements, Colmenares Campos and Pérez Arizpe were simply transferred—in what appears to be a cover-up—to other federal bases, Colmenares to Tlaxcala and Pérez Arizpe to Tlalnepantla, where both were assigned to surveillance duties.

Some of the seven federal officers also took part in the stopping of the Avispones' bus, near the state courthouse, just as the attack against the *normalistas* was being carried out. After letting them go, a few miles down the road, the Avispones' bus was shot at by high-caliber weapons.

I have been able to collect documentary evidence proving the fact that officers at the federal police base had been monitoring the students since at least September 25, when they attempted their "money collection" outside Iguala. In report 1348/2014, dated September 25, Deputy Chief Dorantes Macías informed his superiors that federal officers kept an eye on fifty trainee teachers, traveling in an Estrella de Oro bus on the Iguala–Mezcala highway, for three hours. "Iguala remains under remote surveillance by this station in order to forestall acts of violence, and likewise counts on the presence and help of the state police," Macías reported, later noting that the *normalistas* left the area at 15:00. Another report listed "Immediate actions: we maintain personnel from this station in readiness along the highway stretch, in coordination with state authorities for preventive operations."

On September 26, along with the Army and the state police, Colmenares Campos and other federal officers monitored the Estrella de Oro 1568 bus, starting at 20:00, when the students arrived at toll booth #3 at the entrance of Iguala.

As another report, titled "Disturbances Due to Ayotzinapa Students in the City," number 1369/2014, demonstrates, at 21:55, state police officer Erik Nazario Hernández, from the Iguala C4, informed the federal police base that "students from the Ayotzinapa Normal Rural School, on board two Estrella de Oro buses, have been causing a disturbance at the intersection of Juan N. Álvarez and Periférico against officers of the municipal police."

It wasn't until after this information was received at the federal police base that federal officers were seen by witnesses both outside the state courthouse and on Juan N. Álvarez Street. Further evidence, from two Iguala officers' testimonies taken on September 27, mentions the presence of federal police at one (at least) of the crime scenes.

Iguala police officer Alejandro Andrade de la Cruz, who was in patrol vehicle 028, declared before the State Prosecutor's Office:

"I parked my vehicle across the Periférico to provide security and I stayed there a few minutes listening to calls for assistance from the Chipote Bridge, in front of where the state courthouse is located, and so I told my *compañeros* to get in the truck to go help out at the Chipote Bridge, and arriving at said location I did the same, providing rearguard security by cross-parking the vehicle, and I saw that there were other trucks, maybe five or six . . . and from there I saw two federal patrols arrive, as well as a ministerial police truck."

Officer Nicolás Delgado Arellano, who was on board Andrade de la Cruz's patrol number 028 that night, testified: "I don't remember the exact time because I don't wear a watch, when they called for help and we went to the location in front of the state courthouse on the national Mexico–Acapulco highway. Captain Alejandro Andrade de la Cruz told me that a brawl had been reported, but [when we arrived] at the location there was almost nobody around. We met a federal police vehicle, and then we left to continue patrolling."

Attorney Vidulfo Rosales affirmed in a March 21, 2015 interview: "[The students] don't explicitly refer to seeing federal police firing at them, but they were certainly there, the federal police were there! That much is clear. [The students] are clear about that."

Another eyewitness told me in interview that during the attack on Juan N. Álvarez Street, two federal police pickup trucks blocked the street to facilitate the action.

Despite the many reports and incriminating indications, six of the seven federal agents were not summoned to testify before the PGR until May 11, 2015. The deputy chief of the federal police base, Luis Antonio Dorantes Macías, was not called until September 11, 2015. In his brief statement he failed to mention that the federal police had been monitoring the students ever since they got near to Iguala, hours before the first attack, and that federal officers participated, on his own orders, in the events unfolding in front of the state courthouse as well as in Juan N. Álvarez Street. He also neglected to mention his phone conversation with Iguala's chief of police, Felipe Flores Vázquez, stating only that he learned of the commandeering of the buses at 21:50 and that he notified the Directorate of Operations and Regional Security at the Command Center in Mexico City. This information, however, was not mentioned by Enrique Galindo, the then head of Mexico's federal police.

Dorantes Macías admitted that besides the two Chevrolet Cheyennes, the federal force also possessed two pickup trucks, though he didn't recall their license or vehicle numbers. Curiously, when the Ministry inquired who had occupied those vehicles, he responded that they didn't go out that night. In his second declaration, Dorantes Macías admitted that in the run-up to September 26, the federal police had been alerted to the commandeering of vehicles by Ayotzinapa students, but he claimed not to remember the dates or locations, "since no complaints were made to the authorities." This was a lie, however, as the Estrella de Oro bus line had filed a formal complaint on September 25 about the taking of some of their buses, including the two that the students were riding in on September 26. Asked if the federal police ever employed tear gas, he responded, "None of our units have that kind of equipment."

Federal officer Colmenares Campos also lied to the PGR, altering the time line and omitting the fact that he had been tracking the *normalistas*. He claimed that between 22:15 and 22:30 Dorantes Macías summoned him and Pérez Arizpe to the federal police base on Highway 95, near the Iguala city entrance. Looking at a map of the town, this trip would have taken them directly past the state courthouse at the time the bus driver overheard his exchange with municipal police ("Okay, that's fine!"), just as the students were being kidnapped.

Not mentioning the incident, Colmenares Campos claimed that, once back at the federal base, Dorantes Macías sent them to city hall to question Chief of Police Felipe Flores regarding the shooting the PGR had flagged up. Colmenares Campos said that Flores told him that there had been gunfire in the center of Iguala and that when local police arrived on the scene they were attacked by the *normalistas*, "who were traveling on an Estrella de Oro bus, sparking a chase that ended in front of the state courthouse, which is located on the Cuernavaca–Chilpancingo highway [municipal jurisdiction], leaving said bus at the scene." So went the report Colmenares Campos wrote about the conversation, not mentioning that he had himself been at that very location, and falsely stating that the courthouse lies within municipal jurisdiction.

After interviewing Felipe Flores, Colmenares Campos claims to have returned to the federal police base. After midnight, he said, six agents in patrol vehicles 09908, 11744, 11740, and 09910 left the base for the scene of the attack against the Avispones, which took place on a highway likewise within federal jurisdiction. Later, the state deputy prosecutor, Ricardo Martínez Chávez, arrived with two aides.

Pérez Arizpe, who was riding in the same vehicle as Colmenares Campos, spun his own string of lies about the timing of the joint operation with the state police. Pérez Arizpe also refrained from mentioning that they had been monitoring the *normalistas* and presented an inaccurate description of their encounter with the Avispones. He claimed that on arrival at the Santa Teresa turn-off, "we ensured their security and called emergency services." But, according to the Red Cross, it was a taxi driver who called the ambulance. An aide accompanying deputy prosecutor Martínez Chávez described the scene to the PGR in a declaration submitted on October 29, 2014: "It was raining, and neither the army nor the federal police had offered [the victims] any assistance."

While taking statements from Colmenares Campos and Pérez Arizpe, PGR officials did not ask a single question. Only after Gregorio Jaimes, the bus driver, identified both men as being at the scene and speaking with local police officers did the PGR open an investigation into "abuse of authority and the improper exercise of public service" against them. The status of the investigation is unknown.

Colmenares and Dorantes: Dark Histories

From November 2014, I delved into the key role that federal officers Colmenares Campos and Dorantes Macías played on the fateful night. Through the Transparency Law I obtained the history of arrests and sanctions taken against both men by the federal police and the Secretariat of Public Service.

Colmenares Campos joined the federal highway police in 1987, by order of Commander Enrique Harari Garduño, who in 2000 was arrested for presumed links to organized crime. Since the beginning of his career, Colmenares Campos has accumulated dozens of sanctions, lasting hours and days, and was even the subject of an investigation led by the Higher Audit Office of Mexico in relation to his stints in Baja California Norte, Texcoco, and Iguala. Among his many offenses were absenteeism, operational failures, not writing out reports, abandoning his post, disobedience, lack of super-vision of officers under his command, not returning arms after service, driving his private car without plates, "making improper use of the radio equipment during security and surveillance activities," "lack of discipline in the office," and "participating in a brawl in a den of vice, resulting in damage to the premises."

In 2003, the Office of Internal Affairs of the Federal Police opened a file on him when he was working in Texcoco. He was accused of filching a colleague's medical file and altering a document—"printing the words 'HIV (AIDs)' in the Diagnosis column"—and enjoining other officers "not to tell anyone about it." This earned him a thirty-day suspension.

In 2014, when he was already in Iguala, the Audit Office accused Colmenares Campo and four other agents of arresting, and subsequently handing over to the National Institute of Migration, an Ecuadorian citizen they picked up on the outskirts of Morelos without authority to do so. The federal police rallied around him, however, and on September 9, 2014, just weeks before the disappearance of the *normalistas*, he was absolved by the office of internal affairs.

Dorantes Macías also accumulated a long list of irregularities during his career in the federal police, including "poor performance in security work," "lack of development," "incorrectly filling out the gasoline voucher register," absenteeism, failing to consult the database of stolen cars, not following orders, and neglecting to search vehicles transporting petroleum products, as well as "disciplinary lapses on police premises." On October 23, 2014, he presented his "irrevocable" resignation to the federal police.

Cover-Up and Censorship in the PGR

On March 4, 2016, the Special Office for the Iguala Case of the CNDH sent a letter to Eber Omar Betanzos Torres, the deputy prosecutor of the PGR's Office of Human Rights and Crime Prevention, requesting the arrest of Colmenares Campos and Pérez Arizpe, who they accused of involvement in the disappearance of the students. The case against them was expounded in a document signed by José Trinidad Larrieta, head of the Special Office, titled "Report on the Investigation Focused on the Participation of Federal Police Officers in the Events of Iguala."

In April 2016 the CNDH publicly released its report and demanded that the PGR charge, or at least issue a detainer against, the two officers. And yet, by November 2016, the PGR had taken no action, merely acknowledging that they were investigating the participation of the federal police as well as of the local police force of Huitzuco. The federal police, meanwhile, defensively claimed that to date there had been no proof of wrongdoing on its part.

The CNDH gave the following particulars:

"In the report it is confirmed that [Colmenares Campos and Pérez Arizpe] were reassigned outside of Guerrero a few days after the events, plausibly indicating an attempt to distance them from the events and conceal their responsibility . . . It is relevant to this line of investigation that two of the federal police officers involved in the events, in their respective official declarations and in their own reports, suspiciously omit reference to any circumstance that would put them at the site of the events that took place near the Chipote Bridge."

The CNDH asked the PGR to launch a "comprehensive and thorough investigation" of the officers, including any links to organized crime, money laundering, and illicit enrichment. The organization also urged the PGR to investigate the checkpoint jointly installed by federal and local Iguala police nearby the state courthouse, in order to "determine its role in the disappearance of the students, and the potential responsibility of federal police officers."

The Untouchable Police of Huitzuco

The report sent by the CNDH to the PGR states that Gregorio Jaimes Reyna, the driver of one Estrella de Oro bus, informed the company's lawyers of what he'd seen, including the participation of the federal police. These lawyers "advised him not to relay that information to the ministerial authorities, arguing that it was a delicate issue.

318

He was better off keeping quiet and staying out of trouble." That's why the driver didn't mention the federal police in his first statement.

Jaimes Reyna also told the CNDH that he heard one of the Iguala police officers tell another that no more students would fit in the police vehicle, and the second officer replied, "Don't worry, the guys from Huitzuco are on their way," and soon after more blue and white patrol cars arrived, into which the students were loaded. The driver made the same claim to the Interdisciplinary Group of Independent Experts (GIEI) team in September 2015. Even so, the local police of Huitzuco remain untouchable. As we saw, this is the fief of the Figueroa family, epitomized by Rubén Figueroa Alcocer, *El Tigre de Huitzuco*.

In June 2016, I went to Huitzuco, where the entrance to the city was guarded by two local police officers armed with Beretta assault rifles. One of them, Jesús Sánchez, with seven years of service, confirmed that the Huitzuco force is connected to the Iguala C4, which means that in emergency situations Huitzuco police are called for support.

We know that in the Iguala C4 building were military personnel, state police, Iguala police, and Civil Protection officers and that the network was connected in real time with the PGR base in Iguala as well as with the federal police base and the Huitzuco police station. All of these agencies received live information about the events.

Jesús Sánchez, the Huitzuco officer I spoke with, said he was working on the night of September 26, stationed in Huitzuco's town center, and didn't see anything out of the ordinary. "I was here on night shift. We're here one day, and one day we're out on patrol. That time it was my turn, with eight *compañeros*, because we're supposed to help each other out at night. You won't see many [officers] now, but at night there are more. That time it was raining, we were wearing rain jackets."

He told me that, before the attacks in Iguala, there were around ninety Huitzuco police officers, and now there are only around sixty. Many of them quit voluntarily soon after September 26, 2014; others were let go after failing their trust-worthiness exams. Despite the fact that the Huitzuco force is connected to the Iguala force through the C4, the Guerrero state prosecutors never interrogated Huitzuco officers, and their weapons were not forensically tested. More than a year after the attacks, the PGR finally did so.

Among the Huitzuco police officers who resigned was the chief of police, Javier Duarte Núñez, along with his son. The CNDH and the GIEI both recommended that they be inter-viewed, but they have gone missing.

Talking to people in Huitzuco about the powerful Figueroa family underlines that the only "boss" in town is the powerful Rubén Figueroa, the governor of Guerrero who was removed after the Aguas Blancas massacre, and is a close friend of that other ex-governor, Ángel Aguirre. Norberto Figueroa, another family member, was mayor of Huitzuco when his local police force allegedly collaborated in the disappearance of the *normalistas*.

Sánchez told me that the PGR only called on him and his colleagues to make statements in February 2016, asking if they had assisted the Iguala police on the night of the attacks. He maintained that they did not. A few weeks before I spoke with him, PGR officers came to Huitzuco to conduct tests on their weapons, one year and eight months after the disappear-ance of the *normalistas*.

12

The True Night of Iguala

"The Head of the Office of Investigation is instructed to relay orders to whom it may concern to broaden the investigation into Captain José Martínez Crespo, inquiring into the accusations made against him in regard to possible ties to organized crime, the result of said investigation to be delivered to the Specialized Investigations on Organized Crime (SEIDO).

"The Head of the Office of Investigation is instructed to relay orders to whom it may concern so that, in accordance with Article 13, last paragraph, of the Political Constitution of the United Mexican States ['Civilians involved in military crimes or faults shall be put on trial before the competent civil authority'], there may be an evaluation of the negligence and dereliction of duty of which Secretariat of National Defense (SEDENA) personnel of from the 27th Infantry Battalion, based in Iguala, Guerrero, may have been guilty in the events of September 26 and 27, 2014, when students of the Raúl Isidro Burgos Normal Rural School of Ayotzinapa and other civilians were attacked; and, should sufficient information and evidence emerge, to broaden the investigation into the illicit activity that may be imputed to such officers, including possible Cover-up, Abuse of Authority, or any other improper action undertaken in the fulfillment of their duties."

So read the "general recommendations" of a draft of the "Technical Juridical Assessment" issued by the PGR ombudsman, the Visitaduría or Inspectorate General, led by César Alejandro Chávez Flores, to evaluate the preliminary investigation dossier AP/PGR/SDPDS/01/001/2015 opened by Attorney General Jesús Murillo Karam, which gathers all the investigations related to the disappearance of the forty-three *normalistas*.

The preliminary conclusions from the Inspectorate, as well as the results of investigation DGAI/510/CDMX/2016 conducted by the same Inspectorate into the head of the Criminal Investigation Agency (AIC), Tomás Zerón de Lucio, for his actions at the San Juan River in Cocula, Guerrero, ultimately obliged Chávez Flores to submit his resignation on September 12, 2016.

The Inspectorate General's Investigation

When Arely Gómez came to head the Attorney General's Office (PGR), replacing Jesús Murillo Karam, in April 2015, the agency's Inspectorate General—the body charged with investigating irregularities in preliminary inquiries (including those committed by Public Ministry prosecutors, official experts, and federal ministerial police officers)—was led by the lawyer César Chávez Flores, forty-one, originally from Chihuahua and with significant experience in internal reviews and corruption investigations.

Given the toll the Ayotzinapa case had taken on the PGR, Gómez and Chávez Flores together agreed to conduct a "technical and juridical assessment" of the preliminary investigations. This would entail reviewing each of the actions undertaken by the PGR and determining whether, from the outset, the Attorney General's Office had acted lawfully and in line with international standards of human rights. Their internal review would hold the agency to "the highest international standards in terms of investigating forced disappearance."

This internal review had already been planned when the GIEI submitted its final report on April 24, 2016, in which they laid out the tampering with evidence that occurred at the supposed crime scene near the San Juan River, and the possible planting of human remains by Zerón. The parents of the disappeared demanded an investigation into Zerón, imposing the condition of a quick turnaround if they were going to continue dialoguing with the PGR.

In his defense, Zerón showed a video of himself with the builder Agustín García Reyes, one of the detained suspects, by the San Juan River, before ministerial proceedings on the site began. The video, however, further incriminated Zerón, publicly demonstrating the irregularities surrounding the supposed discovery of the black plastic bags.

Unfortunately for Zerón and his team, Chávez Flores is not a man to take things lightly. While at the Inspectorate, he broke the record for leveling sanctions against PGR officials: in just a year and a half he prosecuted 170 public officers and sacked more than 200.

As the affair escalated into an international scandal, Chávez Flores warned Arely Gómez that the Mexican state was embroiled in a case that could end up before the Inter-American Court of Human Rights, or even the International Criminal Court, so that their own internal review would have to be absolutely rigorous. The attorney general accepted the challenge to investigate all the way, notwithstanding that Zerón was an appointee and protégé of President Peña Nieto. Since taking the top PGR job, all her efforts to remove him had been quashed at the highest level.

The Inspectorate didn't limit itself to the day in October 2014 when the remains were allegedly found by the river; it also looked into the manner in which García Reyes and the other suspects had been detained and the process of investigating the Cocula trash dump.

The internal review wrapped up on August 18, 2016, as per the agreement with the parents. However, on the eve of formally presenting the conclusions to the families, Arely Gómez asked Chávez Flores not to sign it until Peña Nieto had approved the disquieting report. This enraged family members of the disappeared, who promptly broke off all communication with the Peña Nieto government.

Chávez Flores Resigns

"Faced with the choice between doing the right thing and remaining in my job, I have just handed in my resignation," Chávez Flores announced in front of the stunned faces of dozens of colleagues in the Visitaduría offices. He didn't say so explicitly, but it was common knowledge that he stepped down because of the conclusions he had drawn regarding the untouchable Tomás Zerón. "Those of us who work in this Inspectorate have an obligation to cleanse the justice system of our country. What we do here has a transcendent value— we try to bring better institutions and governance to Mexico," the young lawyer added.

When the emotional speech was over, his colleagues gave him an ovation. In the midst of dozens of PGR officials who for almost two years had engaged in acts of torture, illegal detention, and manipulation of the evidence during the investigation into the disappearance of the forty-three, here was one man who chose to do what was right.

For months, as Arely Gómez, other PGR prosecutors, and Zerón himself pressured Chávez Flores to alter the conclusions of his inquiry into the scene at the San Juan River—he also received multiple written threats—Chávez Flores hadn't wavered. The inspector explained to Arely Gómez the negative repercussions of ignoring the irregularities: sooner or later, maybe even under the scrutiny of an international court, they would come to light. Nevertheless, President Peña Nieto had the last word. Instructing Arely Gómez to corner Chávez Flores into resigning, he also told her to keep the report's unwelcome findings a secret. Soon enough he would move his right-hand man, Zerón, to a more useful position.

"They're saying that the problem is you, because you don't want to change your conclusions," Zerón told Chávez Flores during the tense days of their tussle. "I can't do that, Tomás, you know I can't," Chávez Flores responded, reminding him that he'd kept him and other officials informed of his progress every step of the way.

The conclusions he had drawn, pointing the finger at Zerón, were no surprise to anyone, and yet it was the inspector who seemed to have gotten into trouble. One PGR source I spoke with told me, "To have problems with Tomás is to have problems with the president."

Though the Peña Nieto administration tried to keep the reports under wraps, I was able to see the "Final Conclusions" section of the Inspectorate review, as well as the "Preliminary Conclusions" section of the legal audit of the early inquiries in the Iguala case, coordinated by the same Visitaduría. Only now, in the framework of the present work of investigative journalism, have the contents of these reports become available to the public.

These reports are of critical public interest not only because of the victims' right to truth—a fundamental human right—but because they shed light on Mexico's most important case of forced disappearance in decades.

The investigation into Zerón shows how all of his actions along the San Juan River invalidated his own conclusions and corrupted crucial evidence. In short, the "historical truth" that the Peña Nieto administration had been staunchly defending (at a lesser political cost, Los Pinos reckoned, than if the truth were known), is brought crashing down by Cháves Flores's report.

The legal audit urged SEIDO to rethink its entire investigation. In order to find the students and those responsible for their disappearance, priority should be given to the role of the Guerrero state police, the federal police, and 27th Infantry Battalion, and to what happened to the two Estrella de Oro buses.

Weeks after Arely Gómez pressured Chávez Flores to step down, her own turn came. On October 25, 2016, Peña Nieto removed her from the top job at the PGR and sent her to the Civil Service Secretariat. The word in the PGR was that her demotion was punishment for authorizing investigations into Zerón and into the preliminary inquiries. For Los Pinos, it was essential to ensure that the results of the inspector general's inquiry did not see the light of day or have any legal consequences. Humberto Castillejos, legal advisor to Peña Nieto and a key figure in the cover-up of the Ayotzinapa case, recommended his cousin Raúl Cervantes Andrade to replace Gómez. The administration didn't just expect him to sweep the disaster under the carpet; they wanted him to guarantee impunity all round.

Over more than two years of research, more than 100 interviews, the review of thousands of PGR documents and classified reports obtained from information requests, extensive field research, and access to a particular source, I was able to reconstruct a version of the attacks that corresponds to the observations made by the Inspectorate General's legal audit, as well as to the basic mechanics of the case.

It Was the Army

On the night of September 26, 2014, a high-level drug trafficker with much business in Guerrero, who happened to be in Iguala, was informed that students from the Ayotzinapa Normal School were riding in two buses containing a hidden stash of heroin worth at least $2 million. The *normalistas* knew nothing of the precious cargo, nor that their fate would be linked to it.

Although the trafficker dealt in large quantities of heroin, the amount in the buses was not insignificant, and he couldn't let a robbery pass, even if it was an accident. If he didn't respond, he would lose control of his *plaza* or market.

"If people kill for twenty thousand dollars, then how about two million? That's the way it works. The recuperation of the merchandise was about the money, and about authority. If you let one robbery pass, more will come later," my source explained to me. I was able to authenticate the credibility of this source and held several meetings with him over the course of fifteen months.

The trafficker in question had been working his turf for over eight years, pushing drugs into the US in association with Arturo Beltrán Leyva—not as a subordinate, but as a minor partner who, even while keeping a low profile (his name never arose in prosecutions brought against other chiefs of that cartel, such as Édgar Valdez Villarreal or Gerardo Álvarez Vázquez), has gained in power over the years. In 2009, when Arturo Beltrán Leyva was killed in Cuernavaca, the capo decided to continue operating on his own, using Guerrero as his base. To maintain his grip on the zone, he kept soldiers from the 27th and 41st Infantry Battalions on the payroll, along with federal police, state investigative police, federal ministerial police, Iguala municipal police, and various local politicians, both in urban areas and in the mountains where the poppy was grown and the heroin processed.

When he found out that he had lost a valuable consignment, the capo made a call to Colonel José Rodríguez Pérez, commander of the 27th Infantry Battalion—the Army was the security agency with the most authority in the region—asking him to retrieve the merchandise at any cost. "Leading the operation to retrieve the drugs was the Army," my source told me.

The ballistic tests conducted, as well as the crime scene analysis, point to the Estrella de Oro buses 1531 and 1568 as the principal targets of attack. The first bus was stopped at the intersection of Juan N. Álvarez and Periférico Norte, and the second in front of the state courthouse, by a mixture of Iguala, Huitzuco, and Cocula police, with backup from federal police and Guerrero state police. In accordance with this version, as the soldiers were removing the drugs from the compartments, the *normalistas* on board saw what was happening—hence the sudden need to get rid of them permanently, in order to leave no witnesses.

My source explained that the capo only wanted to retrieve his property and did not order the disappearance. From his experience working in the Beltrán Leyva cartel, he knew that

328

excessive violence was bad for business. When he learned of what happened that night in Iguala, according to my source, he was concerned and angry with the Army: they had "heated up the *plaza*," attracting undue attention to a hitherto peaceful market, and forcing him to put the brakes on business in Guerrero.

As the capo apparently told his confidants, his people didn't take part in the operation—they left everything in the hands of the Army. He himself didn't know where the students ended up, but someone told him that at least some of them were taken to the 27th Infantry Battalion base. "I never meant for so many fuckers to get killed, they overdid it," the capo is said to have fumed. Ironically, he was not among the "culprits" arrested by the PGR.

As I learned while researching this book, in Guerrero many drivers of long-distance buses collaborate with criminal organizations to move drugs. Usually, thanks to the protection of corrupt officials, the transport goes without a hitch. According to my source, Iguala had recently turned into an important hub for heroin—harvested and processed in the rural mountains of the state, which has supplanted the Golden Triangle (the states of Sinaloa, Durango, and Chihuahua) as the region in Mexico with the highest poppy cultivation. Control of Iguala had become vital for the heroin trade.

I compared this version of events with the testimonies of victims and witnesses, as well as with the official declarations made by officers from the 27th Battalion and the federal police—though what was most consistent in those declarations was their inconsistency—and with the content of the Inspectorate General's audit of the preliminary inquiries.

The National Drug Threat Assessment Summary published by the Drug Enforcement Administration (DEA) in 2015 underscores the fact that most of the heroin consumed in the US comes from Mexico (next on the list is Colombia), with Mexico increasingly dominant in the production of "white heroin." The summary explains that the consumption of the drug tripled in the US between 2007 and 2013, making it a thriving concern. The level of "purity" is also increasing, which compounds the mortality rate among consumers. All of which leads to the conclusion that white heroin represents, after opioids, the most serious drug threat to the country.

According to the DEA, Guerrero remains under the control of the Beltrán Leyva cartel and its associates, though there is also a small presence of the Sinaloa cartel. It is worth noting that the DEA summary does not devote a single line to either the Guerreros Unidos or Los Rojos, the only organizations cited in the PGR's investigation into the disappearance of the forty-three students. My source explained that while the Guerreros Unidos or Los Rojos do have a presence in Guerrero, they operate on a small scale, well below the level of the drug boss whose cargo was retrieved from the buses.

"Who the hell is this asshole?"

As part of the conclusions drawn in their final report of April 2016, the GIEI team pointed to the Estrella Roja bus, from which *normalistas* were violently evicted in front of the state courthouse, as a possible "means of transport of heroin produced in the region, which would explain the magnitude of the operation launched to prevent the buses from leaving." The team of experts denounced the "opacity" of the PGR with regard to that vehicle and noted contradictions in the driver's testimony. The Estrella Roja bus, which was directly behind the Estrella de Oro 1531, received not a single bullet impact, and all of the students riding on that bus survived. The evidence uncovered in my own research does not support the notion that the Estrella Roja may also have been used to transport drugs.

The statements made by the driver of that bus changed over the two years following the disappearance. In one, he claimed that the students voluntarily got off the bus because it had mechanical problems; but in a signed letter, dated September 26, 2014, he said that federal police officers stopped the bus, pulled the *normalistas* off at gunpoint, and then escorted the bus to the highway so he could continue on his route.

All of the *normalistas* (except for Fernando Marín) riding in the two Estrella de Oro buses that became marooned in traffic were disappeared. As the GIEI team note in their first report (September 2015), the drivers of the Estrella de Oros "suffered more brutal treatment than the drivers of the other three buses that started from the bus terminal." Even if "the drivers of the Costa Line buses endured some police aggression, being fired on along with their passengers . . . they were not detained. The driver of the Estrella Roja bus was not attacked."

The driver of the Estrella de Oro 1568, stopped on Juan N. Álvarez, was beaten and taken to the cell at the Iguala police station, to be eventually released. The driver of the Estrella de Oro 1531, stopped in front of the courthouse, explained in his statement to the PGR that he was taken to a house in the Jacarandas neighborhood, where "they sat me down between two masked policemen, and a gentleman in a white shirt and black pants came in, you could tell it was the body of someone who works out (he looked about forty), who said, 'Who the hell is this asshole?' The police told him, 'He's the bus driver,' and the gentleman said, 'Well, take him to you know where,' and went back towards his truck, which I couldn't see very well, and then he yelled, 'Let him go!' "

The physical description of the "gentleman" who ordered the release of the bus driver matches that of the capo who lost his drug shipment.

In November 2014 I was able to verify that at least four of the five buses had been left abandoned in Iguala's Grúas Meta junkyard, without any sort of protective isolation to conserve potential evidence. It wasn't until the middle of November that the PGR conducted its first forensic tests on the buses. As pointed out in the inspector general's review, despite the fact that the buses formed part of the crime scene they were returned, in defiance of standard protocol, to the Estrella de Oro and Estrella Roja companies. Not until September 2015 did officials check to see if there were any alterations to the body of the buses.

From the Inspector General's report: "The MP [ministerial police] waited seventeen months after the events to conduct an inspection on the buses to check if they had compartments installed to transport drugs. When they finally did so, the buses had already long been returned to the companies and had even been repaired by them, so that the checks were pointless and need not have been ordered."

Given the importance of the Estrella de Oro buses, the inspector general recommended that the drivers be summoned again, to provide additional testimony.

The Army Took Early Control

Before passing the police trustworthiness exams in April 2013 and becoming deputy chief of the Cocula force, thirty-six-year-old César Nava González served in the Panamerican Protection Service for more than ten years. He is currently on trial, accused of involvement in the disappearance of the forty-three students.

On the night of September 26, 2014, after the first attacks against the students on Juan N. Álvarez Street, and before the students were disappeared, the 27th Infantry Battalion had "command and control" of the city of Iguala, according to Nava González's testimony given in December 2015 before the First District Court of Federal Criminal Proceedings in Tamaulipas.

Nava González claimed that he was on his day off when, at 21:30, he received a call on his cell phone from a private number. The caller identified himself as the deputy director of Public Security in Iguala (i.e., deputy police chief) and asked for Salvador Bárcenas, Cocula's chief of police. Nava González responded that the chief had the day off and he, Nava, was in Iguala where he lived with his family, and then asked "what I could do for him, because I was deputy chief César Nava. [The caller] identified himself as [Salgado] Valladares, [and] said . . . that it was he . . . who supported us in regards to public security by patrolling the borders between our two cities, Cocula and Iguala. Now he needed support from all the neighboring cities, like Taxco, Tepecoacuilco, Huitzuco, and Cocula, since armed men had come into Iguala and were shooting guns off in multiple neighborhoods, and could we help with backup as it seemed there was a lot of them."

Nava González said that he would need authorization from Bárcenas and that Salgado should call him directly. Twenty minutes later Nava González heard from Bárcenas, with the instruction to provide support. The deputy chief then called

Ignacio Aceves, an officer over in Cocula, to pass on the order. He also phoned his wife, to let her know what was going on, and then went to the center of Iguala to collect his two daughters and take them home. He put on his uniform before Aceves arrived from Cocula to pick him up, with three police vehicles and eleven officers, leaving just two officers behind in Cocula to guard the station. Another call came from Salgado Valladares, asking if he had gotten permission to help out, and he told him that they were already reconnoitering the streets of Iguala.

Continuing to describe the scene, Nava González said that on Periférico, near the Pemex gas station, traffic had halted and there were the flashing lights of police and ambulances. "We stopped at Álvarez, where there was a local Iguala patrol vehicle, a Ford Ranger, blocking said street." The Cocula officers exited their vehicles and asked what was happening. "The Iguala officers informed us that a group of armed men were riding in the buses that were stopped by the patrol cars, and that their colleagues had been shot at in the center of town, which was why they were blocking [the street]."

Nava Gonzalez observed the bullet impacts on the bus and the crashed police truck with the shattered windshield. The Iguala officers said that some of the men in the bus had fled, while others remained inside.

"Seeing us there [the *normalistas*] started to yell from behind one of the buses, asking for help because one of them was injured and they yelled at me for help. They had their faces covered with their shirts, and I wanted to get closer to see what was going on and who was hurt," Nava González said, adding that he went as far as the corner to ask what they wanted. His account accords with testimonies from the *normalistas* who were riding in the first bus and were asking for help for *Pulmón* (Miguel Ángel Espino).

"They shouted at me to come over to them, because one of them was wounded, I asked if they were armed and they told me no, just please help. I wanted to approach, but the Iguala police said to me, 'They're going to kill you, they're armed.' The occupants of the bus were so insistent that I yelled back that I would come over, but they mustn't shoot . . . 'I'm going to help whoever's wounded, but don't shoot,' and they shouted, 'We're not armed.' I wanted to go with my *compañeros* but they [the students] shouted, 'No, come by yourself.' I told them that wasn't possible, that they were my protection unit, I began to think they really did mean to hurt me and I retreated."

Nava González tried to persuade the students to bring the wounded one out to where he was, but they refused. "They wouldn't stop yelling at me to help them. Seeing the desperation of these people, I decided to make a deal." The *normalistas* brought their wounded *compañero* halfway, and Nava González, Aceves, and another officer went to retrieve him.

"We didn't know if they were armed or not," Nava González said. "I ordered Captain Aceves to call an ambulance," which was only a block away, but the driver refused to come nearer "because it was dangerous."

"I should say," Nava González added, "that since we arrived on scene there was no aggression against us, no firing of any weapons." They checked over the injured man, Miguel Ángel Espino, and couldn't see any visible wounds, but *Pulmón* was having trouble breathing. They put him in the back of one of the Cocula trucks and drove him to the ambulance. The paramedics said that he was having an asthma attack and that they would take care of him. Nava

González then returned to the corner of Periférico and Juan N. Álvarez.

"I received a third call from . . . Mr. Valladares, from the same private number, and he told me that soldiers from the 27th Infantry Battalion were at the local police station . . . and that they had already taken command and control of the station . . . and that they were conducting land patrols. [He said] thanks for the support, and that we should withdraw."

Over the Iguala police radios Nava González also heard someone say, "Withdraw, and say thanks to the [outside] police who came to provide backup, and send them back to their own stations." He and his fellow officers therefore boarded their vehicles and left the scene. Nava González ordered Aceves to go fetch the officer he'd left guarding his house, and then they would "reconvene at the exit towards Cocula." He recalled that they kept alert from Mextitlán to the entrance to Cocula, "in case the people who were shooting up Iguala had gone to Cocula." Later, back at their station, they washed their vehicles "as usual," and Nava González asked some of his officers to take him back to his Iguala home, where he arrived at six in the morning. He then slept until four in the afternoon.

Nava González testified that he later received another call from Salvador Bárcenas, who ordered him to change the license plates on his patrol trucks "to avoid possible retaliation against us personally," and that he transmitted the order to Aceves. He said that work went on as normal until October 13, when he left Guerrero because they were planning to arrest him. On November 15, 2014, men in civilian clothes detained him in Colima and flew him, along with his wife and a cousin, to Mexico City. According to PGR's official version, however, he was arrested in Mexico City while in possession of a firearm.

When he was taken before the Public Ministry at the PGR, they tried to force him to sign a confession previously written by the prosecutor. One of the agents pressuring him was a woman, "Maestra Blanca," who also tortured him and threatened to harm his wife. Listed on the preliminary investigation is Ministry official Blanca Alicia Bernal Castilla. She and other PGR staff wanted him to sign a statement that confessed to having kidnapped the *normalistas*. They wanted me to say, Nava González explained, "that I handed the students over to some assassins I can't remember the names of, they were written out, and that I, wearing civilian clothes, provided security to a criminal gang." He repeatedly refused to sign the confession. "Maestra Blanca was really angry, she ripped up the pages and then had to print them a third time . . . Scared and fearing for my family, there was nothing I could do but sign."

In this forced confession, Nava González explains how, after sending *Pulmón* to the hospital, he went to the Iguala police station where Salgado Valladares asked him to help him transport ten students to Loma de los Coyotes. Arriving there at around 23:00, the pair handed them over to Iguala police officers.

Francisco Salgado Valladares joined the parachute brigade when he was in the Military College and served for ten years. In 1999 he enlisted with the Iguala police, remaining there for the next fourteen years. His sister told me in an interview that he had only recently been promoted to deputy chief. A local functionary said, "Everybody knows that it was Salgado Valladares, not Flores Velázquez, who ran the police."

According to Valladares's sister, he wasn't even working on the night of September 26. That evening he was with his family at the presentation given by María de los Ángeles

Pineda Villa, the mayor's wife: "A lot of people saw my brother there," his sister told me.

When the shooting began, she called her brother twice. The first time he told her he wasn't aware of what was happening. The second time, he was putting on his uniform to go to the station. Afterwards, Salgado Valladares would allegedly tell her that the Army and the federal police were responsible for the disappearance of the *normalistas*.

According to the logbook at the Iguala police station, Salgado Valladares was indeed on call that night. In an interview, another of his brothers said that he was on duty, but only the night shift, and that he did attend the Pineda Villa presentation earlier. His mother would also corroborate that he was at the presentation.

According to his official testimony given on May 8, 2015, Salgado Valladares confessed to having a connection with the Guerreros Unidos since 2012. At 20:30 on the night in question, he said, he heard the C4 reporting over the Matra radio that students had taken a few buses and had beaten a driver. At 22:00 he received a call from Chief of Police Flores, instructing him to go to the station, where he found four individuals in the cell and eight others being held in the patio, handcuffed and with t-shirts over their faces. Prison magistrate Ulises Bernabé García was about to book them when, at 23:30, the deputy chief of Cocula police, César Nava arrived, and took the students away to an undisclosed location.

I was able to interview Salgado Valladares over the phone; he was being held in the Cefereso #4 prison in Tepic. During our ten-minute conversation he gave me a version of events that contradicted, at times, that of his own family. He said that he wasn't the Iguala deputy chief at all; he was in charge of security at the central market (in front of the station where the *normalistas* commandeered three buses). He remained at his post there from eight in the morning on September 26 until eight in the morning on September 27.

The following is an extract of our interview.

ANABEL HERNÁNDEZ: Were you present when the students came to take the buses?

FRANCISCO SALGADO VALLADARES: No, because when the radio operator told us . . . The market is huge, it starts at the bus station and goes all the way to the Bodega Aurrerá. We were at the other end when the radio operator informed us that they had taken the buses and had already headed towards the city center.

AH: So what did you do?

FSV: I answered [the operator] saying that we were there, but we didn't go to the bus station because, like I said, they'd already left.

AH: Did you see any soldiers that night, participating in the events?

FSV: No, I was in the central market. I didn't get in any police vehicles, I couldn't move from there.

AH: There is a statement made by the chief of the Cocula Police, César Nava, in which he claims that after assisting the Iguala police he spoke with you, and that you told him to withdraw because the Army had the situation under control. Is that what happened?

FSV: No, that's not true.

AH: Did you speak with Mr. Nava that night?

FSV: No, I did not.

AH: But you attended the event held by Mrs. Abarca and her husband?

FSV: No, I repeat, I was in the central market, I couldn't leave my post.

AH: But your family tells me, Mr. Salgado, that you were there.

FSV: That I was at the event?

AH: Yes.

FSV: How could my family know that, when I was working?

(His mother and brother, sitting next to me as I was conducting this interview on speakerphone, looked surprised and uncomfortable.)

AH: Because they saw you there, right?

FSV: I was working in the central market. At no point could I have left my post.

AH: Did you go to the local station? Did you see the students there?

FSV: No. That is completely false.

AH: There is a statement you made, in which you apparently confess to going to the local police station where you saw César Nava take the students away. How was this declaration made?

FSV: That official statement was written by the social rep [of the PGR] who was in charge of me.

AH: You were in the military once. Who really controlled security in Iguala? What corporation had the greatest command over the city? The local police, the federal police, and the Army were there. Which of the three had the most power in Iguala?

FSV: As far as I know, the Army has the most control. In fact I've noticed that copies of all the schedules, from every service, are sent to the Army.

Individuals directly involved with the PGR's investigation have assured me that, without any doubt, it is the Army who had control of the situation on that night in Iguala.

340

Rodríguez Pérez Gave the Orders

In his statement made to the PGR, Lieutenant Colonel Benito Cegueda Hernández, second-in-command of the 27th Infantry Battalion, claimed that Colonel José Rodríguez Pérez ran the operation on the night of September 26, from the arrival of the *normalistas* in Iguala until the next morning. It was Rodríguez Pérez who first alerted the base to the presence of the *normalistas* at 19:00 at the toll booth and ordered them to be tracked. At around 22:30, he also sent out two squads to patrol the streets due to the disturbances caused by the commandeering of the buses.

Meanwhile, as we now know, Captain José Martínez Crespo, in his declaration to the PGR, claimed that Rodríguez Pérez reached the 27th Infantry base at around 23:20 to run the operations of that night. Cegueda Hernández told the PGR that Martínez Crespo only gave the colonel a verbal report of his doings, because "These events did not require an official report to higher command, since no military personnel were involved." Thus, no written account exists of the captain's movements and activities up until the early hours of September 27.

And yet, in his testimonies from December 4, 2014 and March 2, 2015, Rodríguez Pérez said nothing about the points raised by Cegueda Hernández and Martínez Crespo. In his second declaration, Rodríguez Pérez claimed that, on September 28, he let state prosecutor Elmer Rosas Asunción, as well as investigator Daniel Soto Mota, into the 27th Battalion base for an inspection. After showing them the preventive detention area, he asked them "if they would like to see any other part of the building, and they said there was no need, and left the base." In an eighty-one-page report, however, Rosas Asunción claimed otherwise.

At 11:00 on that same day, September 28, as part of the search for the students, the state prosecutor Elizabeth López Peña ordered a complete inspection of the 27th Infantry Battalion base, the Center for Strategic Operations of the PGR, the federal police base in Iguala, and both the state and local police stations. The brief was to "verify whether said bases were or were not holding any detainees in the secure or custody areas," as well as to review the "registries or log books, and obtain a list of all who are currently detained." The inspection was to take place in the cells, "as well as the rest of the buildings such as offices, barracks, mess halls." Should CCTV exist, the instruction was to "secure the videos from the dates of September 26, 27, and 28." From the beginning, based on past experience, the families and comrades of the disappeared students feared that the forty-three *normalistas* were being held in a federal government building.

In his report, Elmer Rosas Asunción said that he went to the 27th and 41st Infantry Battalion bases with two witnesses. They were received by Colonel Rodríguez Pérez, who assured them that "the buildings that the battalions occupy have no secure detention area, because the moment any detainees arrive they are sent directly to the appropriate agencies."

And yet, the prosecutor was not allowed to make a thorough inspection. Rodríguez Pérez explained that, for reasons of "national security," he couldn't show them the entirety of the base. In order to see more, they would need to submit an official request to the 35th Military Zone in Chilpancingo.

Rodríguez Pérez assured the prosecutor that on the night of September 26 he called the Iguala chief of police, Felipe Flores Velázquez, to ask if he had any issues with the students that he needed assistance with, but the chief said no. Family members of Flores Velázquez, however, claim that it was he who asked the colonel for help, only to be told that there weren't enough available personnel. In reality, the Army had begun monitoring the students that day before they even got to Iguala. (Flores was arrested on October 21, 2016.)

The Inspectorate General's review highlights the inconsistencies between the statements of military officers and the rest of the evidence and stresses the need to obtain more information from the military. It recommends finding out why the civilian investigators were not allowed to search the bases, why soldiers didn't remain at the Cristina Clinic to protect the students, and the precise content of the communications between Rodríguez Pérez and Flores Velázquez.

In November 2015, Colonel Rodríguez Pérez was reassigned to manage the General Infantry Directorate; in February 2016, he was named chief of vehicle repair workshops and promoted to the rank of brigadier general, an appointment that, by law, must be approved by the president.

According to the time line that I have reconstructed for this investigation, it would seem that at the start of the night it was nobody's intention to disappear the students, merely to take back the buses. After all, at around 22:30, the Iguala and Cocula police came to the aid of three wounded youths— Aldo Gutiérrez, Jonathan Maldonado, and Fernando Marín— helped the asthmatic Miguel Ángel Espino, and sent them to the General Hospital. After 22:30, however, there was a complete change of tack, and soon afterwards the *normalistas* were disappeared.

The Inspector General determined that, based on the military's own declarations, "it emerges that the 27th Infantry

Battalion of the SEDENA was aware at all times of what was occurring with the *normalista* students. Moreover, [its soldiers] were circumstantially present at various stages of the events."

The Scene of the Crime: The Army's Bullet Shells

The State Prosecutor's Office conducted ballistic tests on four student buses (excluding the Estrella Roja) and the soccer team's bus, to determine the caliber of the weapons used and the trajectory of the projectiles. The results, dated September 30, 2014, of which we have a copy, reveal that the attack was concentrated on the Estrella de Oro 1568 and the Castro Tours bus, which were both white with green stripes and appear nearly identical.

Estrella de Oro 1568 received at least twenty-nine impacts from 7.62-caliber weapons, which include AK-47, FN FAL, and G3 rifles—none of which are used by the Iguala or Cocula police. In not one of the "confessions" signed by the police did they describe using AK-47, FN FAL, or G3 rifles. The only force in the region that uses such weapons is the Army; the soldiers themselves described carrying G3 rifles. The shots that were fired at the 1568 bus came from behind, or from a position of pursuant attack, from right to left, and "from slightly up to down."

The Castro Tours bus (on the highway to Chilpancingo) received eighty-three impacts, both frontal and from behind, as in an ambush. The bullets were principally .223-caliber, corresponding to the HK G36 and Beretta weapons carried by Iguala and Cocula police officers, as well as to the Bushmaster assault rifles carried by the federal police. Some of the bullets were 7.62-caliber, corresponding once more to military G3 rifles.

Estrella de Oro 1531, stopped in front of the state court-house, did not receive any bullet impacts, but its tires were punctured, pointing to the priority in stopping this bus. This was the only one containing traces of tear gas: the attackers resorted to drastic measures just to get the *normalistas* off the bus. Costa Line 2012 received six .223-caliber impacts (corresponding to both local and federal police), and the other Costa Line received nine impacts, from both .223- and 7.62-caliber bullets.

On October 8, 2014, the Guerrero State Prosecutor's Office reexamined the 149 bullet shells that had been collected on Juan N. Álvarez Street, at the Santa Teresa turn-off, and in vehicles present at the crime scenes, to identify the caliber and the type of weapon they had been fired from. According to its findings, sixty-seven of these bullets were .223-caliber and had been fired from seventeen separate rifles. Of these sixty-seven shells, only eighteen could be traced back to weapons used by the Iguala police. Of the five 9mm shells, which came from four different weapons, three could be traced back to pistols used by the Iguala police. Fifty-eight 7.62 × 39mm shells, "typically fired from AK-47s," corresponded to six different weapons. Fourteen were 7.62 × 51mm shells shot by two different rifles, "typically fired from G3 rifles," eight of which were PPUs and seven of which were FCs (different brands of ammunition). According to a source within the Army, FC stands for Fábrica de Cartuchos (Cartridge Factory), a manufacturer belonging to SEDENA.

My request for further information was rebuffed by SEDENA, on grounds that the type and number of munitions produced by FC was "classified." However, the above-mentioned source and data in the public domain confirmed that the factory makes 7.62 × 51mm shells for the G3 rifle. The ammunition is produced by the General Directorate of Military Industry, which holds the patent. SEDENA did, however, clarify that the products of its cartridge factory are for the exclusive use of the Army and "cannot be obtained by civilians."

Yet another ballistic report released by the Attorney General's Office found 195 shells at the crime scenes: seventy-seven 7.62 × 39-caliber (from AK-47s), eighty-six .223-caliber (from HK G36s, Berettas, and Bushmasters), eighteen 7.62 × 51-caliber (from G3s), six 9mm, one .22-caliber, one .38 super caliber, and six .380-caliber shells.

Guerrero state police officers were called in to testify to the PGR in April 2016. At least two officers admitted to being present at the scenes while the attacks were taking place. Javier Bello Orbe, coordinator of the ministerial police of Guerrero, claimed that at 22:00, after receiving word of the commandeering of the buses, he went to offer backup in "intercepting [the action] along with officer Eliohenay Salvador Martínez Hernández." He said he saw a bus and three Iguala police vehicles. One local officer "indicated to him verbally that everything was under control and that he should leave." Bello Orbe then allegedly left the scene and went to Juan N. Álvarez Street. Another state police officer, Fabián Guerrero Núñez, confirmed that the authority in charge of the C4 cameras was the Army.

The Violations of Tomás Zerón and the End of the "Historical Truth"

I have read the complete "Conclusions" of the internal review by the Inspectorate General (Visitaduría), dated August 18, 2016 and still not released to the public at the time of writing.

In designing his approach, Inspector General César Alejandro Chávez Flores ruled that to ascertain whether irregularities had taken place by the San Juan River on October 28, 2014, the investigation needed to go right back to the detention of the "confessed" gang members. This set off alarm bells in the SEIDO and the AIC, which were soon moving heaven and earth to derail the investigation. If its conclusions were to be publicly divulged, this would not only expose the irregularities committed by the head of the AIC, Tomás Zerón; it would also refute, from within the PGR itself, the so-called "historical truth."

When Chávez Flores presented his conclusions in a meeting with deputy attorneys at the PGR, he was surprised by their reaction: they presented a counterproposal via PowerPoint, suggesting that Tomás Zerón be fired and proceedings initiated against him and that a veil be drawn over the rest of the irregularities committed at the San Juan River.

Attorney General Arely Gómez had been trying for some time to get Peña Nieto to replace Zerón as the head of the AIC. She saw him as a thorn in her side: from his position in the Criminal Investigations Agency, Zerón controlled almost a third of the PGR (the federal ministerial police; forensic investigative services; and the National Center of Planning, Analysis, and Information to Combat Crime [CENAPI]). She wanted him out by any means possible, but without having the Ayotzinapa case collapse.

In the internal review, Chávez Flores concluded that the arrests of the construction workers Agustín García Reyes, Patricio Reyes Landa, Jonathan Osorio Cortés, and four others along with them "were carried out in an illegal and arbitrary manner." The PGR had violated not only the Mexican constitution but also the American Convention of

Human Rights and the International Covenant on Civil and Political Rights.

The Visitaduría supplied the following particulars: Blanca Alicia Bernal Castilla of the Public Ministry, who played a prominent role in the case, ordered García Reyes, Osorio Cortés, and Reyes Landa to be found and presented to the PGR, which occurred on October 27, 2014. Without taking their official statements, based solely on the accounts of the arresting Navy officers, Bernal Castilla ordered them to be detained on grounds of "flagrancy" (caught red-handed), after they supposedly "volunteered" the information that they were members of Guerreros Unidos.

The review pointed out that Bernal Castilla never justified the offense of flagrancy:

"The conduct of Blanca Alicia Bernal Castilla in the detention of all those involved is in prejudicial contradiction to the principle of legality and justice . . . Not one of the detainees was required to make a declaration about the facts behind their search and capture. . . . The agent of the Public Ministry, Blanca Alicia Bernal Castilla, in total contravention of good ministerial faith, took advantage of her public office to order the search and capture of the subjects, in full awareness that such a procedure would satisfy no legitimate end, instead abusing her power to restrict a fundamental right and leave the defendants altogether helpless."

Further, Bernal Castilla never informed the three detainees why they were taken into custody. The review observed that if the arrest of these supposed principal actors in the alleged murder and incineration of the forty-three students was illegal, it has the effect of corrupting all the testimonies taken from them, as well as the evidence collected during and after their arrest, rendering these elements legally void.

On October 27, 2016, Bernal Castilla illegally signed off on García Reyes's medical report at the time of his presentation by the marines, when in reality she had not seen it; the report, describing severe lesions on his body, was not completed until the next day.

The Inspector noted that the PGR conducted a second medical evaluation, in which García Reyes presented with wounds different from those already described by the Marines. "Currently it is not possible to precisely determine when they were caused," the review reads, inferring that they were inflicted between his detention by the marines and his period of custody in the PGR. Noting the difficulty of ascertaining whether marines or PGR staff were responsible, the text continues: "The absence of certainty in the sequence of events that produced the wounds prevents the accurate determination . . . of the possible commission of ill-treatment or torture."

Also ruled illegal was the removal of García Reyes from his cell at the SEIDO facility, which occurred on October 28, 2014, before he was temporarily handed over to Zerón. It was Bernal Castilla herself who "ordered the temporary cessation of guard and custody," permitting García Reyes to be illegally passed on to Zerón and his team. Bernal Castilla claimed that the custody transfer was to conduct "various proceedings of a ministerial nature," but her report did not describe the conditions, manner, or place of such proceedings, nor the names of the personnel who would be responsible for his custody. Nor did Bernal Castilla call García Reyes's lawyer to inform him or have him accompany him in such "proceedings."

Chávez Flores concluded that "the omissions which plague these proceedings were not the outcome of failings on the part of Ministry official Blanca Alicia Bernal Castilla, but were a deliberate course of action . . . [which] infringed the minimum standard of human dignity owed to all persons deprived of their liberty, in whatever form, including ministerial detention. Such behavior is intolerable by any measure in a constitutional state under the rule of law."

On top of it all, the transfer of custody was not included in the PGR's final dossier, and it seems to have been Bernal Castilla herself who omitted it.

The internal review noted that it was prosecutor Jorge García Valentín who illegally oversaw the transfer of custody of García Reyes from the SEIDO cells. But despite the fact that there were witnesses to the transfer, when García Valentín was questioned about it, he stated: "I don't recall that Agustín García Reyes ever left the facility."

As regards Peña Nieto's right-hand man, Zerón himself, the Visitaduría accuses him of trampling on the victims' right to the truth. "There exists convincing and relevant data to adduce the likely responsibility of the head of the Criminal Investigations Agency for the commission of irregular actions in the investigation he carried out in the vicinity of the San Juan River, in Cocula, Guerrero, on October 28, 2014, where he proceeded without oversight from an officer of the Public Ministry." The report also points out that Zerón "failed to place a formal report of the actions taken on October 28, 2014 in the preliminary inquiry" case file. All of it amounted to a violation of the victims' "right to the truth."

"The right to the truth means not only the elucidation of the facts, but also the transparency of the conclusions and of the criminal and investigative process, such that the victims can freely participate in these, within the terms of the legal requirements," the Inspector summarized. "It is further concluded that the aforementioned official detrimentally undermined Agustín García Reyes's right to be legally represented in his defense," because he was taken to the San Juan River without an attorney.

The Inspector General identified four "main protagonists" of the irregular actions undertaken on October 28: Tomás Zerón de Lucio, Abraham Eslava Arvizu, Bernardo Cano Muñozcano (Zerón's chief of staff), and Jaime David Díaz Serralde.

The review found that the forensic experts who were present at the San Juan River on October 28 violated the rules for securing a crime scene, as well as basic chain of custody rules. Even though Zerón claimed to have ordered secure isolation of the crime scene, the forensic experts who were present "did not produce any documentary evidence that they secured the location, or the names of the agency officers who performed the task." According to a source within the PGR, this means that the crime scene was tampered with and that the actions performed were illegal. By the same token, the evidence supposedly obtained from the scene, including the remains of Alexander Mora, is invalid. Given that these remains are the only evidence of the supposed death of the *normalistas* and that they have been contaminated, no judge could rule them admissible in court. This was one of the most contentious points of the Inspector's conclusions and a major reason why Arely Gómez wanted Chávez Flores to modify them.

The Inspector also concluded that Bernal Castilla wrote contradictory dates and times into the report she submitted along with the reconstruction of events of October 29, 2016, the day on which the black plastic bag with the remains of Alexander Mora was supposedly found. As the official responsible for recording the discovery, she claimed to have been at the river from 08:00 on October 29 until the morning of October 31. According to her minutes, at 08:50, in her presence, Navy divers found a bag with carbonized human remains. Bernal Castilla wrote that the Argentine forensic team and officers from SEIDO did not arrive until after the discovery.

And yet, at the same time that Bernal Castilla claimed to have been at the San Juan River, she also signed nine significant memos or orders which say she was in the SEIDO offices of Mexico City. One of these orders, signed at 09:00, was to designate the forensic investigators that would go to the San Juan River. Another, signed at 14:00 on the same day, authorized detainees Osorio Cortés and García Reyes to be taken from the SEIDO building to assist in the reconstruction of events at the river.

Planting Evidence

Forensic investigator Luis Daniel Hernández Espinoza received an order to go to the San Juan River at 17:00 on October 28, three hours after Tomás Zerón and his team videotaped the plastic bags that had allegedly been pointed out by García Reyes.

According to Hernández Espinoza, he was told to look for trash bags thrown in the river. Although in the GIEI video the bags are visible during Zerón's inspection, Hernández Espinoza claimed that that same day another forensic field expert searched the location "looking for any element requiring further study of the matter, and found nothing."

The Inspector General's internal review accused forensic investigators Mauricio Cerón Solana and Patricia Gómez

Ramírez of "illegal disturbance of evidence, traces, or vestiges of a felony, its instruments or products," "failure to preserve evidence," "failure to examine," and violation of the "chain of custody."

On October 29, Cerón Solana was again present at the river and recalls "there were already Navy divers, federal ministerial police, Center for Investigation and National Security, and Public Ministry officials on site." It was the divers who "brought to light" a trash bag that contained human bone fragments "with signs of exposure to fire." The bag was open.

Inspector Chávez Flores interviewed García Reyes, who maintained that the bags were already in the river when they arrived. This accords with what his wife would describe to me in an interview in May 2016.

On June 24, 2016, García Reyes told Chávez Flores: "I was detained in the SEIDO [building], I was in a cell and then they took me out and just put me in a helicopter, and in the helicopter they said we were going to the San Juan River and there were some bags there that I needed to point out, and that if I didn't do it they were going to torture me, and so I answered yes, and we flew to the bridge at the San Juan River and when we were landing on the soccer field they asked if I knew the place and they said [*sic*] that I did and then we were there and they took me out and told me I better not forget what they'd told me and then they took me to where some plastic bags were, and then one of them dressed in black holding me by the neck told me that if I tried to run they'd shoot me and we got to where the bags were [and] I did what they'd told me to do."

García Reyes explained that all this happened in front of Zerón de Lucio, the boss of those who threatened him and told him what to say. Asked if a public or private lawyer had accompanied him, he said, "No, nobody, there were only *wachos*," slang for Navy personnel.

The PGR's internal review recommended the removal of prosecutor Blanca Alicia Bernal Castilla, forensic coordinator Mauricio Cerón Solana, forensic expert Patricia Gómez Ramírez, and prosecutor Jorge García Valentín. Given that Zerón de Lucio was not subject to the regulatory norms of other PGR officers, the Inspectorate proposed that he be sanctioned under the Federal Law of Administrative Responsibility of Public Servants. Chávez Flores also urged an investigation into potential criminal acts committed by other personnel at the San Juan River.

The "Conclusions" of the Technical and Juridical Assessment were never officially signed. It seems that it was Peña Nieto who shielded Zerón de Lucio, refusing to formally authorize the document or put its recommendations into practice. However, so that the PGR could not make it disappear, the document was included in Chávez Flores's work delivery reception record when he left his post.

The Army and the Federal Police Must Be Investigated

Some of the most trenchant conclusions of the Inspector General's audit of the more than 1,000 pages of the PGR's preliminary investigations show that these were plagued by malpractice, rendering them null and void. In particular, lines of inquiry pointing to the Army, the federal police, the federal ministerial police, and the Guerrero state and ministerial police were set aside. The report underlines that "the investigation [into the disappearance of the *normalistas*] was not carried out in a serious, impartial, or effective manner by the legally responsible agencies towards the specific goal of establishing the truth." In sum, "they did not proceed in a manner fit to uncover the truth and bring about justice."

The Inspectorate found that federal and state investigators prioritized inculpating the Guerreros Unidos and organized crime, criminally indicting as many people as possible, "leaving as a secondary priority of the Mexican state any systematic and rigorous search for the missing students." They should have opened an investigation into forced disappearance, instead of kidnapping and organized crime.

Based on statements made by soldiers, who admitted that they did not intervene during the night of September 26 to stop the attacks, the Inspector General's review determined that "the negligence committed by military personnel of the 27th Infantry Battalion during the events of September 26 and 27 in the city of Iguala had fatal consequences for the students from the Raúl Isidro Burgos Normal Rural School of Ayotzinapa and members of the Avispones de Chilpancingo soccer team." Moreover, "there are grounds to investigate whether SEDENA officers at the 27th Infantry Battalion base, in Iguala, Guerrero, incurred some type of criminal responsibility" in the events. The review suggested that SEDENA's Office of Internal Control initiate such proceedings.

As regards the C4 and the military personnel who controlled the security cameras, there was "a lack of regulation in the functional operation [of the cameras] and a lack of supervision, which led to the possible manipulation of the logbooks, videos, and registries" of the C4.

With respect to the federal police, whose former commissioner, Enrique Galindo, denied their participation in the attacks, the review emphasized: "It is crucially important to evaluate the participation of the federal police of Iguala in the events of 26 and 27 September."

Noting that a preliminary investigation had already been opened into federal agents Víctor Manuel Colmenares Campos and Emmanuel Pérez Arizpe, for "abuse of authority and wrongful exercise of public service," the review urged "widening the investigation into the potential nonfeasance" of federal forces in Iguala. The federal police commissioner should be required "to hand over all the firearms that its agents had in their possession" in order to conduct tests. As we have seen, most of the bullet shells found at the crime scenes were not from Iguala and Cocula police weapons, while the federal police carry guns that use the same caliber of bullet.

The declarations made by federal police officers, the Visitaduría pointed out, exhibited "confusion and little clarity." For example, the statement of Colmenares Campos claimed that the federal police vehicles did not have GPS, while the statement of Pérez Arizpe said they did—information potentially critical to establishing their movements on that night, and how many vehicles and officers were present at the scenes of the attacks.

"The first authority to have knowledge of the events related to the students from the Raúl Isidro Burgos Normal Rural School of Ayotzinapa was the Attorney General's Office of Guerrero, which, on September 26, 2014, opened case file AC/PGR/GRO/IGU/I/256/2014 at 21:45," the internal review notes.

Accordingly, "there should have been immediate action from the local and federal authorities responsible for law enforcement, as the pieces of evidence obtained in the first hours following the crime have the greatest probative value." The Visitaduría's audit found that the federal ministerial police officers Romeo Ortiz Valenciana, José Manuel Dirzo

Correa, and Enrique Ramírez Hernández "failed to fulfill their obligation of a detailed investigation of the facts," while the Ministry's César Iván Pilares Viloria committed "negligence by failing to at once refer the case upwards and open a preliminary inquiry."

The review further explained that "having performed an irregular initial investigation, [authorities] failed to guarantee the certainty, legality, objectivity, impartiality, efficiency, honor, fidelity, discipline, and respect towards the legal order and the human rights of the perpetrators and the direct and indirect victims."

The Iguala police station, to which the PGR claimed the *normalistas* were taken, was not properly maintained as part of a crime scene, nor was the Cocula trash dump where the students were supposedly killed and incinerated. The detainees were subjected to invasive procedures, and errors were committed during the "genetic profiling" of the family members of the disappeared: there were errors in twenty-two of the 134 tests conducted at the PGR's Forensic Genetics lab, whose ultimate head is Tomás Zerón.

The review also ordered "the investigation of negligent conduct" on the part of personnel at Guerrero's Secretariat of Public Security, for potential cover-up and abuse of authority.

Finally, the Visitaduría's internal review concluded that the ministerial declarations taken from witnesses, in particular from the military, were not up to standard, given the lack of "direction and supervision by personnel with authority over Public Ministry staff."

The detentions of the following persons were ruled illegal: Osvaldo and Miguel Ángel Ríos Sánchez; Carlos Pascual Cervantes Jaimes; Ramiro Ocampo Pineda; Rosario Manuel

Borja; brothers Luis Alberto and Juan Estrada Montes de Oca; Raymundo Salvador Bernal; David Hernández Cruz; Carlos Canto Salgado; Elmer Nava Orduña, alleged cousin of *Gil*; Iguala police officers Esteban Ocampo Landa, José Alfredo Leonardo Arellano Landa, Justo Neri Espinoza, Ubaldo Toral Vences, Gerardo Delgado Mota, Jorge García Castillo, Matías González Domínguez, and Natividad Elías Moreno; laborers Agustín García Reyes, Patricio Reyes Landa, and Jonathan Osorio Cortés; also Darío Morales Sánchez, Salvador Reza Jacobo, Benito Vázquez Martínez, and the ex-mayor of Cocula, Carlos Peñaloza Santana.

In view of the audit's findings, the Inspector General recommended that ninety-five Istanbul Protocols should be initiated to investigate the possible torture of detainees. He also opened a brief to examine "probable unlawful procedures" undertaken against the ex-mayor of Iguala José Luis Abarca and his wife, María de los Ángeles Pineda, by federal police officers Agustina Calvo Suriano, José Hugo Espejel Carrillo, Daigoro Herrera Ojeda, and María Lucerito López Martínez.

Among the Public Ministry staff responsible for improper arrests were Juan Eustorio Sánchez Conde, Blanca Alicia Bernal Castilla, Ignacio Quintana Candelario, Norma Angélica García Zúñiga, and Lourdes López Lucho.

The Normalistas' Three Paths

Witnesses of the attacks mention that they saw at least three groups of people, presumably *normalistas*, being transported in various vehicles. One witness claimed to have seen, at around midnight, police vehicles with their lights flashing, blocking federal highway 51, which runs from Iguala to

Ciudad Altamirano, under the ramp bridge linking to the Cocula road. Other units, meanwhile, were transferring people who may have been students into a cargo truck. This was not in Loma de Coyotes, but on the highway.

Another witness saw, at around one in the morning on September 27, a group of police trucks with people in the beds driving at high speed on the highway towards Huitzuco, between the junctions of Tepecoacuilco and Tlaxmalac.

A third witness said that at approximately four in the morning he saw three white pickup trucks (similar to those used by state ministerial police and the PGR's federal ministerial police) driving down the Periférico in the direction of the Taxco highway bridge. From his vantage point on the second floor of a building, he could make out people stacked on top of each other in the beds of the trucks, but he couldn't tell if they were alive.

Epilogue

M ore than 100 people have been arrested on suspicion of involvement in the attacks against the Ayotzinapa students and the disappearance of forty-three of them. And yet, the Mexican government has been unable to explain the truth of what happened on that terrible night in Iguala; nor has it been able to find the disappeared *normalistas*. Far from offering a degree of certainty, the remains of Alexander Mora inspire us with profound disquiet.

The lessons of this case must not be forgotten. Any one of us who live in Mexico could find themselves among the next forty-three, or among the many who are arbitrarily detained and ruthlessly tortured every day. It is imperative to find the disappeared *normalistas* and to bring the guilty to justice: those who ordered, executed, and covered up the murders and disappearance, as well as those in the highest ranks of government who protected the perpetrators and the enablers. This is not merely a question of justice for the families who continue to desperately search for their loved ones. It also means offering an example of justice to a country that needs to pull itself out of an abyss of corruption, impunity, and violence.

The right to the truth is a fundamental one. We must fight for it every day.

Time Line

September 26, 2014

13:00

The *normalistas* arrive in Chilpancingo to try to commandeer buses. The city's bus station is surrounded by troops and state police officers. There is an altercation, and the students return to their campus in Ayotzinapa.

16:30–17:00

Back in Ayotzinapa the students decide to go to Iguala to make another attempt. The organizer is Bernardo Flores Alcaraz, or *Cochiloco*, the school committee member in charge of bus transportation to the October 2 annual protest in Mexico City.

17:59

The Chilpancingo C4 is notified of more than 100 *normalistas* leaving Ayotzinapa in two buses, the Estrella de Oro 1568 and 1531. The Chilpancingo C4 passes the information on to the Iguala C4, where all levels of law enforcement converge: state police, federal police, Iguala municipal police, the PGR, and the Army's 27th Infantry Battalion.

The Army is responsible for controlling the security cameras. There are more than twenty cameras installed throughout the city, though only four are operational, according to the officer in charge of the C4 on this night. From the four working cameras, only a few minutes of recording from two of the cameras are saved; the rest are erased.

18:30

In Iguala's central plaza, María de los Ángeles Pineda Villa, the wife of Mayor José Luis Abarca, presents her second report as president of the city's Integral Family Development program (DIF).

19:30–19:45

Bus 1568 drives towards the Cuernavaca–Iguala toll booth. Bus 1531 stops in front of La Palma restaurant on the Chilpancingo–Iguala highway at Rancho del Cura. Soon after 1568 arrives at the toll booth, Guerrero state police, federal police, and soldiers from the 27th Infantry Battalion show up.

20:00

Pineda Villa's presentation ends.

20:30 (approximately)

At Rancho del Cura, about ten students stop a passenger bus. The driver refuses to give up the vehicle, but he promises that once he has dropped off his passengers at the Iguala terminal, they can have it.

The mayor and his family leave the Iguala central square and go for tacos at a street stall on the edge of town.

21:00 (approximately)

The bus with ten *normalistas* arrives at the Iguala station and the bus driver gets off, locking the students inside. The students phone their *compañeros* for help. Students on the 1568 and 1531 buses decide to head to the station. The state police, the Army, and the federal police keep a constant watch on their movements. Soldiers from the 27th Infantry Battalion follow them.

21:16

At the Iguala station, the ten trapped students are freed. They abandon that bus, but Bernardo Flores Alcaraz orders them to seize a few more: they take two Costa Lines and one Estrella Roja. The students are now riding in five buses.

21:20

Through the C4, the law enforcement agencies and the Army are aware of the taking of the new buses. Felipe Flores Velázquez himself, chief of Iguala's municipal police, updates Luis Antonio Dorantes Macías, head of federal police in Iguala.

The two Costa Line buses and the Estrella de Oro 1568 take the wrong exit out of the bus station and get stuck in traffic in central Iguala. The Estrella de Oro 1531 and the Estrella Roja take the correct exit and head towards the Iguala–Chilpancingo highway.

21:30

First Attack: Gunfire erupts at the corner of Bandera Nacional and Galeana streets. Witnesses later confirm that local Iguala police officers were shooting into the air. Nobody is wounded. More shooting breaks out on the corner of Emiliano Zapata and Juan N. Álvarez (Galeana becomes Juan N. Álvarez). Witnesses see military-looking men arrive in an SUV, begin shooting, and chase one student.

Another civilian vehicle arrives with men resembling soldiers; they start picking up bullet shells. According to testimony from Colonel José Rodríguez Pérez, his men are keeping him informed of events in real time. The Iguala C4 reports on the attacks.

21:40

Second Attack: At the corner of Juan N. Álvarez and Periférico, an Iguala police truck blocks the way of the three buses that took the wrong exit.

Heavy gunfire blasts the Estrella de Oro 1568 bus. According to witnesses, the assailants are local police, state police, and men in civilian clothes. Another witness sees two federal police vehicles block the street a few blocks behind the bus, to facilitate the attack, and federal police vehicles can be seen in cell phone videos. *Normalistas* Aldo Gutiérrez and Jonathan Maldonado are shot and injured.

21:45

The Iguala PGR's office opens a file after receiving news of the shootings from the C4. Federal ministerial police from the Criminal Investigations Agency (AIC) head out. According to their own statements, AIC officers are present at the scenes of the attacks.

22:30

Fernando Marín, *Carrillas*, on Estrella de Oro 1568, is wounded. Officers bring him and his *compañeros* off the bus. According to Marín, both local and state officers are involved.

Officers threaten to kill him, but in the end they call an ambulance. The last sight Marín has of the scene is around twenty of his classmates lying on the sidewalk in police custody. Neighbors will confirm that two federal police vehicles have blocked off Álvarez Street while the attacks unfold.

Third Attack: At the same hour, local and federal police officers stop the Estrella de Oro 1531 and the Estrella Roja bus on the Iguala–Chilpancingo highway, in front of the state courthouse. Motorists stopped on the road will confirm that federal police officers aim at the students and pull them off the Estrella Roja bus, while other officers throw tear gas inside the Estrella de Oro, forcing the students off.

At least one soldier from the 27th Infantry Battalion will admit to being present during the attack, under orders from Colonel José Rodríguez Pérez.

Normalistas call their comrades in Ayotzinapa to ask for help. A group of students leaves the campus and drives towards Iguala.

According to soldiers' testimonies, a squad of fourteen soldiers armed with G3 rifles, under command of Lieutenant Roberto Vázquez Hernández, enters the General Hospital to check the names of casualties, though their departure from the base is not registered in the official logbook. Supposedly, after leaving the hospital, the squad returns to the base.

22:30–22:40

Twelve officers from the Cocula Police Department, commanded by César Nava González, arrive on the corner of Juan N. Álvarez and Periférico in three patrol vehicles. They provide assistance to Miguel Ángel Espino, *Pulmón*, and deliver him to a Red Cross ambulance.

22:50–23:00

The students riding in the Estrella de Oro buses 1568 and 1531 are disappeared. In cell phone videos from surviving *normalistas,* federal police remain at the scene as local police leave.

The driver of the Estrella de Oro 1531 will later testify to the National Committee on Human Rights that federal police, as well as Iguala and Huitzuco local police, are present at the moment of the disappearance in front of the state courthouse. The driver identifies two federal police officers: Víctor Manuel Colmenares Campos and Emmanuel Pérez Arizpe.

22:50–23:00

César Nava González later testifies that the Iguala police commander, Francisco Salgado Valladares, phones him to say that they can return to their station in Cocula, now that the Army has taken control of the situation. According to Army Captain José Martínez Crespo, this is when Colonel José Rodríguez Pérez arrives at the Army base.

23:00

According to soldiers' testimonies, Lieutenant Vázquez Hernández leaves the base again with his squad to go to the scene of the attack at the Santa Teresa turn-off, though it had not yet happened: the squad heads to the scene *before* the attacks begin.

23:00–23:10

Local Iguala and Cocula police leave the area of Juan N. Álvarez Street.

23:00

Guerrero's prosecutor general, Iñaki Blanco Cabrera, receives orders from Governor Ángel Aguirre to head to Iguala to investigate the attacks in the city. However, Secretary of State Public Security Leonardo Vázquez Pérez later testified that he was first notified of the attacks at 22:00.

The Center for Investigation and National Security (CISEN) in Guerrero learns of the attacks.

23:40

Fourth Attack: Armed men attack the Avispones soccer team's Castro Tours bus. The players explain who they are when their attackers attempt to pull them off the bus, and the latter quickly leave. Blanca Montiel, David Josué García, and Víctor Manuel Lugo are killed. The Castro Tours bus closely resembles the Estrella de Oro buses.

23:50–24:00

Captain Martínez Crespo and fourteen soldiers leave the Army base. According to their testimonies, they go directly to the state courthouse. According to jail magistrate Ulises Bernabé García, however, at 23:30 the captain and his squad entered the Iguala police station to search it, which would mean that the squad was out on the streets before the captain, in his official testimony, claimed they left the barracks.

September 27, 2014

00:00, Fifth Attack: The surviving *normalistas* and the students recently arrived from Ayotzinapa regroup to hold a press conference. CISEN officers are present. Armed men fire into the gathered crowd. Students Daniel Solís and Julio César Ramírez are wounded and left lying on the pavement.

00:05

Captain Martínez Crespo and his squad arrive outside the state courthouse and inspect Estrella de Oro 1531.

00:10

Around twenty *normalistas* flee from the attack on the press conference. Some manage to rescue one of their *compañeros*, who was shot in the face, and take him to the nearby Cristina Clinic. Other students scatter; one of them is Julio César Mondragón.

00:30–00:40

Captain Martínez Crespo and his men drive by the corner of Juan N. Álvarez and Periférico. Some of the soldiers alight, aiming rifles at and then kicking the moribund Solís and Ramírez. They offer no assistance.

The squad enters the Cristina Clinic and threatens the students who have taken refuge there.

02:40

Corporal Juan Carlos Peralta calls the Public Ministry to inform of the discovery of the bodies of Daniel Solís and Julio César Ramírez.

09:30

The Army notifies the Ministry of the discovery of a corpse near the Iguala C4. It belongs to Julio César Mondragón, the third *normalista* to be slain on that terrible night in Iguala.

Appendix

Officials in the Enrique Peña Nieto Administration Investigated for the Torture of Detainees (AP/PGR/SDHPDSC/OI/001/2015).

Jesús Omar Maciel Álvarez (in offense against David Cruz Hernández, alias *el Chino*, and fourteen Cocula police officers).

Miguel Ángel Romero Hernández (in offense against David Cruz Hernández, alias *el Chino*, and fourteen Cocula police officers).

Ángel Alfredo Gutiérrez Chagoya (in offense against fourteen Cocula police officers).

Arturo Martínez Pérez (in offense against fourteen Cocula police officers).

Luis Nicasio Díaz Elizalde (in offense against fourteen Cocula police officers).

Javier Rosete Torres (in offense against fourteen Cocula police officers and eight Iguala police officers).

Román Almazán Hernández (in offense against fourteen Cocula police officers).

David Vargas Briseño (in offense against fourteen Cocula police officers).

Josefina de la Cruz Rosales (in offense against fourteen Cocula police officers and eight Iguala police officers).

Sergio Hernández Carranza (in offense against fourteen Cocula police officers).

Israel Ruiz Rodríguez (in offense against fourteen Cocula police officers and eight Iguala police officers).

Jesús Rudimiro Rodríguez Reyes (in offense against fourteen Cocula police officers and eight Iguala police officers).

Miguel Ángel Pita Casco (two investigations were opened against him: one for torture in offense against ten Cocula police officers and another for torture in offense against eight Iguala police officers).

José Eduardo Lavariega (in offense against fourteen Cocula police officers).

Carlos Antonio Hernández Campos (in offense against fourteen Cocula police officers and eight Iguala police officers).

Julio César Ramos Lorenzana (in offense against fourteen Cocula police officers and eight Iguala police officers).

Rodrigo Refugio Hernández García (in offense against ten Iguala police officers).

Carlos Espinosa Martínez (in offense against ten Iguala police officers).

Julio Pablo Cárdenas Ugalde (in offense against ten Iguala police officers).

Daniel Cabello Vargas (in offense against ten Iguala police officers).

César Albarrán Beltrán (in offense against ten Iguala police officers).

Julio César Herrera Sánchez (in offense against ten Iguala police officers).

Jorge Basurto Vargas (in offense against Raúl Javier Crespo).

Alejandro Pérez Berni (in offense against Raúl Javier Crespo).

Rubén Alejandro Betanzos Huerta (in offense against Raúl Javier Crespo).

Aristeo Martínez Carrillo (in offense against Raúl Javier Crespo).

Armando Torres Romero (in offense against eight Iguala police officers).

José Jorge González Valdespino (in offense against eight Iguala police officers).

Víctor Alonso Godínez Jurado (in offense against eight Iguala police officers).

Víctor Hugo Miranda Lima (Navy). (In September 2015 the PGR determined that he engaged in "conduct constituting a crime" in offense against Salvador Reza Jacobo and Benito Vázquez Martínez.)

Alcibiades Marcelino Ayodoro (Navy). (In September 2015 the PGR determined that he engaged in "conduct constituting a crime" in offense against Salvador Reza Jacobo and Benito Vázquez Martínez.)

Celso Mario Rendón Mejía (Navy). (In September 2015 the PGR determined that he engaged in "conduct constituting a crime" in offense against Ramiro Ocampo Pineda, alias *El Chango*, and Rosario Manuel Borja.)

Reynel Calvo Molina (Navy). (In September 2015 the PGR determined that he engaged in "conduct constituting a crime" in offense against Ramiro Ocampo Pineda, alias *El Chango*, and Rosario Manuel Borja.)

Ezequiel Peña Cerda (federal ministerial police) (in offense against Carlos Canto Salgado).

Agustín Castillo Reyes (Navy) (in offense against Carlos Canto Salgado).

Vidal Vázquez Mendoza (Navy). (Two investigations were opened against him for torture in offense against Miguel Ángel and Osvaldo Ríos Sánchez, Carlos Pascual Cervantes Jaimes, and Agustín García Reyes, alias *El Chereje*. In September 2015 the PGR determined that he committed the crime of torture against García Reyes.)

Jazmín Edith García Martínez (Navy). (In September 2015 the PGR determined that she committed the crime of torture in offense against Agustín García Reyes.)

Jazmín Galicia Guzmán (federal ministerial police) (in offense against Osvaldo and Miguel Ángel Ríos Sánchez and Carlos Pascual Cervantes).

Carlos Villaseñor de la Rosa (federal ministerial police) (in offense against Osvaldo and Miguel Ángel Ríos Sánchez and Carlos Pascual Cervantes).

Omar Evaristo Vega Leyva (federal ministerial police) (in offense against Osvaldo and Miguel Ángel Ríos Sánchez and Carlos Pascual Cervantes).

Jairo Antonio Flores Hernández (Navy) (in offense against Osvaldo and Miguel Ángel Ríos Sánchez and Carlos Pascual Cervantes).

Ruben Edison Irraestro (Navy) (in offense against Osvaldo and Miguel Ángel Ríos Sánchez and Carlos Pascual Cervantes).

David Ramírez Alcaraz (Navy). (In September 2015 the PGR determined that he engaged in "conduct constituting a crime" in offense against Raúl Núñez Salgado, alias *Camperra*.)

Carlos Gutiérrez Silva (Navy). (In September 2015 the PGR determined that he engaged in "conduct constituting a crime" in offense against Raúl Núñez Salgado, alias *Camperra*.)

Jesús Emanuel Álvarez Alvarado (federal police). (In September 2015 the PGR determined that he engaged in "conduct constituting a crime" in offense against Jonathan Osorio Cortés, Patricio Reyes Landa, and Darío Morales Sánchez.)

José de Jesús Palafox Mora (federal police). (In September 2015 the PGR determined that he engaged in "conduct constituting a crime" in offense against Jonathan Osorio Cortés, Patricio Reyes Landa, and Darío Morales Sánchez.)

Jorge Edmundo Samperio Rodríguez (federal police). (In September 2015 the PGR determined that he engaged in "conduct constituting a crime" in offense against Jonathan Osorio Cortés, Patricio Reyes Landa, Darío Morales Sánchez, and Jorge Luis Poblete Aponte.)

Artemio Navarro Jiménez (federal police). (In September 2015 the PGR determined that he engaged in "conduct constituting a crime" in offense against Luis Alberto and José Juan Estrada Montes de Oca and de Raymundo Salvador Bernal.)

Ramiro Cruz de Jesús (Navy). (In September 2015 the PGR determined that he engaged in "conduct constituting a crime" in offense against Luis Alberto and José Juan Estrada Montes de Oca, and Raymundo Salvador Bernal.)

Ricardo Alfredo Díaz Ambriz (Navy). (In September 2015 the PGR determined that he engaged in "conduct constituting a crime" in offense against Luis Alberto and José Juan Estrada Montes de Oca and Raymundo Salvador Bernal.)

Jorge Nieto Alonso (federal police). (In September 2015 the PGR determined that he engaged in "conduct constituting a crime" in offense against Jorge Luis Poblete Aponte.)

Agustina Calvo Suriano (federal police). (In September 2015 the PGR determined that she engaged in "conduct constituting a crime" in offense against José Luis Abarca Velázquez and María de los Ángeles Pineda Villa.)

Hugo Espejel Carrillo (federal police). (In September 2015 the PGR determined that he committed "conduct constituting a crime" in offense against José Luis Abarca Velázquez and María de los Ángeles Pineda Villa.)

Daigoro Herrera Ojeda (pf). (In September 2015 the PGR determined that he engaged in "conduct constituting a crime" in offense against José Luis Abarca Velázquez and María de los Ángeles Pineda Villa.)

María Lucerito López Martínez (pf). (In September 2015 the PGR determined that she engaged in "conduct constituting a crime" in offense against José Luis Abarca Velázquez and María de los Ángeles Pineda Villa.)

The PGR has ruled that nineteen officers on this list committed the crime of torture. As of publication, none of them has been sentenced.

Index

27th Infantry Battalion, 3, 8, 13, 19, 57, 64, 82–83, 115–17, 166, 225; at attack, 278, 281, 343–44; in control of Iguala, 333, 336; dereliction of duty, 321; and disappearances, 326; on drug trade payroll, 328; families demand investigation of, 229; inspection refused by, 103–4, 230, 309, 341–42; OBI (Information Search Organ), 264, 279, 295–97; parents of victims blame, 152; protection not offered by, 283; real-time updates before attack, 263; response to attack, 292, 303; responsible for attack, 355; students at base of, 329; testimony of, 88–89, 281, 294–95. *See also* Army; military

41st Infantry Battalion, 82; on drug trade payroll, 328; inspection refused by, 103–4

42nd Infantry Battalion, 8

102nd Infantry Battalion, 60

Abarca Velázquez, José Luis, 105–49, 123, 239, 250; absence of incriminating evidence against, 137, 139–40, 149; accusation against, 111–14, 122, 130–33, 148; and Aguirre Rivero, 124–25; arrest of, 133–37; background of, 106–8; blamed for attack, 64, 87, 105–6, 164, 199–200, 234; escape of, after attack, 129–32; fertilizer affair, 118–21; first interview with, 140–44; first report of attack to, 126–27, 140–41, 145; gold business of, 105–7; and Guerreros Unidos, 196, 201; home of, 148; indictment of, 149; investigation focuses on, xxiii; and María de los Ángeles Pineda Villa, 108; orders arrest of *normalistas*, 174, 187; and Pineda Villa brothers, 111; political beginnings of, 114–15; PRD asks for media protection money, 127–28; real estate of, 108–9; resignation of, 128–29;